The Canadian Settlers' Guide

Catherine Parr Traill

THE

CANADIAN

SETTLERS' GUIDE.

𝔓𝔲𝔟𝔩𝔦𝔰𝔥𝔢𝔡 𝔟𝔶 𝔄𝔲𝔱𝔥𝔬𝔯𝔦𝔱𝔶.

TENTH EDITION, CONSIDERABLY ENLARGED.

LONDON:
EDWARD STANFORD, 6 CHARING CROSS.
1860.

[*Price Five Shillings, Post Paid.*]

226. f. 48.

LONDON: PRINTED BY W. CLOWES AND SONS, STAMFORD STREET.

PREFACE TO THE TENTH EDITION.

THE value attached to this little work may be estimated in some degree by its having already reached a Tenth Edition.

The testimony borne to its worth and utility to actual and intending settlers, by persons so well entitled to give an opinion of its merits as William Hutton, Esq., Secretary to the Board of Agriculture and Statistics; Frederic Widder, Esq., Resident Commissioner of the Canada Company, and A. C. Buchanan, and A. B. Hawke, Esqrs., the Government Emigration-Agents at Quebec and Toronto, has doubtless given it an importance which it otherwise might not have attained.

The matter in the first portion of the book is written by Mrs. Traill, after a residence of twenty-five years in the Colony, a considerable portion of which has been in those "Backwoods of Canada," so vivid and interesting a description of which she gave to the public through the medium of Knight's Shilling Volumes.

The second part consists of official documents.

The third part consists of a republication of several letters, written from one friend in Canada to another in England, and are reprinted by request, but do *not* form any portion of the work which claims to be official, though it is believed to give correct information.

Much valuable official information will be found in the Appendix.

The growing interest felt in Canadian matters at home, and the prospect of an extensive Emigration to this Province in the approaching year, have caused a large demand for the work from Great Britain and other parts of Europe; and with a view therefore to make it more useful and acceptable, a very large and valuable addition has been made to it, selected from the works and "endorsed" by the opinions of some of the most eminent authorities in Canada.

These various documents comprise an amount of information, the result of actual experience, and bearing the stamp of official authority, upon which the utmost reliance may be placed; and they are published with a view to the instruction and guidance of Settlers *of all classes* who may contemplate a residence in this thriving Colony, whose onward progress exceeds that of any other dependency of the British Crown.

The population of Canada is now estimated at nearly three millions, being an increase since 1851-2 of above thirty-three per cent.

The information given hereinafter is intended chiefly for the guidance of those who intend to settle upon land, the class most likely to succeed just now, if possessed of some little capital. A demand for labourers and mechanics would soon follow.

The Publisher has carefully abstained from giving any account of the Province more favourable than the one borne out by official returns as to fertility and climate.

London, October, 1860.

CONTENTS.

	PAGE
ALIENS, naturalization of . .	200
America, arrival in . . .	46
Assessments, how made . .	160
BANKING system, security afforded by	159
Banks in Canada	159
Blocks of land, conditions of sale	195
Bonds, government, county, municipal	159
Book post to Canada . . .	202
Bureau of Agriculture, reports of	133, 140
CANADA and Illinois compared	141
Canada, Upper and Lower, difference between . .	169
Canals, abolition of tolls on .	87
Cattle-breeding, neglect of .	170
Christmas, a song for . . .	74
Christmas-day in the backwoods	70
Churches and schools . . .	37
Clearing and logging wild land	30

	PAGE
Climate of Canada . . .	211
Clothing and necessaries . .	8
Coins, English, value of . .	102
Country gentlemen, enviable life of	166
,, lack of, in Canada	166
Currency and cents, equivalent value of	112
Currency and sterling, table for calculating . . .	113
Customs Act of 1859 misunderstood in England . .	124
DAIRY products, neglect of .	170
Debt, National, of Canada .	121
Deeds, registration of . . .	160
Draining, neglect of . . .	167
Dress, advice about . . .	10
EASTERN townships . . .	98
,, ,, easy access to markets	98
Emigrants, inducements to .	36
,,. protection to . .	102

PAGE

Emigrants, notice to . . . 103
     ,,   agents, list of . . 103
Emigration, diminution of, ac-
          counted for . 173
     ,,   Report of Select
          Committee on . . . 197
Exports and imports . . . 124

FARM operations, diary of . . 181
Feudal tenure, abolition of . 119
Field notes, how made . . 196
Fisheries, Lower Canada . . 98
     ,,   Upper Canada . . 99
Flax and hemp, culture of . 136
Free goods 125
Free grants 96
     ,,   conditions of ob-
          taining 96
     ,,   direct and colla-
          teral advantages of . 178
     ,,   results of . . . 179
Free ports 87
Fruits and flowers 14

GALT, Honourable A. T., ex-
     tracts from pamphlet of 86
Game, list of 191
Goods, exports, imports, and
     duties on 126
Grains, standard weight of . 200

HARVEST prospects . . . 125
Hedge-rows, want of . . . 164
Home, adornment of . . . 13
House, choosing site for . . 33
Husbands and fathers, address
     to 1
Hutton's, Mr., pamphlet . . 141

PAGE

ILLINOIS and Canada compared 141
     ,,   comparative cost of
          farming in . . . 151
     ,,   inferior to Canada in
          all respects . . . 141
     ,,   district, American opi-
          nion of 171
     ,,   want of water, ague
          and fever in . . . 153
Imports and exports . . . 124
Indian summer 75
Indians, some anecdotes of . 165
Institutions, educational, cha-
          ritable, etc. etc. 121
     ,,   scientific, munici-
          pal 121

LAND agents, names of . . 106
Land jobbers, improvements
          retarded 163
     ,,   ,, , denounced .
Land, price of Government,
          much reduced . . 195
     ,,   regulations . . . 196
     ,,   value of 95
Lands for sale, where situated 106
Letters from Canada . . . 156
Log house, building and fur-
          nishing 18

MANUFACTORIES, lamentable
     want of 19
Manure from fish offal, enor-
     mous supply of . . . 190
Map, new, of Canada . . . 174
     „ free grant roads and
          blocks of land shown in 174
Minerals, list of . . 117, 190

	PAGE
Minerals, where found	114
Money, best mode of remitting	176
„ lent, undoubted security for	176
Months in Canada	49
OCCUPATION, choice of	11
Ottawa	203
Outfit required	47
POSTAGE, book	202
„ letter and newspaper	111
Prairie farming in Illinois	141
,, Caird's pamphlet on, admirably answered	141
„ „ fallacies of Caird's report thereon	193
QUALITY of land, how ascertained	80
Quarantine regulations	200
RECIPROCITY Act	176
Registration of deeds	160
„ how made available as security	160
Rent of farms in Canada	172
„ „ England and Canada compared	175
Rice, Indian	66
Roads, free grant, list of	96
Routes, rates of passage, etc.etc.	110
SAGUENAY, splendid fishing in	192
„ salmon rivers in, to be let	128

	PAGE
Salmon Fisheries of Lower Canada	128
„ „ where situate, and description of	129
„ „ regulations for their preservation	131
„ „ laws relating to	131
„ „ map of	131
Schools and churches	37
Securities for money lent	159
Seed time and harvest	180
Servants, duties of	7
Servants, female, much wanted, etc.	10
Settlement, former and present, contrasted	16
Settlement, new, description of	28
Sheep and wool	139
Soil, capabilities of	94
Sporting in Canada	191
Statistics, commercial	101
Sterling and currency, tables to calculate	113
Sugar-making	61
Surveyed lands, where situate	196
TAXATION, direct and indirect, all low	123, 175
Temperance, its great importance	22
Temperature, table of mean, monthly and annual	93
Timber, what kinds exported, where grown	155
Tolls, abolition of canal	87
Trade and revenue	99
Trees of Canada, a list of	78
„ localities in which found	155

x CONTENTS.

PAGE

VALUE of land 26, 95
Vessel, choice of 24
Vines, culture of 68
Voyage, etc., etc., preparations
    for 39, 45

WAGES, mechanics' . . . 104
Wild land, clearing of . . 32

PAGE

Wives and daughters, address to 2
Woods, natural productions of 34
Working class, wives of the,
    strangeness of their new
    duties 5

YANKEES and Canadians, best
    feeling between . . 176

INTRODUCTORY REMARKS.

BEFORE the master of the household fully decides upon taking so important a step as leaving his native land, to become a settler in Canada, let him first commune with himself and ask the important question, Have I sufficient energy of character to enable me to conform to the changes that may await me in my new mode of life ?—Let him next consider the capabilities of his partner—her health and general temper; for a sickly, peevish, discontented person will make but a poor settler's wife, in a country where cheerfulness of mind and activity of body are very essential to the prosperity of the household.

In Canada, persevering energy and industry, with sobriety, will overcome all obstacles, and in time will place the very poorest family in a position of substantial comfort that no personal exertions alone could have procured for them elsewhere.

To the indolent or to the intemperate man, Canada offers no such promise; but where is the country in which such a person will thrive or grow wealthy? He has not the elements of success within him.—It is in vain for such a one to cross the Atlantic; for he will bear with him that fatal enemy which kept him poor at home. The active, hardworking inhabitants who are earning their bread honestly by the sweat of their brow, or by the exertion of mental power, have no sympathy with such men. Canada is not the land for the idle sensualist. He must forsake the errors of his ways at once, or he will sink into ruin here as he would have done had he stayed in the old country. But it is not for such persons that our book is intended.

B

To Wives and Daughters.

As soon as the fitness of emigrating to Canada has been
fully decided upon, let the females of the family ask God's
blessing upon their undertaking; ever bearing in mind that
"unless the Lord build the house, their labour is but lost
that build it; unless the Lord keep the city, the watchman
waketh but in vain." In all their trials let them look to
Him who can bring all things to pass in His good time,
and who can guard them from every peril, if they will only
believe in His promises, and commit their ways to Him.

As soon, then, as the resolution to emigrate has been fixed,
let the females of the house make up their minds to take a
cheerful and active part in the work of preparation. Let
them at once cast aside all vain opposition and selfish regrets,
and hopefully look to their future country as to a land of
promise, soberly and quietly turning their attention to making the necessary arrangements for the important change that
is before them.

Let them remember that all practical knowledge is highly
valuable in the land to which they are going. An acquaintance with the homely art of baking and making bread—which
most servants and small housekeepers know how to practise,
but which many young females that live in large towns and
cities, where the baker supplies the bread to the family, do
not—is necessary to be acquired.

Cooking, curing meat, making butter and cheese, knitting,
dressmaking and tailoring—for most of the country people
here make the every-day clothing of their husbands, brothers
or sons—are good to be learned. By ripping to pieces any
well-fitting old garment, a suitable pattern may be obtained
of men's clothes; and many a fair hand I have seen occupied
in making garments of this description. For a quarter of a
dollar, 1s. 3d., a tailor will cut out a pair of fine cloth trousers;
for a coat they charge more; but a good cloth is always
better to have made up by a regular tailor: loose summer
coats may be made at home, but may be bought cheap, ready-
made, in the stores.

My female friends must bear in mind that it is one of the
settler's great objects to make as little outlay of money as
possible. I allude to such as come out to Canada with very
little available capital, excepting what arises from the actual

labour of their own hands, by which they must realize the means of paying for their land or the rental of a farm. Everything that is done in the house, by the hands of the family, is so much saved or so much earned towards the paying for the land, or building houses and barns, buying stock, or carrying on the necessary improvements on the place : the sooner this great object is accomplished, the sooner will the settler and his family realize the comfort of feeling themselves independent.

The necessity of becoming acquainted with the common branches of household work may not at first be quite agreeable to such as have been unaccustomed to take an active part in the duties of the house. Though their position in society may have been such as to exempt them from what they consider menial occupations, still they will be wise to lay aside their pride and refinement, and apply themselves practically to the acquirement of such useful matters as those I have named—if they are destined to a life in a colony —even though their friends may be so well off as to have it in their power to keep servants, and live in ease and comfort. But if they live in a country place, they may be left without the assistance of a female servant in the house, a contingency which has often happened from sudden illness, a servant's parents sending for her home, which they will often do without consulting either your convenience or their daughter's wishes ; or some act on the part of the servant may induce her to be discharged before her place can be filled : in such an emergency the settler's wife may find herself greatly at a loss, without some knowledge of what her family requires at her hands. I have before now seen a ragged Irish boy called in from the clearing by his lady-mistress, to assist her in the mystery of making a loaf of bread, and teaching her how to bake it in the bake-kettle. She had all the requisite materials, but was ignorant of the simple practical art of making bread.

Another who knew quite well how to make a loaf and bake it too, yet knew nothing of the art of making yeast to raise it with ; and so the family lived upon unleavened cakes, or dampers, as the Australians call them, till they were heartily tired of them : at last a settler's wife calling in to rest herself, and seeing the flat cakes baking, asked the servant why they did not make raised bread : " Because we have no yeast, and do not know how to make any here in these horrible back woods," was the girl's reply. The neighbour, I dare say

B 2

was astonished at the ignorance of both mistress and maid; but she gave them some hops and a little barm, and told the girl how to make the yeast called hop-rising; and this valuable piece of knowledge stood them in good stead : from that time they were able to make light bread; the girl shrewdly remarking to her mistress, that a little help was worth a deal of pity. A few simple directions for making barm as it is here practised, would have obviated the difficulty at first.   As this is one of the very first things that the housewife has to attend to in the cooking department, I have placed the raising and making of bread at the beginning of the work. The making and baking of REALLY GOOD HOUSEHOLD BREAD is a thing of the greatest consequence to the health and comfort of a family.

As the young learn more quickly than the old, I would advise the daughters of the intending emigrant to acquire whatever useful arts they think likely to prove serviceable to them in their new country. Instead of suffering a false pride to stand in their way of acquiring practical household knowledge, let it be their pride—their noble, honest pride—to fit themselves for the state which they will be called upon to fill —a part in the active drama of life; to put in practice that which they learned to repeat with their lips in childhood as a portion of the Catechism, " To do my duty in that state of life, unto which it may please God to call me." Let them earnestly believe that it is by the will of God that they are called to share the fortunes of their parents in the land they have chosen, and that, as that is the state of life they are called to by his will, they are bound to strive to do their duty in it with cheerfulness.

There should therefore be no wavering on their part; no yielding to prejudices and pride. Old things are passed away. The greatest heroine in life is she who, knowing her duty, resolves not only to do it, but to do it to the best of her abilities, with heart and mind bent upon the work.

I address this passage more especially to the daughters of the emigrant, for to them belongs the task of cheering and upholding their mother in the trials that may await her. It is often in consideration of the future welfare of their children, that the parents are, after many painful struggles, induced to quit the land of their birth, and the home that was endeared to them alike by their cares and their joys; and though the children may not know this to be the main-spring that urges them to make the sacrifice, in most cases it is so; and this consideration should have its full weight, and induce the children to do all in their power to repay their parents for the love that urges them to such a decision.

The young learn to conform more readily to change of country than the old. Novelty has for them a great charm : and then hope is more lively in the young heart than in the old. To them a field of healthy enterprise is open, which they have only to enter upon with a cheerful heart and plenty of determination, and they will hardly fail of reaching a respectable state of independence.

The wives and daughters of the small farmers and of the working class should feel the difficulties of a settler's life far less keenly than any other, as their habits and general knowledge of rural affairs have fitted them for the active labours that may fall to their lot in Canada. Though much that they have to perform will be new to them, it will only be the manner of doing it, and the difference of some of the materials that they will have to make use of : inured from childhood to toil, they may soon learn to conform to their change of life. The position of servants is much improved in one respect : their services are more valuable in a country where there is less competition among the working class. They can soon save enough to be independent. They have the cheering prospect always before them :—It depends upon ourselves to better our own condition. In this country honest industry always commands respect : by it we can in time raise ourselves, and no one can keep us down.

Yet I have observed with much surprise that there is no class of emigrants more discontented than the wives and daughters of those men who were accustomed to earn their bread by the severest toil, in which they too were by necessity obliged to share, often with patience and cheerfulness under privations the most heartbreaking, with no hope of amendment, no refuge but the grave from poverty and all its miseries. Surely to persons thus situated, the change of country should be regarded with hopeful feelings ; seeing that it opens a gate which leads from poverty to independence, from present misery to future comfort.

At first the strangeness of all things around them, the loss of familiar faces and familiar objects, and the want of all their little household conveniences, are sensibly felt ; and these things make them uncomfortable and peevish : but a little reasoning with themselves would show that such inconveniences belong to the nature of their new position,

and that a little time will do away with the evil they complain of.

After a while new feelings, new attachments to persons and
things, come to fill up the void : they begin to take an interest
in the new duties that are before them, and by degrees conform to the change; and an era in their lives commences,
which is the beginning to them of a better and more prosperous state of things.

It frequently happens that before the poor emigrant can
settle upon land of his own, he is obliged to send the older
children out to service. Perhaps he gets employment for
himself and his wife on some farm, where they can manage
to keep the younger members of the family with them, if
there is a small house or shanty convenient, on or near the
farm on which they are hired. Sometimes a farmer can
get a small farm on shares; but it is seldom a satisfactory
mode of rental, and often ends in disagreement. As no
man can serve two masters, neither can one farm support
two, unless both parties are, which rarely happens, quite
disinterested, and free from selfishness, each exacting no
more than his due. It is seldom these partnerships turn
out well.

There is an error which female servants are very apt to fall
into in this country, which, as a true friend, I would guard
them against committing. This is adopting a free and easy
manner, often bordering upon impertinence, towards their
employers. They are apt to think that because they are
entitled to a higher rate of wages, they are not bound to
render their mistresses the same respect of manners as was
usual in the old country. Now, as they receive more, they
ought not to be less thankful to those who pay them well, and
should be equally zealous in doing their duty. They should
bear in mind that they are commanded to render " honour to
whom honour is due." A female servant in Canada, whose
manners are respectful and well-behaved, will always be
treated with consideration and even with affection. After all,
good-breeding is as charming a trait in a servant as it is in a
lady. Were there more of that kindly feeling existing
between the upper and lower classes, both parties would be
benefited, and a bond of union established, which would
extend beyond the duration of a few months or a few years,
and be continued through life : how much more satisfactory
than that unloving strife where the mistress is haughty and
the servant insolent.

But while I would recommend respect and obedience on the part of the servant, to her employer I would say, treat your servant with consideration: if you respect her she will also respect you; if she does her duty, she is inferior to no one living as a member of the great human family. The same Lord who says by the mouth of his apostle, "Servants obey your masters," has also added, "and ye masters do ye also the same, forbearing threatening; knowing that your master also is in heaven, and that with him there is no respect of persons."

Your servants, as long as they are with you, are of your household, and should be so treated that they should learn to look up to you in love as well as reverence.

If they are new comers to Canada, they have everything to learn; and will of course feel strange and awkward to the ways of the colony, and require to be patiently dealt with. They may have their regrets and sorrows yet rankling in their hearts for those dear friends they have left behind them, and require kindness and sympathy. Remember that you also are a stranger and sojourner in a strange land, and should feel for them and bear with them as becomes Christians.

Servants in Canada are seldom hired excepting by the month;—the female servant by the full calendar month: the men and boys' month is four weeks only. From three to four dollars a month is the usual wages given to female servants; and two, and two dollars and a half to girls of fourteen and sixteen years of age, unless they are very small, and very ignorant of the work of the country; then less is given. Indeed, if a young girl were to give her services for a month or two, with a good clever mistress, for her board alone, she would be the gainer by the bargain, in the useful knowledge which she would acquire, and which would enable her to take a better place, and command higher wages. It is a common error in girls coming direct from the old country, and who have all Canada's ways to learn, to ask the highest rate of wages, expecting the same as those who are twice as efficient. This is not reasonable; and if the demand be yielded to from necessity, there is seldom much satisfaction or harmony, both parties being respectively discontented with the other. The one gives too much, the other does too little in return for high wages.

Very little if any alteration has taken place nominally in the rate of servants' wages during twenty-one years that I have lived in Canada, but a great increase in point of fact.* Twenty years ago the servant-girl gave from 1s. 6d. to 2s. 6d. a yard for cotton prints, 10s. and 12s. a pair for very coarse shoes and boots: common white calico was 1s. and 1s. 3d. per yard, and other articles of clothing in proportion. Now she can buy good fast prints at 9d. and 10d., and some as low as 7½d. and 8d. per yard, calicoes and factory cottons from 4½d. to 9d. or 10d.; shoes, light American-made, and very pretty, from 4s. 6d. to 7s. 6d., and those made to order 6s. 3d. to 7s. 6d.; boots 10s.; straw bonnets from 1s. 6d., coarse beehive plat, to such as are very tasteful and elegant in shape and quality, of the most delicate fancy chips and straws, proportionably cheap.

Thus while her wages remain the same, her outlay is decreased nearly one half.

Ribbons and light fancy goods are still much higher in price than they are in the old country; so are stuffs and merinos. A very poor, thin Coburg cloth, or Orleans, fetches 1s. or 1s. 3d. per yard; mousselin de laines vary from 9d. to 1s. 6d. Probably the time will come when woollen goods will be manufactured in the colony; but the time for that is not yet at hand. The country flannel, home-spun, home-dyed, and sometimes home-woven, is the sort of material worn in the house by the farmer's family when at work. Nothing can be more suitable to the climate, and the labours of a Canadian settler's wife or daughter, than gowns made of this country-flannel: it is very durable, lasting often two or three seasons. When worn out as a decent working dress, it makes good sleigh-quilts for travelling, or can be cut up into rag-carpets, for a description of which see the article—*Rag-Carpets :* and for instructions in dyeing the wool or yarn for the flannel see *Dyeing.* I have been thus minute in naming the prices of women's wearing apparel, that the careful wife may be enabled to calculate the expediency of purchasing a stock of clothes, before leaving home, or waiting till she arrives in Canada, to make her needful purchases. To such as can prudently spare a small sum for buying clothes, I may point out a few purchases that would be made more advantageously in England or Scotland than in Canada: 1st. A stock, say two pairs a piece for each person, of good shoes.—The leather here is not nearly so durable as what is prepared at

* Since the above statement was written the wages both of men and women have borne a higher rate; and some articles of clothing have been raised in price. See the tables of rates of wages and goods for 1860.

home, and consequently the shoes wear out much sooner, where the roads are rough and the work hard. No one need encumber themselves with clogs or pattens: the rough roads render them worse than useless, even dangerous, in the spring and fall, the only wet seasons: in winter the snow clogs them up, and you could not walk ten yards in them; and in summer there is no need of them: buy shoes instead; or, for winter wear, a good pair of duffle boots, the sole overlaid with india-rubber or gutta-percha.

India-rubber boots and over-shoes can be bought from 4s. to 7s. 6d., if extra good, and lined with fur or fine flannel. Gentlemen's boots, long or short, can be had also, but I do not know at what cost. Old women's list shoes are good for the house in the snowy season, or good, strongly-made carpet shoes; but these last, with a little ingenuity, you can make for yourself.

Flannel I also recommend, as an advisable purchase: you must give from 1s. 9d. to 2s. 6d. for either white or red, and a still higher price for fine fabrics; which I know is much higher than they can be bought for at home. Good scarlet or blue flannel shirts are worn by all the emigrants that work on land or at trades in Canada; and even through the hottest summer weather the men still prefer them to cotton or linen.

A superior quality, twilled and of some delicate check, as pale blue, pink, or green, are much the fashion among the gentlemen: this material, however, is more costly, and can hardly be bought under 3s. 6d. or 4s. a yard. A sort of over-shirt made full and belted in at the waist, is frequently worn, made of homespun flannel, dyed brown or blue, and looks neat and comfortable; others of coarse brown linen, or canvas, called logging-shirts, are adopted by the choppers in their rough work of clearing up the fallows: these are not very unlike the short loose slop frocks of the peasants of the Eastern Counties of England, reaching no lower than the hips.

Merino or cottage stuffs are also good to bring out, also Scotch plaids and tweeds, strong checks for aprons, and fine white cotton stockings: those who wear silk, had better bring a supply for holiday wear: satin shoes are very high, but are only needed by the wealthy, or those ladies who expect to live in some of the larger towns or cities; but the farmer's wife in Canada has little need of such luxuries—they are out of place and keeping.

ON DRESS.

It is one of the blessings of this new country, that a young person's respectability does by no means depend upon these points of style in dress; and many a pleasant little evening dance I have seen, where the young ladies wore merino frocks, cut high or low, and prunella shoes, and no disparaging remarks were made by any of the party. How much more sensible I thought these young people, than if they had made themselves slaves to the tyrant fashion. Nevertheless, in some of the large towns the young people do dress extravagantly, and even exceed those of Britain in their devotion to fine and costly apparel. The folly of this is apparent to every sensible person. When I hear women talk of nothing but dress, I cannot help thinking that it is because they have nothing more interesting to talk about; that their minds are uninformed, and bare, while their bodies are clothed with purple and fine linen. To dress neatly and with taste and even elegance is an accomplishment which I should desire to see practised by all females; but to make dress the one engrossing business and thought of life is vain and foolish. One thing is certain, that a lady will be a lady, even in the plainest dress; a vulgar-minded woman will never be a lady, in the most costly garments. Good sense is as much marked by the style of a person's dress, as by their conversation. The servant-girl who expends half her wages on a costly shawl, or mantilla, and bonnet, to wear over a fine shabby gown, or with coarse shoes and stockings, does not show as much sense as she who purchases at less cost a complete dress, each article suited to the other. They both attract attention, it is true; but in a different degree. The man of sense will notice the one for her wisdom; the other for her folly. To plead fashion, is like following a multitude to do evil.

CANADA A FIELD FOR YOUNGER WORKING FEMALES.

Quitting the subject of dress, which perhaps I have dwelt too long upon, I will go to a subject of more importance: the field which Canada opens for the employment of the younger female emigrants of the working class. At this very minute I was assured by one of the best and most intelligent of our farmers, that the township of Hamilton alone could give immediate employment to five hundred females; and most other townships in the same degree. What an inducement to young girls to emigrate is this! good wages, in a healthy and improving country; and what is better, in one where idleness and immorality are not the characteristics of the inhabitants: where steady industry is sure to be rewarded by marriage with young men who are able to place their wives in a very different station from that of servitude. How many young women, who were formerly servants in my house, are now farmers' wives, going to church or the market-towns with their own sleighs or light waggons, and, in point of dress, better clothed than myself!

Though Australia may offer the temptation of greater wages to female servants; yet the discomforts they are exposed to must be a great drawbreak; and the immoral, disjointed state of domestic life, for decent, well-conducted young women, I should think, would more than counterbalance the nominal advantages from greater wages. The industrious, sober-minded labourer, with a numerous family of daughters, one would imagine, would rather bring them to Canada, where they can get immediate employment in respectable families; where they will get good wages and have every chance of bettering their condition and rising in the world, by becoming the wives of thriving farmers' sons or industrious artizans; than form connexions with such characters as swarm the streets of Melbourne and Geelong, though these may be able to fill their hands with gold, and clothe them with satin and velvet.

In the one country there is a steady progress to prosperity and lasting comfort, where they may see their children become land-owners after them, while in the other, there is little real stability, and small prospect of a life of domestic happiness to look forward to. I might say, as the great lawgiver said to the Israelites, "Good and evil are before you, choose ye between them."

Those whose destination is intended to be in the Canadian towns will find little difference in regard to their personal comforts to what they were accustomed to enjoy at home. If they have capital they can employ it to advantage; if they are mechanics, or artizans, they will have little difficulty in obtaining employment as journeymen. The stores in Canada are well furnished with every species of goods: groceries, hardware, and food of all kinds can also be obtained. With health and industry, they will have little real cause of complaint. It is those who go into the woods and into distant settlements in the uncleared wilderness that need have any fear of encountering hardships and privations; and such persons should carefully consider their own qualifications, and those of their wives and children, before they decide upon embarking in the laborious occupation of backwoodsmen in a new country like Canada. Strong, patient, enduring, hopeful men and women, able to bear hardships and any amount of bodily toil, (and there are many such,) these may be pioneers to open out the forest-lands; while the old-country farmer will find it much better to purchase cleared farms, or farms that are partially cleared, in improving townships, where there are villages and markets and good roads: by so doing they will escape much of the disappointment and loss, as well as the bodily hardships that are too often the lot of those who go back into the unreclaimed forest lands.

Whatever be the determination of the intended emigrant, let him not exclude from his entire confidence the wife of his bosom, the natural sharer of his fortunes, be the path which leads to them rough or smooth. She ought not to be dragged as an unwilling sacrifice at the shrine of duty from home, kindred, and friends, without her full consent: the difficulties as well as the apparent advantages, ought to be laid candidly before her, and her advice and opinion asked; or how can she be expected to enter heart and soul into her husband's hopes and plans? Nor should such of the children as are capable of forming opinions on the subject be shut out from the family council; for let parents bear this fact in mind, that much of their own future prosperity will depend upon the exertion of their children in the land to which they are going; and also let them consider that those children's lot in life is involved in the important decision they are about to make. Let perfect confidence be established in the family: it will avoid much future domestic misery and unavailing repining. —Family union is like the key-stone of an arch: it keeps all the rest of the building from falling asunder. A man's friends should be those of his own household.

Woman, whose nature is to love home and to cling to all home ties and associations, cannot be torn from that spot that is the little centre of joy and peace and comfort to her, without many painful regrets. No matter however poor she may be, how low her lot in life may be cast, home to her is dear, the thought of it and the love of it clings closely to her wherever she goes. The remembrance of it never leaves her: it is graven on her heart. Her thoughts wander back to it across the broad waters of the ocean that are bearing her far from it. In the new land it is still present to her mental eye, and years after she has formed another home for herself she can still recall the bowery lane, the daisied meadow, the moss-grown well, the simple hawthorn hedge that bound the garden-plot, the woodbine porch, the thatched roof and narrow casement window of her early home. She hears the singing of the birds, the murmuring of the bees, the tinkling of the rill, and busy hum of cheerful labour from the village or the farm, when those beside her can hear only the deep cadence of the wind among the lofty forest-trees, the jangling of the cattle-bells, or strokes of the chopper's axe in the woods. As the seasons return she thinks of the flowers that she loved in childhood; the pale primrose, the cowslip and the bluebell, with the humble daisy and heath-flowers; and what would she not give for one, *just one* of those old familiar flowers! No wonder that the heart of the emigrant's wife is sometimes sad, and needs to be dealt gently with by her less sensitive partner; who if she were less devoted to home, would hardly love her more, for in this attachment to home lies much of her charm as a wife and mother in his eyes. But kindness and sympathy, which she has need of, in time reconciles her to her change of life; new ties, new interests, new comforts arise; and she ceases to repine, if she does not cease to love, that which she has lost: in after life the recollection comes like some pleasant dream or a fair picture to her mind, but she has ceased to grieve or to regret; and perhaps like a wise woman she says—"All things are for the best. It is good for us to be here."

ADORNMENT OF HOME.

What effect should this love of her old home produce in the emigrant-wife? Surely an earnest endeavour to render her new dwelling equally charming; to adorn it within and without as much as circumstances will permit, not expending her husband's means in the purchase of costly furniture which would be out of keeping in a log-house, but adopting such things as are suitable, neat, and simple; studying comfort and convenience before show and finery. Many inconveniences must be expected at the outset; but the industrious female will endeavour to supply these wants by the exercise of a little ingenuity and taste. It is a great mistake to neglect those little household adornments which will give a look of cheerfulness to the very humblest home.

Nothing contributes so much to comfort and to the outward appearance of a Canadian house as the erection of the verandah, or stoup, as the Dutch settlers call it, round the building. It affords a grateful shade from the summer heat, a shelter from the cold, and is a source of cleanliness to the interior. It gives a pretty, rural look to the poorest log-house, and as it can be put up with little expense, it should never be omitted. A few unbarked cedar posts, with a slab or shingled roof, costs very little. The floor should be of plank; but even with a hard dry earthen floor, swept every day with an Indian broom, it will still prove a great comfort. Those who build frame or stone or brick houses seldom neglect the addition of a verandah: to the common log-house it is equally desirable; nor need any one want for climbers with which to adorn the pillars.

SHADE PLANTS.

Among the wild plants of Canada there are many graceful climbers, which are to be found in almost every locality. Nature, as if to invite you to ornament your cottage-homes, has kindly provided so many varieties of shade-plants, that you may choose at will.

First, then, I will point out to your attention the wild grape, which is to be found luxuriating in every swamp, near the margin of lakes and rivers, wreathing the trees and tall bushes with its abundant foliage and purple clusters. The fox-grape and the frost-grape * are among the common wild varieties, and will produce a great quantity of fruit, which, though very acid, is far from being unpalatable when cooked with a sufficiency of sugar.

From the wild grape a fine jelly can be made by pressing the juice from the husks and seeds, and boiling it with the proportion of sugar usual in making currant-jelly, i.e., one pound of sugar to one pint of juice. An excellent home-made wine can also be manufactured from these grapes. They are not ripe till the middle of October, and should not be gathered till the frost has softened them; from this circumstance, no doubt, the name of frost-grape has been given to one species. The wild vine planted at the foot of some dead and unsightly tree, will cover it with its luxuriant growth, and convert that

* There are many other varieties of wild grapes, some of which have, by careful garden cultivation, been greatly improved. Cuttings may be made early in April, or the young vines planted in September or October.

which would otherwise have been an unseemly object into one of great ornament. I knew a gentleman who caused a small dead tree to be cut down and planted near a big oak stump in his garden, round which a young grape was twining : the vine soon ascended the dead tree, covering every branch and twig,. and forming a bower above the stump, and affording an abundant crop of fruit.

The commonest climber for a log-house is the hop, which is, as you will find, an indispensable plant in a Canadian garden, it being the principal ingredient in making the yeast with which the household bread is raised. Planted near the pillars of your verandah, it forms a graceful drapery of leaves and flowers, which are pleasing to look upon, and valuable either for use or sale.

The Canadian ivy, or Virginian creeper, is another charming climber, which if planted near the walls of your house, will quickly cover the rough logs with its dark glossy leaves in summer, and in the fall delight the eye with its gorgeous crimson tints.

The wild clematis or traveller's joy may be found growing in the beaver meadows and other open thickets. This also is most ornamental as a shade-plant for a verandah. Then there is the climbing fumatory, better known by the name by which its seeds are sold by the gardener, "cypress vine." This elegant creeper is a native of Canada, and may be seen in old neglected clearings near the water, running up the stems of trees and flinging its graceful tendrils and leaves of tender green over the old grey mossy branches of cedar or pine, adorning the hoary boughs with garlands of the loveliest pink flowers. I have seen this climbing fumatory in great quantities in the woods, but found it no easy matter to obtain the ripe seeds, unless purchased from a seedsman : it is much cultivated in towns as a shade-plant near the verandahs.

Besides those already described I may here mention the scarlet-runner, a flower the humming-birds love to visit ; the wild cucumber, a very graceful trailing plant ; the major convolvulus or morning glory ; the wild honeysuckle, sweet-pea and prairie-rose: These last-named are not natives, with the exception of the wild or bush honeysuckle, which is to be found in the forest. The flowers are pale red, but scentless ; nevertheless it is very well worth cultivating.

I am the more particular in pointing out to you how you may improve the outside of your dwellings, because the log-house is rough and unsightly; and I know well that your

comfort and cheerfulness of mind will be increased by the care
you are led to bestow upon your new home in endeavouring to
ornament it and render it more agreeable to the eye. The
cultivation of a few flowers, of vegetables and fruit, will be a
source of continual pleasure and interest to yourself and
children, and you will soon learn to love your home, and cease
to regret that dear one you have left.

I write from my own experience. I too have felt all the
painful regrets incidental to a long separation from my native
land and my beloved early home. I have experienced all
that you who read this book can ever feel, and perhaps far
more than you will ever have cause for feeling.

Contrast now to Period of, Early Settlement.

The emigrants of the present day can hardly now meet with
the trials and hardships that were the lot of those who came
to the province twenty years ago, and these last infinitely less
than those who preceded them at a still earlier period.

When I listen, as I often do, to the experiences of the old
settlers of forty or fifty years' standing, at a time when the
backwoodsman shared the almost unbroken wilderness with the
unchristianized Indian, the wolf, and the bear; when his seed-
corn had to be carried a distance of thirty miles upon his
shoulders, and his family were dependent upon the game and
fish that he brought home till the time of the harvest : when
there were no mills to grind his flour save the little handmill,
which kept the children busy to obtain enough coarse flour to
make bread from day to day ; when no Sabbath-bell was ever
heard to mark the holy day, and all was lonely, wild, and
savage around him :—then my own first trials seemed to sink
into utter insignificance, and I was almost ashamed to think
how severely they had been felt.

Many a tale of trial and of enterprise I have listened to with
breathless interest, related by these patriarchs of the colony,
while seated beside the blazing log-fire, surrounded by the
comforts which they had won for their children by every
species of toil and privation. Yet they too had overcome the
hardships incidental to a first settlement, and were at rest, and
could look back on their former struggles with that sort of
pride which is felt by the war-worn soldier in fighting over
again his battles by his own peaceful hearth.

These old settlers and their children have seen the whole
face of the country changed. They have seen the forest dis-

appear before the axe of the industrious emigrant; they have seen towns and villages spring up where the bear and the wolf had their lair. They have seen the white-sailed vessel and the steamer plough those lakes and rivers where the solitary Indian silently glided over their lonely waters in his frail canoe. They have seen highways opened out through impenetrable swamps where human foot however adventurous had never trod. The busy mill-wheels have dashed where only the foaming rocks broke the onward flow of the forest stream. They have seen God's holy temples rise, pointing upwards with their glittering spires above the lowlier habitations of men, and have heard the Sabbath-bell calling the Christian worshippers to pray. They have seen the savage Indian bending there in mute reverence, or lifting his voice in hymns of praise to that blessed Redeemer who had called him out of darkness into his marvellous light. And stranger things he may now behold in that mysterious wire, that now conveys a whispered message from one end of the province to the other with lightning swiftness; and see the iron railway already traversing the province, and bringing the far-off produce of the woods to the store of the merchant and to the city mart.

Such are the changes which the old settler has witnessed; and I have noted them for your encouragement and satisfaction, and that you may form some little notion of what is going on in this comparatively newly-settled country; and that you may form some idea of what it is likely to become in the course of a few more years, when its commerce and agriculture, and its population shall have increased, and its internal resources shall have been more perfectly developed.

In the long-settled portions of the province a traveller may almost imagine that he is in England: there are no stumps to disfigure the fields, and but very few of the old log-houses remaining: these have for the most part given place to neat painted frame, brick or stone cottages, surrounded with orchards, cornfields and pastures. Some peculiarities he will notice, which will strike him as unlike what he has been used to see in the old country; and there are old familiar objects which will be missed in the landscape, such as the venerable gray tower of the old church, the ancient ruins, the old castles and fine old manor-houses, with many other things which exist in the old country. Here all is new; time has not yet laid its mellowing touch upon the land. We are but in our infancy; but it is a vigorous and healthy one, full of promise for future greatness and strength.

c

FURNISHING LOG-HOUSE.

In furnishing a Canadian log-house, the main study should be to unite simplicity with cheapness and comfort. It would be strangely out of character to introduce gay, showy, or rich and costly articles of furniture into so rough and homely a dwelling. A log-house is better to be simply furnished. Those who begin with moderation are more likely to be able to increase their comforts in the course of a few years.

Let us see now what can be done towards making your log parlour comfortable at a small cost. A dozen of painted Canadian chairs, such as are in common use here, will cost you 2l. 10s. You can get plainer ones for 2s. 9d. or 3s. a chair; of course you may get very excellent articles if you give a higher price; but we are not going to buy drawing-room furniture. You can buy rocking chairs, small at 7s. 6d.; large, with elbows, 15s.: you can cushion them yourself. A good drugget, which I would advise you to bring with you, or Scotch carpet, will cover your rough floor; when you lay it down, spread straw or hay over the boards; this will save your carpet from cutting. A stained pine table may be had for 12s. or 15s. Walnut or cherry wood cost more; but the pine with a nice cover will answer at first. For a flowered mohair you must give five or six dollars. A piece of chintz of suitable pattern will cost you 16s., the piece of twenty-eight yards. This will curtain your windows: and a common pine sofa stuffed with wool, though many use fine hay for the back and sides, can be bought cheap, if covered by your own hands. If your husband or elder sons are at all skilled in the use of tools, they can make out of common pine boards the frame-work of couches, or sofas, which look, when covered and stuffed, as well as what the cabinet-maker will charge several pounds for. A common box or two stuffed so as to form a cushion on the top, and finished with a flounce of chintz, will fill the recess of the windows. A set of book-shelves stained with Spanish brown, to hold your library.—A set of corner shelves, fitted into the angles of the room, one above the other, diminishing in size, form an useful receptacle for any little ornamental matters, or for flowers in the summer, and gives a pleasant finish and an air of taste to the room. A few prints, or pictures, in frames of oak or black walnut, should not be omitted, if you can bring such ornaments with you. These things are sources of pleasure to yourselves, and of interest to others. They are intellectual luxuries, that even the very poorest man regards with delight, and possesses if he can, to adorn his cottage walls, however lowly that cottage may be.

I am going to add another comfort to your little parlour—a clock : very neat dials in cherry or oak frames, may be bought from 7s. 6d. to 20s. The cheapest will keep *good time*, but do not strike. Very handsome clocks may be bought for ten dollars, in elegant frames ; but we must not be too extravagant in our notions.

I would recommend a good cooking-stove in your kitchen : it is more convenient, and is not so destructive to clothes as the great log fires. A stove large enough to cook food for a family of ten or twelve persons, will cost from twenty to thirty dollars. This will include every necessary cooking utensil. Cheap stoves are often like other cheap articles, the dearest in the end : a good, weighty casting should be preferred to a thinner and lighter one ; though the latter will look just as good as the former : they are apt to crack, and the inner plates wear out soon.

There are now a greater variety of patterns in cooking-stoves, many of which I know to be good. I will mention a few :—' The Lion,' ' Farmers' Friend,' ' Burr,' ' Canadian Hot-Air, ' Clinton Hot-Air ;' these two last require dry wood ; and the common ' Premium ' stove, which is a good useful stove, but seldom a good casting, and sold at a low price. If you buy a small-sized stove, you will not be able to bake a good joint of meat or good-sized loaves of bread in it.

If you have a chimney, and prefer relying on cooking with the bake-kettle, I would also recommend a roaster, or bachelor's oven : this will cost only a few shillings, and prove a great convenience, as you can bake rolls, cakes, pies, and meat in it. An outside oven, built of stones, bricks, or clay, is put up at small cost, and is a great comfort.* The heating it once or twice a week, will save you much work, and you will enjoy bread much better and sweeter than any baked in a stove, oven, or bake-kettle.

Many persons who have large houses of stone or brick, now adopt the plan of heating them with hot air, which is conveyed by means of p pes into the rooms. An ornamented, circular grating admits the heated air, by opening or shutting the grates. The furnace is in the cellar, and is made large

* Two men, or a man and a boy, will build a common-sized clay oven in a day or less, if they understand the work and prepare the materials beforehand.

enough to allow of a considerable quantity of wood being put
in at once.

A house thus heated is kept at summer heat in the coldest
weather; and can be made cooler by shutting the grates in
any room.

The temperature of houses heated thus is very pleasant,
and certainly does not seem so unhealthy as those warmed
by metal stoves, besides there being far less risk from fire.

Those who wish to enjoy the cheerful appearance of a fire
in their sitting-room, can have one; as little wood is required
in such case.

The poorer settlers, to whom the outlay of a dollar is often
an object, make very good washing-tubs out of old barrels, by
sawing one in half, leaving two of the staves a few inches
higher than the rest, for handles. Painted washing-tubs
made of pine, iron hooped, cost a dollar; painted water-pails
only 1s. 6d. a piece; but they are not very durable. Owing
to the dryness of the air, great care is requisite to keep your
tubs, barrels, and pails in proper order. Many a good vessel
of this kind is lost for want of a little attention.

The washing-tubs should be kept in the cellar, or with
water in them. Those who keep servants must not forget to
warn them of this fact.

In fitting up your house, do not sacrifice all comfort in the
kitchen, for the sake of a best room for receiving company.

If you wish to enjoy a cheerful room, by all means have a
fire-place in it. A blazing log-fire is an object that inspires
cheerfulness. A stove in the hall or passage is a great
comfort in winter ; and the pipe conducted rightly will warm
the upper rooms; but do not. let the stove supersede the
cheering fire in the sitting-room. Or if your house has been
built only. to be heated by stoves, choose one that, with a
grate in front, can be opened to show the fire. A handsome
parlour-stove can now be got for twelve dollars. Tanned and
dyed sheep-skins make excellent door-mats, and warm hearth-
rugs. With small outlay of money your room will thus be
comfortably furnished.

A delightful easy-chair can be made out of a very rough
material—nothing better than a common flour barrel. I will,
as well as I can, direct you how these barrel-chairs are made.
The first four or five staves of a good, sound, clean flour
barrel are to be sawn off, level, within two feet of the ground,
or higher, if you think that will be too low for the seat: th s
is for the front: leave the two staves on either side a few

inches higher for the elbows; the staves that remain are left to form the hollow back: auger holes are next made all round, on a level with the seat, in all the staves; through these holes ropes are passed and interlaced, so as to form a secure seat: a bit of thin board may then be nailed, flat, on the rough edge of the elbow staves, and a coarse covering, of linen or sacking, tacked on over the back and arms: this is stuffed with cotton-wool, soft hay, or sheep's wool, and then a chintz cover over the whole, and well-filled cushion for the seat, completes the chair. Two or three of such seats in a sitting-room, give it an air of great comfort at a small cost.

Those settlers who come out with sufficient means, and go at once on cleared farms, which is by far the best plan, will be able to purchase very handsome furniture of black walnut or cherry wood at moderate cost. Furniture, new and handsome, and even costly, is to be met with in any of the large towns; and it would be impertinent in me to offer advice as to the style to be observed by such persons: it is to the small farmer, and poorer class, that my hints are addressed.

The shanty, or small log-house of the poorer emigrant, is often entirely furnished by his own hands. A rude bedstead, formed of cedar poles, a coarse linen bag filled with hay or dried moss, and bolster of the same, is the bed he lies on; his seats are benches, nailed together; a table of deal boards, a few stools, a few shelves for the crockery and tinware; these are often all that the poor emigrant can call his own in the way of furniture. Little enough and rude enough. Yet let not the heart of the wife despond. It is only the first trial; better things are in store for her.

Many an officer's wife, and the wives of Scotch and English gentlemen, in the early state of the colony have been no better off.—Many a wealthy landowner in Canada was born in circumstances as unfavourable. Men who now occupy the highest situations in the country, have been brought up in a rude log-shanty, little better than an Indian wigwam. Let these things serve to cheer the heart and smooth the rough ways of the settler's first outset in Canadian life.—And let me add that now there is more facility for the incoming emigrant's settling with comfort, than there was twenty or thirty years ago; unless he goes very far back into the uncivilized portions of the country, he cannot now meet with the trials and privations that were the lot of the first settlers in the province. And there is no necessity for him to place himself

and family beyond the outskirts of civilization. Those who
have the command of a little capital can generally buy land
with some clearing and buildings; and the working man can
obtain good employment for his wife and elder girls or boys,
so as to enable them by their united savings, to get a lot of
land for themselves, to settle upon.   This is more prudent
than plunging at once into the bush, without possessing
the experience which is necessary for their future welfare,
almost for their very existence, in their new mode of life.
When they have earned a little money and some knowledge
of the ways of the country, they may then start fair, and
by industry and sobriety, in a few years become independent.

To pay for his land by instalments, is the only way a poor
man can manage to acquire property : to obtain his deed is
the height of his ambition : to compass this desirable end all
the energies of the household are directed.   For this the
husband, the wife, the sons and the daughters all toil : each
contributes his or her mite : for this they endure all sorts of
privations, without murmuring.   In a few years the battle is
won.   Poverty is no longer to be feared.

The land is their own : with what pride they now speak of
it ; with what honest delight they contemplate every blade of
wheat, every ear of corn, and the cattle that feed upon their
pastures !   No rent is now to be paid for it.   God has blessed
the labours of their hands.   Let them not forget that to Him
is the glory and praise due.

When they have acquired land and cattle, let them not in
the pride of their hearts say—" My hand and the power of my
arm has gotten me all these ;" for it is God that giveth the
increase in all these things.

On Temperance.

With habits of industry long practised, cheered by a
reasonable hope, and with experience gained, no one need
despair of obtaining all the essential comforts of life ; but
strict sobriety is indispensably necessary to the attainment of
his hopes.   Let not the drunkard flatter himself that success
will attend his exertions.   A curse is in the cup ; it lingers
in the dregs to embitter his own life and that of his hapless
partner and children.   As of the sluggard, so also may it be
said of the intemperate—" The *drunkard* shall starve in
harvest."   It is in vain for the women of the household to
work hard and to bear their part of the hardships incidental

to a settler's life, if the husband gives himself up as a slave to this miserable vice.

I dwell more earnestly upon this painful subject, because unfortunately the poison sold to the public under the name of whiskey, is so cheap, that for a few pence a man may degrade himself below the beasts that perish, and barter away his soul for that which profiteth not; bring shame and disgrace upon his name, and bitterness of heart into the bosom of his family. I have known sad instances of this abhorrent vice, even among the women; and they have justified themselves with saying—"We do it in self-defence, and because our husbands set us the example : it is in vain for us to strive and strive : for everything is going to ruin. Alas that such a plea should ever be made by a wife. Let the man remember that God has set him for the support of the wife : he is the head, and should set an example of virtue and strength, rather than of vice and weakness. Let both avoid this deadly sin, if they would prosper in life, and steadfastly resist the temptation that besets them on every side. And not to the poor man alone would I speak; for this evil habit pervades all classes; and many a young man of fair expectations is ruined by this indulgence, and many a flourishing home is made desolate by him who founded it. The last state of this man is worse than the first.

CHOICE OF A VESSEL.

Having determined on his future course, the next point is, the choice of a vessel in which to embark for Canada. Those persons who can afford to do so, will find better accommodations and more satisfaction in the steamers that ply between Liverpool, Glasgow, Plymouth, and Quebec, than in any of the emigrant sailing-ships. The latter may charge a smaller sum per head, but the difference in point of health, comfort, and respectability will more than make up for the difference of the charge. The usual terms are five or six pounds for grown persons ; but doubtless a reduction on this rate would be made, if a family were coming out. To reach the land of their adoption in health and comfort, is in itself a great step towards success. The commanders of this line of ships are all men of the highest respectability, and the poor emigrants need fear no unfair dealing, if they place themselves and family under their care. At any rate the greatest caution should be practised in ascertaining the character borne by the captains and owners of the vessels in which the emigrant is

about to embark: even the ship itself should have a character
for safety and good speed. Those persons who provide their
own sea-stores, had better consult some careful and experienced friend on the subject. There are many who are
better qualified than myself to afford them this valuable
information.

LUGGAGE.

As to furniture, and iron-ware, I would by no means advise
the emigrant to burden himself with such matters; for he
will find that by the time he reaches his port of destination,
the freightage, warehouse room, custom-house duties, and
injury that they have sustained in the transit, will have made
them dear bargains, besides not being as suitable to the
country as those things that are sold in the towns in Canada.
Good clothing and plenty of good shoes and boots, are your
best stores, and for personal luggage you will have no freight
to pay. A list of the contents of each box or trunk, being
put within the lid, and shown to the custom-house officer,
will save a great deal of unpacking and trouble. Any of
your friends sending out a box to you, by forwarding an
invoice and a low estimate of the value of the goods, the
address of the party, and the bill of lading, properly signed
by the captain to whose care it is assigned, to the forwarder
at Montreal, will save both delay and expense.

I now copy, for the instruction of the emigrant, the following advice which was published in the "Old Countryman,"
an excellent Toronto bi-weekly paper:

"EMIGRATION TO CANADA.—The arrangements made by the
Government of Canada for the reception and protection of
emigrants on their arrival at Quebec contrast in a remarkable
manner with the want of such arrangements at New York,
and the other ports of the United States, to which emigrants
are conveyed from Europe. On the arrival of each emigrant
ship in the river St. Lawrence, she is boarded by the medical
officer of the Emigrant Hospital at Grosse Isle, situated a few
miles below Quebec, and, whenever disease prevails in a ship,
the emigrants are landed, and remain at the hospital, at the
expense of the Colonial Government, until they are cured.—
On the ship's arrival at Quebec, Mr. Buchanan, the government agent of emigrants, proceeds at once on board, for it is
his duty to advise and protect each emigrant on his arrival,

He inquires into all complaints, and sees that the provisions
of the Passenger Act are strictly enforced. This he is enabled
to do in a most effectual manner, as under an arrangement
sanctioned by the Commissioners of Emigration in Great
Britain, whenever an emigrant vessel leaves any British port
for Quebec, the emigration officer of that port forwards to
Mr. Buchanan, by mail steamer, a duplicate list of her passengers, with their names, age, sex, trade, &c. This list is
usually received by him two or three weeks before the vessel
reaches Quebec, so that he is not only fully prepared for her
arrival, but is furnished with every particular which may be
useful to him in protecting the emigrants.—If just cause of
complaint exist, he institutes, under a very summary law of
the Province of Canada, legal proceedings against the master :
but so thoroughly are the value and efficiency of this officer
felt, that since a very short period subsequent to his appointment, it has very rarely been found necessary to take such
proceedings. In cases where emigrants have arrived without
sufficient funds to take them to places where employment is
abundant and remunerative, their fares have been paid by
Mr. Buchanan, out of the funds in his possession for the purpose. Emigrants from other than British ports experience
precisely the same protection at the hands of Mr. Buchanan."

" IMPORTANT TO EMIGRANTS.—The many fatal cases of cholera
which have taken place on board emigrant vessels, will
impress upon all who contemplate emigrating the propriety
of adopting the salutary precautions set down by orders of her
Majesty's Land and Emigration Commissioners, and widely
circulated by placard. These precautions state :—That the
sea-sickness, consequent on the rough weather which ships
must encounter at this season, joined to the cold and damp of
a sea-voyage, will render persons who are not very strong
more susceptible to the attacks of this disease.. To those who
may emigrate at this season, the Commissioners strongly
recommend that they should provide themselves with as much
warm clothing as they can, and especially with flannel, to be
worn next the skin ; that they should have both their clothes
and their persons quite clean before embarking, and should be
careful to do so during the voyage—and that they should
provide themselves with as much solid and wholesome food as
they can procure, in addition to the ship's allowance, to be
used on the voyage, and that it would, of course, be desirable,
if they can arrange it, that they should not go in a ship that
is much crowded, or that is not provided with a medical man.".

Owing to the rapid progress made in the province during the last few years in population, trade, agriculture and general improvement, lands have increased in value, and it now requires as many pounds to purchase a farm as formerly it cost dollars.

The growth of towns and villages, the making of roads, gravel, plank and now rail-roads; the building of bridges, the improvement of inland navigation, mills of all sorts, cloth factories, and the opportunities of attending public worship have, under a peaceful government, effected this change; and wise men will consider that the increased value of lands is a convincing proof of the flourishing condition of the people and the resources of the country, and feel encouraged by the prospect of a fair return for capital invested either in land or any other speculation connected with the merchandize of the country.

The crown lands to the Westward, in the newly surveyed counties, are selling at 12s. 6d. currency per acre. The soil is of great fertility : and to this portion of the province vast numbers are directing their steps.: certain that in a few years the value of these bush farms will be increased fourfold; but let none but the strong in arm and will go upon wild land. The giants of the forest are not brought down without much severe toil ; and many hardships must be endured in a back-woodsman's life, especially by the wife and children. If all pull together, and the women will be content to bear their part with cheerfulness, no doubt success will follow their honest endeavours.—But a wild farm is not to be made in one, two, or even five years.—The new soil will indeed yield her increase to a large amount, but it takes years to clear enough to make a really good farm, to get barns and sheds and fences and a comfortable dwelling-house : few persons accomplish all this under ten, fifteen and sometimes even twenty years. I am speaking now of the poor man, whose only capital is his labour and that of his family; and many a farmer who now rides to market or church in his own waggon and with his wife and children, well and even handsomely clad, by his side, has begun the world in Canada with no other capital. It is true his head has grown grey while these comforts were being earned, but he has no parish poor-house in the distance to look forward to as his last resource, or the bitter legacy of poverty to bequeath to his ʼfamishing children and broken-hearted widow. And with so fair a prospect for the future, wives and mothers will strive to bear with patience the trials and toils

which lead to so desirable an end, but let not the men rashly
and unadvisedly adopt the life of settlers in the Bush, without
carefully considering the advantages and disadvantages that
this mode of life offer over any other; next his own capabili-
tiés for successfully carrying it into effect, and also those of
his wife and family: if he be by nature indolent, and in
temper desponding, easily daunted by difficulties and of a
weak frame of body, such a life would not suit him. If his
wife be a weakly woman, destitute of mental energy, unable
to bear up under the trials of life, she is not fit for a life of
hardship—it will be useless cruelty to expose her to it. If
the children are very young and helpless, they can only increase the settler's difficulties, and render no assistance in the
work of clearing; but if on the contrary the man be of a hardy,
healthy, vigorous frame of body, and of a cheerful, hopeful
temper, with a kind partner, willing to aid both within doors
and without, the mother of healthy children, then there is
every chance that they will become prosperous settlers, an
honour to the country of their adoption. The sons and
daughters will be a help to them instead of a drawback, and
the more there are from six years old and upwards to lend a
hand in the work of clearing, the better for them: they will
soon be beyond the reach of poverty. It is such settlers as
these that Canada requires and will receive with joy. To all
such she bids a hearty welcome and God-speed; and I trust
the intelligent wives and daughters of such settlers may derive
some assistance in their household labours from the instruction
conveyed to them as well as to others in the pages of this book,
which is not intended to induce any one to emigrate to
Canada, but to instruct them in certain points of household
economy, that they may not have to learn as many have done,
by repeated failures and losses, the simple elements of Canadian housekeeping.

DESCRIPTION OF A NEW SETTLEMENT.

Extracted from Major Strickland's " Twenty-seven Years' Residence in Canada West."

" On the 16th of May, 1826, I moved up with all my goods and chattels, which were then easily packed into a single-horse waggon, and consisted of a plough-iron, six pails, a sugar-kettle, two iron pots, a frying-pan with a long handle, a tea-kettle, a few cups and saucers,* a chest of carpenter's tools, a Canadian axe, and a cross-cut saw.

" My stock of provisions comprised a parcel of groceries, half a barrel of pork, and a barrel of flour.

" The roads were so bad (in those days when there were no roads) that it took me three days to perform a journey of little more than fifty miles. [This was twenty-eight years ago, let it be remembered, when travelling was a matter of great difficulty.] We, that is my two labourers and myself, had numerous upsets, but reached at last the promised land.

" My friends in Douro turned out the next day and assisted me to put up the walls of my shanty and roof it with basswood troughs, and it was completed before dark. [This shanty was for a temporary shelter only, while working on the chopping, and preparing for the building of a good log-house.]

" I was kept busy for more than a week chinking between the logs, and plastering up all the crevices, cutting out the doorway and place for the window-casing, then making a door and hanging it on wooden hinges. I also made a rough table and some stools, which answered better than they looked.

" Four thick slabs of limestone placed upright in one corner of the shanty, with clay packed between them to keep the fire

* Instead of crockery, the old bush-settlers' plates and dishes, cups, &c., were of tin, which stood the rough travel of the forest roads better than the more brittle ware.

THE CANADIAN SETTLER'S FIRST HOME IN THE BACKWOODS.

off the logs, answered very well for a chimney, with a hole cut through the roof above to vent the smoke.

"I made a tolerable bedstead out of some ironwood poles, by stretching strips of elmwood bark across, which I plaited strongly together to support my bed, which was a good one, and the only article of luxury in my possession.

"I had foolishly hired two Irish emigrants who had not been in Canada longer than myself, and of course knew nothing of either chopping, logging or fencing, or indeed of any work belonging to the country. The consequence of this imprudence was that the first ten acres I cleared cost me nearly 5l. an acre—at least 2l. more than it should have done.*

"I found chopping in the summer months very laborious. I should have underbrushed my fallow in the fall before the leaves fell, and chopped the large timber during the winter months, when I should have had the warm weather for logging and burning, which should be completed by the first day of September. For want of experience it was all uphill work with me.

* * * * * *

"A person who understands chopping can save himself a good deal of trouble and hardwork by making what is called a *Plan*-heap. Three or four of these may be made on an acre, but not more. The largest and most difficult trees are felled, the limbs only being cut off and piled. Then all the trees that will fall in the same direction should be thrown along on the top of the others, the more the better chance of burning well.

"If you succeed in getting a good fallow, the chances are, if your plan-heaps are well made, that the timber will be for the most part consumed, which will save a great many blows with the axe, and some heavy logging.†

"As soon as the ground was cool enough after the burn was over, I made a Logging Bee, at which I had five yoke of oxen and twenty men. The teamster selects a large log to commence a heap—one which is too ponderous for the cattle to draw: against this the other logs are drawn and piled: the

* The usual price for chopping, logging, and fencing an acre of hardwood land is from eleven to twelve dollars; but if the pine, hemlock, and spruce predominate, fourteen dollars is given.

† I have been told that in the western townships, where the land is very heavily timbered, the usual plan now adopted by the settlers is to chop one year, and let the timber lie till the following year when it is fired. The fire burns all up, so that a few charred logs and brands which are easily logged up is all that remain. This lightens the labour, I am told, very much; it is practised in the "Queen's Bush."

men with handspikes roll them up one above the other, until the heap is seven or eight feet high and ten or twelve broad— all the chips, sticks, roots, and other rubbish are thrown up on the top of the heap. A team and four men can pick and log an acre a day if the burn has been good.

"My hive worked well, for we had five acres logged and fired that night. On a dark night a hundred or two of such heaps all on fire at once have a very fine effect, and shed a broad glare of light over the country for a considerable distance.

* * * * * * *

" My next steps towards my house-building was to build a lime-heap for the plastering of my walls and building my chimneys. We set to work, and built an immense log-heap: we made a frame of logs on the top of the heap to keep the stone from falling over the side. We drew twenty cart-loads of limestone broken up small with a sledge hammer, which was piled into the frame, and fire applied below. This is the easiest way in the bush of getting a supply of this useful material.

" I built my house of elm logs, thirty-six feet long by twenty-four feet wide, which I divided into three rooms on the ground floor, besides an entrance-hall and staircase, and three bed-rooms above. I was busy till October making shingles, roofing, cutting out the door and windows, and hewing the logs smooth inside with a broad axe."

" The best time of the year to commence operations is early in April or September. The weather is then moderately warm and pleasant, and there are no flies in the bush to annoy you.

" A log-shanty, twenty-four feet long by sixteen feet wide, is large enough to begin with, and should be roofed with shingles or troughs.* A cellar should be dug near the fire-place commodious enough to contain twenty or thirty bushels of potatoes, a barrel or two of pork or other matters.

" As soon as your shanty is completed, measure off as many acres as you intend to chop during the winter, and mark the boundaries by a blazed-line [notched trees] on each side. The next operation is to cut down all the small trees and brush—this is called under-brushing. The rule is, to cut down

---

* This is a chopper's shanty: a good shelter for those who are clearing in the bush, or lumbering. It should be chinked, and made wind and water tight.

everything close to the ground from the diameter of six inches and under.

"There are two modes of piling, either in heaps or windrows. If your fallow be full of pine, hemlock, balsam, cedar and the like, then I should advise windrows : and when hardwood predominates, heaps are better. The brush should be carefully piled and laid all one way, by which means it packs and burns better.

"The chopping now begins, and may be followed without interruption until the season for sugar-making commences. The heads of the trees should be thrown on the heaps, or windrows ; this a skilful chopper will seldom fail to do.

"The trunks of the trees must be cut into lengths from fourteen to sixteen feet, according to the size of the timber.

*   *   *   *   *   *   *

"The emigrant should endeavour to get as much chopping done the first three years as possible, as, after that time, he will have many other things to attend to. [It is a mistake to clear more wild land than a man and his family can work, as it is apt to get overrun with a second growth of brush and the fire-wood, and give a great deal of trouble, besides making a dirty-looking, slovenly farm.]

"In the month of May, the settlers should log up three or four acres for spring crops, such as potatoes, (which are always a great crop in the new soil,) Indian corn and turnips, which last require to be pitted or stored from the effects of the severe winter frost.

"The remainder of the fallow should be burnt off and logged up in July : the rail-cuts split into quarters and drawn aside ready for splitting up into rails. After the log-heaps are burned out, rake the ashes while hot into heaps, if you intend to make potash.

"As soon as the settler is ready to build, let him if he can command the means. put up a good frame, rough-cast, or a good stone-house. With the addition of £150 in cash, and the raw material, a substantial family-house can be built which will last a vast number of years."

So far my brother. I will now add a few remarks myself. There are many very substantial dwellings now seen on the old clearings, built of stone collected from the surface of the field. These are faced with a proper instrument into form, and in skilful hands are used as a proper building material. They have rather a motley surface, unless the building is rough-cast, but are very warm in winter and cool in summer.

I like the deep recesses which the windows form in this sort
of building; they remind one of some of the old-fashioned
houses at home with low window seats. I enjoy to sit in
these gossiping corners. A good verandah round takes off
from the patchy look of these stone-houses. Then there is the
strip-house, and the vertical clapboard, or plank-house, and
the block-house, either upright or horizontally laid; all these
are preferable in every respect to the common log-house, or to
the shanty; but persons must be guided by their circumstances
in building. But those who can afford a hundred or two
pounds to make themselves comfortable, do so at once, but it
is not wise to expend all their ready money in building a
frame-house at first. Among other reasons I would urge one,
which is :—in building on wild land, owing to the nature of
the forest land, it is very difficult to select a good site for a
house or the best; and it is mortifying to find out that you
have selected the very least eligible on the land for the
residence : it is better to bear with cheerfulness a small evil
for a year or two than have a ceaseless cause of regret for
many years. It is always necessary to have water both for
household purposes and near the cattle-yard. Good chain
pumps can now be bought at a cost of a few dollars ; and for
soft water, tanks lined with water-lime can be constructed to
any size. This is a great comfort if properly finished with a
pump—the coldest water can be obtained ; the expense is pro-
portioned to the size.

In building a house a cellar lined with stone or cedar slabs
or vertical squared posts, and well lighted and ventilated,
is a great object : it will be found the most valuable room in
the house. The comfort of such an addition to the dwelling
is incalculable ; and I strongly commend the utility of it to
every person who would enjoy sweet wholesome milk, butter,
or any sort of provisions. A good house is nothing, wanting
this convenience, and the poorest log-house is the better for it ;
but the access to the under-ground apartment should not be in
the floor of the kitchen or any public passage ; many limbs
are broken yearly by this careless management. An entrance
below the stairs or in some distant corner, with a post and
rail to guard it, is just as easy as in the centre of a floor
where it forms a fatal trap for the careless and unwary.

An ice-house, in so warm a climate as the summer months
present, is also a great luxury. The construction is neither
expensive nor difficult, and it would soon pay itself. Fresh
meat can be hung up for any time uninjured in the ice-

D

house, when it would be spoiled by the ordinary summer heat in any other situation. A lump of ice put into the drinking water, cools it to a delightful temperature, and every one who has experienced the comfort of iced butter, and the luxury of iced creams, will agree with me it is a pity every housewife has not such a convenience at her command as an ice-house.

I have placed my notice of this article in the chapter that is more particularly addressed to the men, because it depends upon them and not upon their wives, having these comforts constructed. A little attention to the conveniences of the house, and to the wishes of the mistress in its fitting up and arrangements, would save much loss and greatly promote the general happiness. Where there is a willingness on the husband's part to do all that is reasonable to promote the internal comfort, the wife on hers must cheerfully make the best of her lot—remembering that no state in life, however luxurious, is without its trials. Nay, many a rich woman would exchange her aching heart and weary spirit, for one cheerful, active, healthy day spent so usefully and tranquilly as in the Canadian settler's humble log-house, surrounded by a happy, busy family, enjoying, what she cannot amid all her dear-bought luxuries have, the satisfaction of a hopeful and contented heart.

NATURAL PRODUCTIONS OF THE WOODS.—HOW MADE AVAILABLE TO THE SETTLER.

When the Backwoodsman first beholds the dense mass of dark forest which his hands must clear from the face of the ground, he sees in it nothing more than a wilderness of vegetation which it is his lot to destroy: he does not know then how much that is essential to the comfort of his household is contained in the wild forest.

Let us now pause for a few minutes, while we consider what raw material is there ready to be worked up for the use of the Emigrant and his family.

Here is timber for all purposes; for building houses, barns, sheds, fencing and firewood.

The ashes contain potash, and the ley added to the refuse of the kitchen is manufactured by the women into soap, both hard and soft: or if spread abroad in the new fallow, it assists in neutralizing the acid of the virgin soil, rendering it more fertile and suitable for raising grain crops. From the young tough saplings of the oak, beech, and iron wood, his boys, by the help of a common clasp knife, can make brooms to sweep the house, or to be used about the doors.—The hickory, oak, and rock-elm supply axe handles and other useful articles. From the pine and cedar he obtains the shingles with which his log-house is roofed. The inner bark of the bass-wood, oak and many other forest trees, can be made into baskets and mats. Dyes of all hues are extracted from various barks, roots, and flowers. The hemlock and oak furnish bark for tanning the shoes he wears. Many kinds of wild fruits are the spontaneous growth of the woods and wilds.

The forest shelters game for his use ; the lakes and streams wild fowl and fish.

The skins of the wild animals reward the hunter and trapper.

From the birch a thousand useful utensils can be made, and the light canoe that many a white settler has learned to make with as much skill as the native Indian.

Nor must we omit the product of the sugar-maple, which yields to the settler its luxuries in the shape of sugar, molasses, and vinegar.

These are a few of the native resources of the forest. True they are not to be obtained without toil, neither is the costly product of the silkworm, the gems of the mine, or even the coarsest woollen garment.

CONCLUDING REMARKS.

In conclusion, having touched upon almost every subject likely to prove useful to the emigrant's wife or daughter, in her Canadian home, I will take my leave, with the sincere hope that some among my readers may derive profit and assistance from the pages, which, with much toil and pains, I have written for their instruction. Very happy I shall be, if I find that my labours have not been entirely fruitless, and that my little book has been indeed, what it professes to be, a Guide and a Friend to the Female Emigrant.

If I have sometimes stepped aside to address the men, on matters that were connected with their department, it has still been with a view to serve their wives, daughters, or sisters ; and such hints I hope may be well taken, and acted upon, for the ultimate benefit and comfort of all. In writing this little book, I have been influenced by no other desire than that of benefiting my countrywomen, and endeavouring

to smooth for them the rough path which I have trodden
before them, and in which, therefore, I may not be an in-
competent guide.

I have urged upon no one the expediency of leaving their
native land; but I have laboured to show them that Canada
is preferable, in many respects, to any other country to which
they might feel inclined to turn their steps.   Here the
capitalist will find safe investment for his surplus wealth:
the agriculturist will find a large field open to him, for the
exercise of his knowledge, with a ready market for his produce,
and the protection of a mild government, under the name o.
her whom Britons delight to call their Queen.   Here the
labour of the poor man is amply rewarded, and he has it in
his power in a few years to become independent, and owe no
man anything but that debt of brotherly love, which all
Christians are bound to pay to each other.

It is a pleasant thing to contemplate the growing prosperity
of a new country.   To see thriving farmers, with well-stored
barns, and sunny pastures covered with flocks and herds;
with fruitful gardens and orchards, extending over spaces
where once lay the trackless and impenetrable forest; and to
reflect that these things have been the result of industry and
well-directed energy;—that by far the greater number of the
men who own these blessings, have raised themselves from a
state of abject poverty to a respectable position among their
fellow-men.

The Irish emigrant can now listen to tales of famine and
misery endured by his countrymen, while he looks round with
complacency and contentment upon his own healthy, well-fed,
well-clothed family, and thinks how different is his lot from
that of his less fortunate brethren at home.

He sees his wife and children warmly clad with the wool
spun from the fleeces of the flock before his door; fed by the
produce of his farm; and remembers the day when he landed
in the strange country, hungry, naked, forlorn, and friendless;
with drooping head and crushed heart—scarcely even daring
to hope that better things were in store for him and that
pale, wasted creature at his side, his partner in misery and
despair.

How many such have I seen and known!   How many of
those who came to this province eighteen years ago, under
such sad circumstances as I have described, were among the
settlers who came forward, with willing mind and liberal
hand, to offer their subscriptions towards the relief of the

famine-stricken Irish peasantry, in those sad years when,a funeral pall seemed to have fallen over their native land. Do not these facts speak well for Canada?

When I cast my eyes over this improving country, and behold such undoubted proofs of the prosperity of its inhabitants, I cannot but rejoice and feel glad in my very heart, that such things are; and naturally wish that the poor among my countrymen and women, were as happily situated as those I have described.

Let me add yet a few words ere we part, on a subject that doubtless is very dear to you—I mean your Church. If your lot be cast as a resident in any of the towns or villages, of which now there are so many; or in the long-cleared and populous portions of the province; you will find churches and ministers of every denomination, with ready access to Sunday-schools, for the better instruction of your children: in the cleared townships services are held at stated times, in the school-houses, of which there are one or more in each section of every township: but you may be far from a church, and your opportunities may be few and far between, of attending divine worship. Nevertheless, suffer not your God to be forgotten in the lonely wilderness; for you have need of his fatherly care over you and yours.—His ear is ever open to hear, and his holy arm stretched over you to save. He is at hand in the desert, as well as in the busy city: forsake him not, and bring up your children in his love and in his ways; so shall his blessing be upon yourselves and your substance.

The first church in which I bent my knee in heartfelt thankfulness to the Almighty, for his saving care over me and my husband, in preserving us from the perils of the great deep, and the perils of the pestilence which had brought me down very low, almost to the very gates of death—was in a log church of the rudest description; and subsequently, it was in a barn, where two of my elder children were baptized by the good rector of Peterboro', long since called away from his pastoral labours by his Heavenly Master. But there was no lack of reverence among the little flock in the wilderness, who were gathered together that day; for they felt that the rudest building can be made holy by the invisible presence of that Great God who has said, "Where two or three are gathered together in my name, there am I in the midst of them."

On that very spot, or within a few yards of it, the walls of a stone church are raised, and it will not be without a missionary of the Church, to administer the holy ordinances:

so you see that while we were yet but a little flock, scattered and without frequent means of obtaining religious instruction, there were those who cared for the spiritual destitution of the poor colonists in the Backwoods; and many liberal donations were sent from the mother-country for the erection of this church: many others, in like manner, have been built by funds supplied from England, and this fact will, I hope, encourage and cheer those whose first settlement may be made in remote and less-favoured situations. It is also encouraging to the poor Canadian emigrants to know that kind and pious hearts care for them.

Much has been effected by the Government with respect to the establishing of schools in every township, and in all the principal towns; and much improvement will yet be made; for we are what the Yankees would call a progressing people, *and must go forward*, till a satisfactory system of education has been established in the country to meet this great want.

And now, farewell; and I trust you will find kind hearts and friends, and much prosperity, in the land of your adoption; never forgetting that you still belong to that land, which is the glory of all lands, and are subjects to a mild and merciful Sovereign, who is no less beloved in her province of Canada, than she is by her loyal people of Britain.

DESIGN FOR A CHURCH AND SCHOOL.

PREPARATIONS NECESSARY FOR THE VOYAGE.

(Extracts from " Work and Wages," by Vere Foster, Esq.)

At Liverpool.

On your arrival at Liverpool or other ports of departure, go straight to your lodging-house, if you have chosen one; if not, go at once to the office where your passage is engaged, or where you wish to engage it, and find out when the ship will sail, where it is, when you should go on board, and when the berths (sleeping-places) will be marked, and take care to be on board at that time, and to get the number of your berth marked on your passage ticket. At many of the offices there is a store where baggage will be taken care of free of charge.

Lodging.

The usual charge for lodging, including use of kitchen fire and cooking utensils, and storing of luggage, is from 4d. to 9d. per night—4d. being a very common price. Children under fourteen years of age are usually charged less, according to agreement; infants nothing. Mind you make an agreement beforehand.

Choice of a Ship.

Choose a ship that is well ventilated—that is to say, go in a ship which has one sleeping-deck for passengers rather than two; be careful that you can not only walk upright on this deck, but that it is at least seven feet from the deck above, as is the case in all the liners, and that the ship has not a great deal of housing on the outside deck to interfere with a proper current of air below. See that the ship has high bulwarks (wooden walls), at least six feet high, at the side of the outside deck, so as to protect passengers from being drenched every time they come on deck by the spray, whenever the sea is a little rough. If you have a family, choose a ship, if possible, which has separate water-closets for males and females, and if possible one of these below, or else at the hindmost end of the vessel on deck; if below, then take with you some chloride of lime got from a chemist, and throw a little into the closet now and then, to stop bad smells.

The weak among my readers—and I would add the very poor but that they cannot afford to choose—should be careful if possible to select a ship in which they are not required to cook for themselves, but are engaged to be supplied daily with enough of cooked provisions. To the richer passengers who can bribe the cooks with half a crown now and then, to pretty women who can coax them with their smiles, or to strong men who can elbow their way with their broad shoulders, such advice is not necessary, as they can have access to the crowded cookhouse at any time, and any number of times daily; but the others have often to wait for hours in the wet, or even all day, to cook a single meal, and the caprice of the cook seldom allows them even then to get a meal properly cooked. They are pushed off to make way for others till the time allowed for cooking is over, or a storm rises to prevent it. The want of properly cooked food especially, and of proper ventilation, are I believe the principal causes of diarrhœa, dysentery, typhus fever, and cholera on board ship.

Note.—*Sailing vessels should be especially avoided.* The average voyage in a steam-ship to Quebec is about twelve days. That of a sailing ship forty-two days. This loss of time represents a sum of thirty dollars lost in wages, being nearly the cost of the journey. A long voyage gives opportunities for gross outrages upon passengers, for which offences against females the New York sailing vessels have been often and disgracefully notorious. The impositions practised upon emigrants in New York are most disgraceful, and no one who values comfort and personal safety will take that route. Scarcely a single death took place upon the steamers from Glasgow and Liverpool *to Quebec* during the last two years.

How to Engage your Passage.

At Liverpool, or any other port of embarkation for America, be careful whom you employ to show you to a shipping office; ask no questions in the street, pay no attention to the offers of services of any one you meet, not even to ask your way to any place or office, as each such question may cost you five or ten

shillings or more ; but, having gone on board a number of
ships, and chosen the one you like best, buy your ticket yourself
at the head agency office of the ship, the address of which will
be posted up in very large letters on board the ship itself ;
or, what will be better still, ask the person to whom you may
have been recommended from home to get the ticket
for you. You will then be more sure of being charged the
market rate for passage. He will probably get it cheaper for
you than what you can get for yourself, and yet make a few
shillings for himself in doing so. When you go to a shipping office or to a shop to make purchases be sure to go in
quite alone, as if any person shows you in or goes in with
you, it will most likely be to get his commission in one way
or another out of increased price to be charged to you. All
the offices and shops pay commissions of from five to seven and
a half per cent., or more, to persons who bring them customers,
and the worse the ship the higher the commission ; it is therefore the interest of persons of no character to induce emigrants to
go in as bad a ship, and pay as high a price for their passage
as possible. When you have got your ticket, mind you keep
it, giving it up to no one except for a moment to the Government officer, who will visit the ship to inspect the passengers
just before you sail, and who will tear off a piece of every
ticket, which serves him as a note of how many passengers
there are on board, their ages, and so on. Keep the ticket
till *after* the end voyage as long as you like, as the law allows,
in order that you may at all times know your rights, and as
an evidence of your agreement in case of your having to seek
redress.

Emigrants should on no account, except when properly
recommended, suffer themselves to be so misguided as to pay
in Europe their passage any further than to the port of arrival
of their ship in America, as it often happens that railroad
or other tickets bought in Liverpool are found to be of no use
in America, and the fare has to be paid over again, and no
redress can be got in America for breach of an agreement
made in England. This especially applies to agreements
about baggage. Of course there are honest persons in this
trade as in others, and much expense and imposition at New
York may be saved by buying tickets from such persons,
who may be heard of by inquiring of the Government Emigration officer at each port. It must be clearly understood that
any recommendation given by me one year or month will not
be good for another, unless renewed.

SEA STORES.

The quantity of ship's provisions which each passenger fourteen years of age gets, or rather is entitled to, without extra payment on the voyage to America, are as follows :—

BRITISH LAW.	AMERICAN LAW.
3 quarts of water daily.	3 quarts of water daily.
2½ lbs. of bread or biscuit weekly.	2½ lbs. navy bread　　weekly.
1 lb. wheaten flour 　　 „	1 lb. wheaten flour　　　„
5 lbs. oatmeal 　　 „	6 lbs. oatmeal　　　　„
2 lbs. rice 　　 „	1 lb. salt pork (free from bone) „
½ lb. sugar 　　 „	½ lb. sugar　　　　„
2 oz. tea, or 4 oz. cocoa or coffee „	2 oz. tea　　　　„
2 oz. salt 　　 „	8 oz. molasses and vinegar　„

According to the British law, a passenger over one and under fourteen years of age gets only half allowance; according to the American law, every passenger over one year old gets full allowance. Of course passengers will get fed according to one scale or the other, not both. The British law provides that certain substitutions may be made at the option of the master of the ship for the oatmeal and rice, and very properly requires that these provisions should be given to the passengers daily, in a cooked state, but this is not attended to one time in a hundred. Each passenger is entitled by law to lodgings and provisions on board from the day appointed for sailing in his ticket, or else to one shilling for every day of detention, and the same for forty-eight hours after arrival in America. As regards extra provisions, they must depend on taste and circumstances. As much as heretofore will not be required if the ship's provisions shall be issued cooked according to law. In my voyage in the "Washington," from Liverpool to New York, which occupied thirty-seven days, I took the following extra provisions, which I found sufficient, and which were the same in quality and quantity as I had been in the habit of supplying previously to passengers whom I had assisted to emigrate to America :—1½ stone wheaten flour, 6 lbs. bacon, 2½ lbs. butter, a 4 lb. loaf *hard baked*, ½ lb. tea, 2 lbs. brown sugar, salt, soap, baking powder. These extra provisions cost 10s. 6d.; I consider them to be plenty, so far as necessary articles are concerned. A ham, a cheese, more *butter*, more flour, some potatoes and onions, and in case of children, many little extras, such as sweet preserves, suet, raisins, preserved milk, treacle, lemons, &c., would be palatable and desirable additions, particularly during the first fortnight, until the stomach gets inured to the motion of the ship. *Remember*, that you cannot, when at sea, run to a shop to get what you want; you must get it beforehand. I also took the following articles for the use of myself and messmate, the prices of which, of the commonest kind, though quite good enough for so temporary a purpose, should be as follows, according to size, for one, two, or more persons;—Tin water-can, 6d., 1s., 1s. 2d.; tin hook saucepan or boiler, 5d., 7d., 10d.; frying-pan, 6d., 8d., 10d., 1s., 1s. 4d.; tin dish or wash basin, 5d., 6d., 9d.; tin kettle, 8d., 1s., 1s. 4d.; tin tea-pot or coffee-pot, 6d., 8d., 10d., 1s.; tin plate, deep, so as not to spill easy, 1½d., 2½d., 3d.; tin pint mug, 1½d.; chamber vessel, 6d.; knife, fork, and spoon, 4½d.; treacle-can for 3 lbs. or 6 lbs., 4d., 6d.; barrel and padlock to hold provisions, 1s. to 1s. 3d.; small calico bags to hold ship's weekly flour, oatmeal, rice, biscuits, tea and sugar; towels and rubbers; straw mattress, length 5 ft. 10 in., 8d. to 1s. 2d. (a better description of do. would cost 1s. 4d. to 2s. 4d.); blankets for one person, 2s., or according to size, per pair, 4s., 6s. 6d., 9s.; rug, 1s., 1s. 4d., 1s. 6d., 1s. 10d.; sheets each, 9½d. Instead of buying a mattress, it would be better to bring an empty tick from home and fill it with straw at Liverpool or other port. A crock will be wanted for the butter, price, holding 3 lbs., 3d. Bring some Epsom salts, or pills, or other purging medicine, with you, and plenty of treacle for children, as rolling in bed and want of occupation during the voyage stops digestion. Families would do well to take with them a tin slop-pail, price 1s. 6d. to 1s. 10d., or japanned, 2s.; also a broom and small shovel. The handles and spouts of all tin articles should be riveted on as well as soldered. The bottoms of trunks should have a couple of stripes of wood nailed on to them lengthwise, one at the front edge and the other at the back edge, to keep them off the damp floor. *See that you get all the articles of sea stores which you pay for.* Almost any sort of clothes will do for the voyage; dirt, grease, tar, and salt water will spoil anything good.

BAGGAGE.

The enormous quantity of unnecessary baggage frequently brought by emigrants causes a heavy expense and a world of trouble, costing them perhaps their value several times over before they get to their journey's end, a very small quantity of baggage being allowed free of charge on railroads, and extra baggage being charged most extravagantly high, to make up for the lowness of passenger fares; besides, there is imposition in cartage and porterage at every stage. Most articles of clothing are as cheap in America as in England; anything woollen, however, and strong boots, may be taken with advantage (shoes may be laughed out of use, especially with plates and nails, which heat the feet, and are not necessary in so dry a climate and on such stoneless roads). Carpenters should bring their light tools, but heavy tools will not be worth the expense of carriage. Pins, tape, needles, and thread should be brought, as they take up little room, and are extremely dear in America. Not many dresses or bonnets should be brought, as the difference of their style from those worn in America may cause them to be laughed out of use, and the money paid for them will have been wasted. All clothing and other baggage not wanted on the voyage should be packed in separate boxes, with the owner's name clearly marked on them.

MONEY.

The best shape in which emigrants can take small sums of money to America is in English gold and silver, which will pass as readily in America as in England, but cannot be changed in England without loss. It will be most safely carried on the person. On account of the risk of loss on the voyage by robbery or other accident, it is better for a passenger to pay any amount he may have over, say 10*l*. or 20*l*., into a well-known bank, taking a certificate of deposit, or a draft on a Canadian bank, in exchange. Assisted emigrants should be provided with means to be paid to them on *arrival in America*, through a banker or the agent of the ship, to enable them to go up the country in search of employment. When an emigrant *pays* gold in America, he should insist, until he gets acquainted with the different bank notes, on *receiving* his change in gold or silver, or he may find himself in possession of worthless bank notes—American banks being very liable to fail. The following table will show the United States and Canadian values of English money :—

English Coins.	U.S. Value.		Canadian Value.		*English Coins.*	U.S. Value.		Canadian Value.	
	Dolls.	Cents.	*s.*	*d.*		Cents.		*s.*	*d.*
A sovereign is worth	4	84	or 24	4	A Shilling is worth	23	or	1	3
Half-sovereign ,,	2	42	or 12	2	Sixpence ,,	11	or	0	7½
Crown ,,	1	20	or 6	1	Fourpence * ,,	7	or	0	5
Half-crown * ,,		60	or 3	1½	Threepence ,,	5	or	0	3½
Florin ,,		46	or 2	6					

* The only Canadian coins yet issued are 20, 10, and 5 cent pieces in silver; and 1 cent pieces in copper.

A sovereign is generally worth about 4 dollars and 84 cents, sometimes 2 or 3 cents more or less; so, for any amount under 1*l.*, it is near enough to calculate a cent and a half-penny as exactly equal. A dollar is composed of a hundred cents, each equal to a halfpenny, and is written thus— $1; a dollar and a half, and a dollar and a quarter, thus— $1 50, $1 25.

LAST THING.

The last thing to do before going on board is to get a few loaves of fresh bread *hard baked*, and a good-sized piece of roasted or boiled fresh meat to eat when cold. An Emigrant's Guide which I have seen contains the following sound advice: "When the time arrives to go on board ship, do so without delay, not allowing yourself to be persuaded by the lodging-house keeper to sleep on shore, as there will be plenty of time in the morning. Such an indulgence has cost many the loss of a passage and a week's delay in Liverpool."

Go on board your ship, if possible, before it moves out of the dock, rather than after it has gone into the river, as in the latter case you may have to stop for hours in the rain on the pier-head waiting for the small steamer which is to take you alongside the ship, and getting your luggage, and provisions, and bedding, for which and yourself there is no shelter, soused and spoiled with the wet, or else have to hire a small boat to take you to the ship at an enormous expense.— Whether you go in the steamer or in a small boat, you will have to get on board in a very scrambling manner, and your baggage may get all knocked to pieces, as often happens. For the cartage or porterage of your baggage from your lodging to your ship, make a clear agreement beforehand with the carter or porter as to what you are to pay, and let that agreement include the carrying of your baggage not only on board the ship, but ALONGSIDE OF YOUR BERTH: "From the moment your luggage gets on board take care that it be well watched; and if you lie in the ship in dock a night, keep a close guard over it, as ships are at such times infested by thieves, who cannot be known from passengers," and whom the officers of the ship are otherwise too busy to look after.

THE VOYAGE.

The berths (sleeping places) are each from six to six and a half feet long, and eighteen inches wide, ranged one over the

other in double shelves along the side of the ship. Single
men are berthed separately from the rest of the passengers.
All clothing and other baggage not wanted at sea should be
put out of the way till the end of the voyage, as the officers of
the ship may direct. Passengers should be particularly cleanly
on board a crowded ship, to prevent ship fever from breaking
out (this is very important), and should keep much on deck
to breathe the fresh air for the same reason, and pay a cheerful obedience to the discipline of the ship. The floor should
be sprinkled with vinegar sometimes to sweeten the air, and
chloride of lime should be sprinkled now and then in the
water-closet, if any between the decks. Be careful of your
sea stores, as your passage may be longer than you expect,
and it is better to have some over at the end than to be short
at sea.

*How Emigrants may secure good treatment for future passengers,
more effectually than can be done by Acts of Parliament,* whose regulations are easily evaded. Whenever it happens, as is sometimes the case, that passengers have received the full allowance of provisions of good quality, for which they have agreed
and paid, and have been otherwise very well treated during
the voyage, they should in justice to the captain or other
officers, before leaving the ship, express their thanks to them
in a written address, have it published in the newspapers
where they land, (for which no charge will in general be
made,) and then post a few copies of those papers to the principal papers in the old country; and the same if they have
been very ill treated.

On Arrival in America.

Do not listen to any one of the numerous persons who will
come on board the ship, or meet you as you go ashore, saying
that they are the agents of the Government, or of this or that
benevolent society, or of a railroad or steamboat company, or
telling you that the person you are asking for is dead, or the
office is closed, and the owners bankrupt; but, as at Liverpool,
ask your way in a respectable shop to the place you wish to
go to. If you are not bound to any particular house, or railroad, or steamboat, one of you, if a party, should look about
for a lodging, while the rest mind the baggage on board. Be
on your guard against extortionate charges for cartage, board
and lodging, contrary even to agreement, against the purchase
of false travelling tickets, or payment of extravagant prices
for the conveyance of yourselves and *baggage* into the interior.

In selecting a lodging-house, be careful not only to find out beforehand what you will have to pay, having it expressly understood that there is to be no *further charge* for *storing your luggage*, but get a printed card of prices, and make your payments daily, at least for the first day or two, in dollars and cents. What is called a shilling in New York is worth only sixpence sterling. A shilling, sterling, is worth 1s. 3d., of Canada money. The lowest expense at emigrant lodging houses in New York is 50 cents for three meals and bed, or from 12½ cents to 18¾ cents for a single meal or bed. In a better kind of house the charge is 1 dollar a day, or 25 cents a single meal or bed. Fruits and green vegetables should be eaten sparingly for some time after landing, and river water should not be drunk excepting boiled as tea, coffee, &c., for fear of diarrhœa. Emigrants should leave the overcrowded cities on the sea coast as soon as possible and go up the country, the further the better, and, leaving the main lines of travel, where emigrants are in each other's way, scatter right and left, inquiring for work on any terms.—The propensity of emigrants to remain about large cities, and especially those on the sea coast, is very much complained of by Americans, and with too much foundation. There they land at the rate of a thousand or more daily throughout the year; many of these loiter days, weeks, and months, wasting their money and idling away their precious time, quietly waiting for Providence to turn up something for them, until their last penny is spent, their trunks are retained by the lodging-house keepers to pay their bills, and they are turned out beggars on the streets. Meanwhile a few hundred miles up the country throughout the spring and summer they are badly wanted, and might at such times, if common labourers, be earning 4s. 2d. sterling a day, boarding themselves, or if good harvesters, even as much as 8s. 4d. sterling, besides their board. —They should not stickle for high wages at first, when their abilities are not known, but care more to learn during the first month how to earn high wages afterwards.

REQUIRED OUTFIT.

The following is a careful estimate of the quantity and cost of provisions required for 12 months, for a man and his wife, and three young children—and also a list of articles required by settlers going into the Bush. The prices are attached at which they can be purchased at the villages near the settlements. The total capital required is about 58l. currency, or 47l. sterling, although very many have succeeded, and are now independent, who had not 10l. in the world upon their first settlement.

PROVISIONS NECESSARY FOR A FAMILY OF FIVE, SAY FOR ONE YEAR.

	£	s.	d.
8 barrels of Flour, at 1l. 15s. per barrel	14	0	0
2 „ of Pork, at 3l. 15s. „	7	10	0
80 bushels of Potatoes, at 2s. per bushel	8	0	0
30 lbs. of Tea, at 2s. 6d. per lb.	3	15	0
1 barrel of Herrings	2	0	0
½ „ of Salt	0	7	6
Cost of Provisions	£35	12	6

SEED.

	£	s.	d.
20 bushels of Potatoes, at 2s. per bushel	2	0	0
3 „ of Wheat, at 7s. 6d. „	1	2	6
10 „ of Oats, at 2s. „ „	1	0	0
Cost of seed	£4	2	6

OTHER NECESSARIES.

	£	s.	d.		£	s.	d.
				Brought over	£3	17	6
1 Axe	0	8	9	1 Kettle	0	5	0
1 Grindstone	0	7	6	1 Fryingpan	0	3	0
1 Shovel	0	1	10	1 Teapot	0	2	6
2 Hoes, at 3s. 6d. each	0	7	0	6 Small Tin Vessels,			
3 Reaping-hooks at				at 4d. each	0	2	0
1s. 6d. each	0	4	6	3 Large Tin Dishes,			
1 Scythe	0	5	0	at 2s. 6d. each	0	7	6
1 Inch Auger	0	5	0	6 Spoons, at 2d. each	0	1	0
1 Inch and a half				6 Knives and Forks	0	5	0
Auger	0	7	6	3 Pairs of Blankets,			
1 Hand-Saw	0	7	6	at 1l. 5s. per pair	3	15	0
2 Water Pails, at 1s.				2 Rugs for Quilts, at			
6d. each	0	3	0	2s. 6d. each	0	5	0
1 Window Sash, and				2 Pairs of Sheets, at			
Glazing	0	5	0	3s. per pair	0	6	0
1 Bake-Oven	0	5	0	1 Smoothing Iron	0	2	6
2 Pots, at 5s. each	0	10	0	1 Pig	0	15	0
					£10	7	1

Carried over	£3	17	6			
Total				£50	2	1
Add, one Cow				5	0	0
Hay for do, 1st year				3	0	0
				£58	2	1
					Currency.	
				Or £47	0	0
					Sterling.	

THE MONTHS IN CANADA.

JANUARY.

THIS month, though we date our new year from its commencement, as in the old country, is not really the first month of our Canadian winter, which often commences as early as the first week in November: some years,,however, it is later, and I have seen fine mild open weather far into December; yet you must not be surprised at snow-showers and severe frosts in those two months, and winter clothing should all be prepared before the chances of a November cold setting in. The month of January forms, as it were, a break in the winter's cold. I have known many new year's days when there was not snow enough on the ground to make sleighing practicable: this present January, for instance, when the earth was brown and bare, and wheeled vehicles alone were seen on the road.

The first new year's day, viz., 1833, that I passed in Canada there was no snow to be seen, and the air was so warm that we sat with the outer door open, the heat of the stoves being too oppressive for comfort. We had had snow showers as early as November the 3rd, but no intense degree of cold till after the 27th of January: after that time we had heavy snow-storms and intense cold all through the month of February and up to the 17th of March, when a warm, rapid thaw set in and cleared the snow off by the middle of April, even in the woods.

. In the year 1846 the new year's day was warm, and we walked on the dead leaves in the woods. This year, 1855, there was snow about the middle of November which lay till the 22nd, then the weather was mild again. We had intense cold the week before Christmas, but a thaw commenced on

E

the 23rd, and the snow disappeared, the ground being bare
till the 13th of January, when a scattering of about an inch
fell, but it was not till the last week in that month that any
quantity of snow fell, greatly to the discomfiture of the farmer,
who reckons on the sleighing season for the easier transport
of his grain to market, and as a season of recreation for his
family.

There is always a January thaw in the early part of the
month, when the December snows melt off. The frost then
relaxes its iron bands, and a moist atmosphere takes the place
of the keen frosts of early winter : rain frequently falls, and
high winds blow. A change is sure to take place again on or
about the 12th of January ; snow again covers the ground.
After heavy snow-storms a cold north-west wind begins to
blow ; the new-fallen snow is sent in clouds like smoke over
the open fields, drifting in high banks on the road sides, filling
up the corners of the rail fences, and blocking the narrow
lanes : the cutting wind plays fantastic tricks on the edges of
these snow-drifts, sweeping them out in hollows and caves,
sculpturing their spotless surfaces in curved lines of the most
graceful forms, so that you would imagine some cunning hand
had chiselled them with infinite care and pains. But while
these changes are going on with the snow-falls in the open
country, in the great forest it is very different. There, un-
disturbed by the war of winds, the snow-flakes fall in ceaseless silent showers till the whole dark unsightly mass of fallen
trees and broken boughs are covered with the spotless deposit.
The thick branches of the evergreens receive the load that
falls from the lofty pines and naked hardwood trees, as moved
by the wind they shake off the feathery burden. Go into the
forest the morning after a heavy snow-storm, and you will behold one of the purest, one of the loveliest scenes that nature
can offer you. The young saplings bent down with the weight
of snow, unable to lift their heads, are bent into the most graceful arches, and hang like bowers of crystal above your path ;
the keen frost has frozen the light branches and holds them
down to the hardening surface, so that these bent trees remain
in this way till the breath of spring sets them once more free,
but often they retain the bent form and never recover the
upright shape entirely. The cedar swamp which is so crowded
with trees, of all ages and sizes, from the tiny seedling, rooted
on the decayed trunks of the old fallen trees, to the vigorous
sapling striving to make its way upwards, and the hoary

trunks, over the bleached and mossy heads of which centuries have passed, now presents a curious aspect, filled with masses of new-fallen snow, which forms huge caverns and curtains lying in deep banks on the prostrate trunks, or adorning the extended fan-like branches with mimic flowers of purest white.

January parties, balls, pic-nics, and sleigh rides, are frequent in the towns and long-settled parts of the country; so that though the cold is often intense, this season is not without its pleasures. The back-woodsman is protected in his drives by the ancient forest, which excludes the wind, and is equal to a second greatcoat in travelling.

No vegetation is to be seen going on in this month: silence and stillness prevail. The bear, the raccoon, the porcupine, the ground-hog, the flying squirrel, and little striped chitmunk or ground-squirrel, with many other smaller animals, lie soundly sleeping in their nests or burrows. The woods are deserted by most of the feathered tribes, a solitary tree-creeper, the little spotted woodpecker, with some of the hardy little birds called Chickadee-dee by the natives, are alone seen on sunny days in the thick shelter of the pines and hemlocks; while around the houses of the settlers the snow-birds in lively flocks whirl hither and thither in the very wildest of the snow-drifts, or a solitary whiskey jack (Canada Jay) ventures to gather up the crumbs which have been swept outside the door. Sometimes the graceful form of a black squirrel may be seen running along the outstretched branch of a tree, his deep sable fur contrasting very remarkably with the glittering silver snow, over which he gambols as gaily as if in the warmth of a July sun.

FEBRUARY.

This is indeed the coldest of the Canadian winter month; and though the lengthening of the days gives you more sunshine, it seems to add little to your warmth. Cold and clear the sun shines out in a blue and often cloudless sky, but the thermometer often indicates a very low temperature, 10, 12, 18, nay, sometimes as low as 28, and even 30 degrees below zero. Warm wrappings are now indispensably necessary to the traveller. In the event of any person finding their ears, hands, or faces frozen, which accident can be seen as well as felt, the part becoming of a livid whiteness, and feeling hard and stiff, the remedy is at hand, and must be applied immediately to the frozen part, viz., snow rubbed on hard till the flesh resumes its former healthy appearance : some apply spirits of turpentine or brandy, or spirits of any kind, after the snow has been rubbed on well.

The care of the cattle and sheep, drawing in firewood, splitting of rails for fencing, and preparing sap troughs, are the usual operations in the settlements during this month.

MARCH.

The early part of March often resembles February, with this difference, the longer days cause a relaxation of the severe cold during the sunshining hours ; the very surface of the snow thaws, patches of bare earth begin to appear towards the middle of the month; the weak but pleasant note of the little song sparrow and the neat snow sparrow, in its quaker-like plumage, may be heard and seen as they flit to and fro, picking the seeds of the rough green amaranth and tall woolly stalked mulliens, which stand faded and dry in the garden patch or on the road side. The equinox is often attended with rough gales and snow-storms : these past, the sun begins to melt off the snow, and a feeling of coming spring is experienced in the soft airs, and a look of life in the bark and birds. The rising of the sap is felt in the forest trees ; frosty nights and sunny days call forth the activity of the settlers in the woods ; sugar-making is now at hand, and all is bustle and life in the shanty.

I have largely entered into the details of this busy season in the earlier part of my book. We will now proceed to April.

APRIL.

April in Canada is not the same month in its general features, as the lovely, showery, capricious April, that month of smiles and tears, of storms and sunshine, in dear old England. It is often cold, stern, and harsh, yet with many hopeful changes that come to cheat us into the belief that winter is gone, and the season of buds and flowers is at hand, and some years it is so; but only once in five or ten years does the Canadian April prove a pleasant genial month.

Some warm, lovely, even sultry days, misty like Indian summer, are experienced, and the snow melts rapidly and a few flies creep out and sport a while in the warm beams of the young sun, but "by-and-by a cloud takes all away." The wind blows chilly, snow-showers fall, and all is cold, cheerless winter again.

In fine Aprils a few blossoms peep out from under the thick carpet of dead leaves, and then you see the pretty snow-flower, or Hepatica, lifting its starry head and waving in the spring breezes on the waysides, on upturned roots and in the shelter of the underwood, where the forest is a little thinned out so as to admit of the warm beams of the sun ; pale pink, blue of two shades, and snowy white are the varieties of this cheerful little flower. Violets, the small white, and a few pale-blue ones, are next seen. The rich rank soil at the edges of your clearing produces the sanguinaria or blood-root—the modest white flower, shrouded at its first breaking the soil in a vine-shaped leaf, veined with orange. The root of this plant affords a bright red dye to the Indians, with which they stain the bark of their mats and baskets. You may know the blood-root, on breaking the leaf or the root, by its red juice.

In low, open, moist ground the mottled leaf of the dog's-tooth violet (erythronium) comes up, and late in April the yellow bells, striped on the outside of the petal with purplish brown, come up in abundance. Spring-beauty, too, is an April flower, a delicate little flower with pale pink striped bells—Claytonia is its botanical name—but we love to call these wild flowers by some simple name, which simple folks may easily remember.

As the snow melts off in the woods, the leaves of various evergreen plants appear still fresh and green. Among these are the pyrolas, or sweet-winter-greens, a numerous and lovely family of Canadian plants ; several varieties of the club-moss, one of which is known as the festoon pine, and is used to make wreaths for ornamenting the settlers' houses with. The wild garlic, too, shows its bright green spear-shaped leaves early in this month. This plant, so eagerly sought for by the cattle, to which it is a very healing medicine, is dreaded by the dairy-maid, as it destroys the flavour of the milk, and spoils the butter.

If the month of April should prove cold, many of the above-named flowers put off their blossoming-time, appearing in the ensuing month of May.

April unlocks the ice-bound lakes and streams ; and it is during this month that the winter snows are dissolved. The

warmth which in sunnier climes brings to perfection the
bulbs, and gives odour to the violet and blue-bell, the pale
primrose, and the narcissus, here must be expended in loosen-
ing the frost-bound earth from its icy fetters and the waters
from their frozen chains. Let us therefore not despise our Canadian April, though she be not as winning and fair as her name-
sake at home.

MAY.

Clear skies, cold and bright, often mark this month: such
weather is useful in drying up the moist earth, saturated by
the snow which April has melted away, and hardening the
soft earth which is to be made ready for the spring crops.

This is a busy month, the busiest in all the year, for the
work of two must be crowded into it.

Ploughing, sowing, planting, goes on incessantly : no time
now for the gardener or the husbandman to be idle. Everything is full of life and activity, from the little squirrel and
tiny titmouse running up and down the trees, gathering its
moss and grey lichens to build its curious oven-shaped nest.

What crowds of birds now visit us! The green frogs are
piping in the creeks and marshes. The ground is now yielding us flowers of every hue. Yellow, blue, and white violets ;
buttercups, anemones, or wind-flowers, the wood daffodil, or
bell-flower. The snow-white trillium, moose-flower, some call
it, wild vetches, blue and white.

Vegetables of all kinds are sown during the month of May ;
and the grain, such as spring wheat, barley, oats, and peas,
with early potatoes, and, later in the month, Indian corn.
must be put in all through May.

The bright skies and sunshine, the singing of the birds, the
bursting out of the leaves and buds of all kinds make May a
charming month. There is far less rain in the Canadian
spring than in the same season in Britain. There is less need
for it, as the earth has received so large a share of moisture in
the form of snow, during the winter months. May is usually
a dry month here—sometimes cold drying winds prevail, and
frosty nights are not uncommon, which often check vegetation.
The new growth of the pine takes place in May.

JUNE.

This month perfects the leafage of the late deciduous trees, such as the oak, butternut, ash, and some others. It is in this month that the forest trees are seen in their greatest beauty, so intensely green, so varied, that the eye is never tired with wandering over their living verdure. Later in the summer, these charming tints seem to lose their youthful freshness, and assume one uniform colour of sober green. There are frequent thunder-storms, and often heavy rains early in June, and sultry heat: the musquitoes and black flies, in situations favourable to them, now appear; but it is in July the musquitoes are the most troublesome, especially in the close pine woods, and near lakes and streams. On open, old cleared parts of the country these pests are less known, and less heeded. Flies always attack the new comers with more virulence than old settlers, who scarcely feel the annoyance.

Some of our most beautiful flowers—I mean the wild flowers —blossom during this month, such as the yellow moccasin (and later the white and purple), the large orange lily, lilies of many kinds, the blue lupin, the splendid euchroma or painted cup, which may be known by the brilliant scarlet colour that tips the leaves and involucrum of the flowers: this beautiful plant is found chiefly on dry sandy soils, or on the open plain lands: it continues from June till September. The sweet-scented, round-leafed, winter-green, called lily of the valley (it should be lily of the woods), with several of the same lovely family, bloom all through June and July.

The evening air at dew-fall is now filled with the perfume of the single red-rose, a dwarf rose with crimson stems and greyish thorns, which grows in vast profusion on the plains. The sweet-scented shrub Ceanothers or New Jersey tea, with white feathery flowers, also adds its perfume along with the sweet-scented Monarda or mountain sweet: but these are only a few, and a very few, of the blossoms that you will find springing in the open fields, the deep forest, or the road-side wastes.

The wild strawberry, which is sure to spring up in old clearings and new meadows, now begins to ripen from the tenth to the end of the month: you will find them red and ripe, and far finer in size and flavour, than any that are to be found in the woods in the old country.

Potatoes are often planted in the early part of this month, and hoeing, both of corn and potatoes, is continued, with other work on the farm.

JULY.

July is the hottest month of the Canadian year: there is often a succession of heavy thunderstorms and showers, which give a sultry heat, which is less bearable than the clear dry atmosphere that marks the harvest month of August. The raspberry and huckleberry ripen during the month of July: the rice comes in flower with many other aquatic plants. On the still-flowing lakes now may be seen vast beds of that most beautiful flower, the large white nymphæa or double white water lily, looking down through the clear water: these flowers may be discovered in every stage of progression, from the soft young bud closely folded up in its oily olive-coloured calyx, to the half-opened blossom, showing its ivory petal, and the nearly full-blown flower still shielding the lemon-tinted anthers, which are seen only fully developed in the perfect blossom which sits as a crown upon the waters, giving out its exquisite odour to the soft breeze that gently stirs the limpid bosom of the lake. The deep golden cup of the yellow nymphæa may also be seen, seldom far removed from the white blossomed; and the arrow-shaped leaves of the blue spiked pondwort, and rosy flowers of the persicaria, form a beautiful sight on hot sunny days.

The meadows are now mowed, and the hay harvest is in full operation; and if the weather have proved sufficiently warm, the earliest sown fall-wheat will now be cradled, i. e., mown with the cradle scythe; an instrument which has quite set aside the old reaping-hook and sickle. A good cradler will cut three acres of heavy wheat in a summer's day: one or more following in his steps to bind and stock up the sheaves.

The cherry, currant, and garden-raspberry, are now ripe— peas and some other vegetables—but early potatoes are still rare, unless care has been taken to plant early kidneys, which should be put in early in May to insure their being fit for table in the middle of July.

Many splendidly-coloured butterflies are seen during the hot months of July and August, some of a superior size to any seen in England. The large brimstone swallow-tail, the great scarlet and black; admirals of several sorts, with a variety of small gay-winged species, and some very fine moths, one of a delicate green with coloured eyes in its wings, red feet, and a thick body covered with white feathery down; besides sphinxes and tiger-moths, with an endless list of dragon-flies, and beetles of various hues appear.

The humming-birds may now be seen, making frequent visits to the flower garden, hovering over the open blossoms of the larkspurs, morning-glories, scarlet bean, and any other honey-yielding flowers. In the forest you may chance to see the gay glancing wings of that shy but splendid bird, the scarlet tanager or summer red-bird; while in the orchard and gardens, the blue-bird and the wild canary, or American gold-finch, dart to-and-fro in the sunshine; and at night, the rapid voice of the whip-poor-will is heard from eve till dawn, es-pecially where there are groves of trees, near the house: you will know the oriole by its orange and black plumage; the cat-bird by its long tail, dark dove-coloured coat, and squalling note, much like that of a cat calling her kittens. The saucy blue or crested jay, calls "thate, thate," and the "Phœbe" repeats its own name in a variety of tones. It is pleasant to know even a bird or a flower by name; and though some of my readers may care for none of these things, there may be others, and perhaps not a few, who may be glad of the in-formation I have given them about the wild flowers and wild creatures of the strange land they may be destined to sojourn in for many years. It may enable them to teach their children the names of the natural productions, and create an interest in their young minds in the new country, which will not be without its beneficial effects upon their minds. Little children love simple knowledge, and ask for it eagerly. To acquire the name of any object that strikes its fancy, is the first step on the young child's ladder to learning.

AUGUST.

Harvest, if not begun in the last-named month, commences the first week in this. The grain now ripens as fast as it can be cut and carried. The weather is generally hot, dry, and clear all through this month, with splendid sunsets; but the nights are often cool—almost chilly. It is during the hot season that agues and other intermittents usually prevail, more than in the moister months of the spring. The heavy dews should be avoided as much as possible. Towards the latter part of August, it is not very unusual to experience slight frosts at night. I have seen a change on some of the forest leaves before this month was out. Some of the earlier sorts of apples may be used now—the early harvest-yellow, harvest and early Joe, with some others.

Sun-flowers of many kinds are now in bloom, with many sorts of fruit. The mandrake or May-apple may now be gathered : the berries of many wild plants are ripe. The flower-garden is in all its glory. Melons ripe, and all kinds of vegetables. Nature is perfecting her great work. Not only is man busy with the harvest, but the wild animals are also garnering up their winter stores. The squirrels are busy from morning till night, gleaning the ripe grain, and laying it up on the rail fences and stumps to dry in the sun before they venture to carry it off to their granaries and burrows : they are a lively, busy race ; ever at work or at play. They seem to me the happiest of all God's creatures, and the prettiest.

The flowers that are most commonly seen now are of the starry or syngenesian class—sun-flowers, asters of many kinds, golden-rod, lion's-foot, liatris or gay-feather, with many others.

SEPTEMBER.

This is one of the most delightful months in the year. The heat is sometimes very great in the first week ; but after that is past, a genial warmth, with a clear air, is felt. The warm rich tints steal by degrees over the trees, especially those that grow at the outer edges of the clearings, and the soft maples and dogwood bushes that skirt the water ; but it is not till the rains of the equinox, and its subsequent frosts, that the glory of the autumnal foliage is seen in all its splendour.

The harvest is now over ; and the fall ploughing has begun with great zeal: by the second week in this month, most of the wheat will have been sown, unless where sickness or other causes have delayed the work. September, like May, is a busy month in Canada. The Indian rice is now ripe, and the squaw goes forth in her light bark canoe, to gather in her harvest—one which, like the birds of the air, she gathers, without having scattered the seed, or toiled for its increase.

OCTOBER.

There is generally a season of rain during the last week of September, lasting until the tenth or twelfth of October. This may be looked for almost as a certainty. The weather generally clears about that time, and frosty nights and mild days ensue. Indian summer, for the most part, succeeds close upon the rainy season. Warm, sultry, hazy days. The autumn foliage is fast covering the earth with a thick carpet of variegated leaves, returning to her bosom that which was derived from her, to be again resumed in due season, to form fresh leaves and buds, and woody fibre. How much wisdom may be imparted to us even by the fall and decay of the leaves of the trees!—and to man alone has been given the privilege of looking upon these things with the eye of faith and reason, that by the small and weak things of earth, his soul may be lifted up to Heaven, to adore God the Creator in all his works.

The last flowers that linger yet are the gentians. These belong to the months of September and October, exclusively, and are among the most beautiful of the Canadian wild flowers. The large, bright blue, fringed gentian, may be seen lifting its azure blue and white fringed bell, by shady banks and open woods, in size varying from the plant of two or four inches in height, to the tall branching one of two and three feet high, with flowers proportionably large. The pitcher-shaped gentian, of deep cerulean blue, closed at the lips, is found in damp spots; not in the close swamps of the forest, however, but in open places, a little marshy, and among small thickets. The pale lilac whorled gentian grows more frequently in half-cultivated fields, and waste lands; while the full, deep-coloured purple of the large bell-flowered gentian, the Calathian violet, is found on dry sandy and gravelly soil. This is one of the most beautiful of all our wild flowers, and is worthy of a place in any garden. I have seen it in conservatories at home, tenderly nursed and guarded with care, while here it braves the first chilling frosts, and may be said to lay its head almost on the lap of winter snows.

The lovely asters, the late everlasting, the golden-rod, and a few more hardy plants, linger on in bloom through the Indian summer, and then wither with the first hard frost.

It is during the fall months that the northern lights are so frequently seen illumining the horizon—a novelty which will attract the attention of the emigrant, and fill him with pleasing admiration. It is seen at times all through the year, but in September, October, and November more frequently, especially before the setting in of the Indian summer.

Early in this month, the root crops are stored, and such trees planted out, as you desire, in the orchard.

NOVEMBER.

Our year is fast drawing to a close: all nature seems preparing for the change. The squirrel and wood-chuck have laid by their stores of nuts and grain and seeds. The musk-rats and beavers have built their houses, and the latter have repaired their dams. The summer birds have left us: the discordant cry of the blue jay is heard only at intervals. Only a few of our old feathered friends abide with us, and they seek the warm shelter of the woods, and doze away the long cold winter in silence and gloom.

November is very unlike the foggy, cheerless, dark, soul-depressing month, bearing that name in Britain: it often, it is true, wears the garb of winter, but this is by no means a certain characteristic of the season. There are often delightful days of sunshine and clear frost; and, in some years, Indian summer falls into this month, and gives an aspect of warmth and loveliness to the very borders of winter's frozen garments.

The plough is now busy preparing the fallows for the ensuing spring crops, that the soil may be mellowed by the winter frost and snow. This work is continued as long as the ground is open. The only plants now of any interest are the winter-greens. The red berries of the cranberries, and the purple clusters of the frost grapes, give liveliness and beauty to the scenery.

DECEMBER.

Sometimes this month is open and fair during the first week or so; but it varies from moderate to intense cold. We must not be surprised at finding the streams ice-bound, the earth hardened into stone, or deep snow covering the earth; but this is according to our climate; and to those who look for its approach, and are in any way prepared for its severity, the Canadian winter is a cheerful season.

I have brought my year to its close. Some will think my sketch too fair a one, because they will experience many changes and discomforts; and seasons are brightened or darkened by our individual feelings and domestic circumstances. To the sad and sorrowful all seasons are alike gloomy.

"To feverish pulse each gale blows chill."

I have chosen a medium year from among those of which I have kept a faithful diary, and I consider it a fair average of the Canadian climate, or of that portion of Canada lying between Toronto and Kingston. Above, it is milder; below, colder, but less variable.

Some decided changes I have marked in my time. The year 1834 the spring came on very early: the snow was all gone in March, and earlier in the sun-exposed clearings: leaves were out in the first week in May; but a severe frost and snow took place on the 14th and 15th of May, and cut off vegetation for a time; nevertheless, we had a long, dry, hot summer, and fine fall.

We then had three successive wet harvests; which, with a visitation of cholera, checked emigration for several years: this, joined to the rebellion, proved a great drawback to the prosperity of the colony. Good, however, sprung out of evil, and many ills and abuses were remedied, which might have remained to this day, but for the attention of the rulers of the people being turned towards them.

We have had winters of comparative mildness, with plenty of snow, but no very intense cold. The spring of 1839 was very early, but the summer was hot and moist; and that year we had a long Indian summer; while some years we have had scarcely any weather corresponding to that uncertain season.

Spring is the most uncertain of our seasons. The fall is the wettest, but often the most delightful of them; but to such as are of a contented spirit, there is good at all seasons, and in everything: for, as the old poet says—

> " Not always fall of leaf, nor ever Spring;
> Not endless night, nor yet eternal day;
> The saddest birds a season find to sing,
> The roughest storms a calm may soon allay:
> Thus with succeeding turns God tempers all,
> That man may hope to rise, yet fear to fall."*

Maple Sugar.

This little volume would be incomplete unless it contained some instruction on the making of maple sugar, though the manufacturing of this Canadian luxury is no longer considered

---

* These lines form a portion of an admirable little poem called " Times Go by Turns," written by Father Robert Southwell, who was the victim of religious persecution during the reign of Queen Elizabeth.

so important a matter as it used formerly to be : the farmer,
considering that his time can be more profitably employed in
clearing his land, will not give his attention to it, for maple
sugar is less an article of trade than it used to be. The West
India sugars are now to be bought at 4d. per lb., or if you pay
a dollar you can get 14 lbs. of good soft sugar. The price of
maple sugar is never less than 3d., but 5d. for many years was
the standard price if it were good, now there is little call for
maple sugar, muscovado being quite as cheap. Still there are
situations and circumstances under which the making of maple
sugar may be carried on with advantage. There will always
be a class of emigrants who, for the sake of becoming the
proprietors of land will locate themselves in the backwoods,
far from the vicinity of towns and villages, who have little
money to expend, and who are glad to avail themselves of so
wholesome and so necessary a luxury at no greater cost than
their own labour.

With the assistance of the children and the females of the
house, a settler may, if he have a good sugar-bush, make several
hundredweight of sugar in a season, besides molasses and
vinegar. Many a stout boy of fourteen or fifteen, with the aid
of the mother and young ones, has made sugar enough to
supply the family, besides selling a large quantity. In the
backwoods the women do the chief of the sugar-making; it is
rough work, and fitter for men; but Canadians think little of
that. I have seen women employed in stronger work than
making sugar. I have seen women under-brushing, and even
helping to lay up and burn a fallow, and it grieved me, for it
was unfit for them.

We will suppose that the settler has resolved upon making
sugar. The first thing is to look out for a good sugar-bush,
where he can be sure of a hundred or two hundred of good
trees, standing not very far from each other. In the centre of
his bush he should fix upon a boiling-place : a fallen pine, or
any large tree should be chosen : if there be not one ready
felled, he must cut one down, as he needs a good lasting back
log against which to build his fire at the boiling time; but
there are other requisites to be attended to : a certain number
of troughs, hollowed out of small pine, black ash, basswood,
and sundry other kinds of wood; one or more troughs to each
tree; if the trees be large, two, and even three troughs are
placed, and so many incisions made in the bark with the axe,
into which spills of cedar are inserted; these are made with a

MAPLE SUGAR-MAKING IN THE BUSH.

hollow sort of chisel; but some do not take much pains, and only stick a flat slip of shingle, slanting from the gash in the bark, to direct the flow of the sap to the trough. The modes of tapping are various: some use the auger and bore a hole, which hurts the tree the least; some cut a chip out across the bark, and cut two sweeping lines down so as to give the sap two channels to flow in; others merely gash the bark with a slanting cut, and insert the spill.

There should be a large trough hewed out almost as big as an Indian canoe, or barrels, placed near the boiling-place for a store trough: into this the sap is collected: as fast as the smaller ones fill, the boys and women empty their contents into pails, and the pails into the large receptacle. The boiling-place is made by fixing two large stout forked posts into the ground, over which a pole is laid, stout enough to support the kettles; iron-wood is good for this purpose; on this the kettles are hung at a certain height above the fire. A hoop, with a piece of clean coarse serge or flannel sewed over it, serves for a strainer; the edge of the pots should be rubbed with clean lard to prevent the sap boiling over. It is a common plan, but I think by no means a nice one, to keep a bit of pork or fat bacon suspended by a string above the sap kettles: when the boiling sap reaches this it goes down: but I think my plan is better, and certainly more delicate. If possible have more than one kettle for boiling down; a constant change from the pots facilitates the work: as the first boiling decreases, and becomes sweeter, keep adding from the others, and filling them up with cold sap. A ladleful of cold sap thrown in at boiling-point, will keep it down. Attention and care is now all that is required. The one who attends to the boiling should never leave his business; others can gather the sap and collect wood for the fires. When there is a good run, the boiling-down is often carried on far into the night. If heavy rain occurs, it is better to empty the sap-troughs, as the sap would be too much weakened for boiling. The usual month for sugar-making is March, though I have known some years in which sugar was made in February. By the middle of April the sap is apt to get sour if kept many hours, and will not grain. If you have sap kept rather long, put salaratus in till it foams a little: but it is seldom that good sugar is made from acid sap. A handful of quicklime, some prefer to cure sour sap. The best run of sap occurs when a frosty night is followed by a warm sunny day. If cold weather set in after the trees have been tapped, it is sometimes necessary to tap them a second time.

After the sap has been boiled down to thin molasses, it is then brought in to be sugared off. The syrup must be carefully strained through a woollen strainer; eggs are then beaten up with the shells, and poured into the cold syrup, which is now ready for boiling into thick syrup, or for sugaring off.

Where the sugar bush is far from the house, some persons prefer having a small shanty put up, of logs, and thatched with bark: it may be built so as to enclose a large stump, to which may be affixed a wooden crane, by means of a socket in which the upright part of the crane can be made to move: to the cross-beam of the crane the pots can be hung, and a fire, with a few large stones or a great log at the back, fixed, lighted beneath. The advantage of the crane is this—that if the syrup boil too fast to be kept down; by aid of a wooden hooked stick, or a bit of chain affixed to the upper limb, it can be moved forward in an instant from the fire.

Care must be taken to watch the syrup, ladle in hand, till the scum is seen to rise in a thick mass, which it does just a minute or two before boiling commences: this scum is then to be taken off with a skimmer or ladle, and if this part of the business be well done, the sugar will be good and bright, and clear-looking. It is the want of care in clarifying the sugar, that gives it the dark look and bitter taste that many persons object to in maple sugar. Keep removing the scum, as it rises from time to time; if it has been well scummed the syrup will look as clear as the finest Madeira wine. Rub the edge of the kettle with clean lard or butter when you first set it over the fire, but do not depend on this preventative for boiling over, as when near sugaring, the liquid is very thick, and rises rapidly. It is prudent always to keep a little cool stuff by you to throw in, should it rise too fast. Towards the close of the boiling, the greatest care and watchfulness is required. When the syrup boils in thick yellow foam, and the whole pot seems nothing but bubbles, the sugar is nearly come; it then drops ropy from the ladle, and experienced sugar-makers can tell by blowing it off the edge of the ladle if it be done; it then draws into long, bright threads that easily stiffen when cool. Others drop a little into a pail of cold water, when, if it hardens, they say it is ready to pour out into pails or pans, or any convenient vessel. Most persons

F

grease the pans or moulds before they pour the syrup into them, that it may turn out easily.

Much maple sugar is spoiled in its quality by being over-boiled. It is true it hardens more readily, but loses in excellence of grain and colour.

In the course of two or three days the sugar will be formed into a solid cake, and may be turned out; but if you wish to have a good fine-grained sugar, after turning it out of the moulds, pierce the bottoms of the cakes, and set them across sticks, over a clean vessel; a sugar-trough will do, and the wet molasses will drain out, which will improve the look or your sugar, render it easier to break up for use, and removes any coarse taste, so that you may put it as a sweetener into cakes, puddings, tea, or coffee, and it will be as nice as the best muscovado.

The larger coarse-grained maple-sugar, which looks like sugar-candy, is made by not over-boiling the syrup, pouring it into shallow pans, and letting it dry slowly in the sun, or a warm room. This I like better than the cake sugar, but it is not so convenient to store. To those who have few utensils or places to put things in, as a sweetmeat for eating, the dark heavy-looking sugar is liked the best, but I prefer the sparkling good-grained sugar, myself, for all purposes.

The Indian sugar, which looks dry and yellow, and is not sold in cakes, but in birch boxes, or mowkowks, as they call them, I have been told, owes its peculiar taste to the birch-bark vessels that the sap is gathered in, and its grain, to being kept constantly stirred while cooling. I have been told that a small bit of lime put into the syrup whitens the sugar. Milk is used to clarify, when eggs are not to be had, but I only made use of eggs. Four eggs I found enough for one boiling of sugar.

INDIAN RICE.

Indian rice is a wholesome and nourishing article of diet, which deserves to be better known than it is at present. It grows in vast beds, in still waters, in a depth from three to eight feet, where there is a great deposit of mud and sand. In many places where there is little current, these beds increase so as to materially fill up the shallow lakes, and impede the progress of boats on their surface.

When the rice begins to show its tender green blade above the water, you would think the lake was studded with low verdant islands. In the months of July and August, the rice comes in flower, and a very beautiful sight it is for those who have an eye to enjoy the beauties of nature. The leaves, which are grassy, attain a great length, and float upon the surface of the water; I have seen the leaves of the rice measured to the amazing extent of eleven, twelve, and thirteen feet. The deer come down at night to feed on the rice-beds, and there the hunter often shoots them. The Indians track them to their feeding-places, and shoot them by torchlight.

In the month of September is the Indian's rice harvest: by that time it is fully ripe and withered. The squaws collect it by paddling through the rice-beds, and with a stick in one

INDIANS GATHERING RICE.

hand, and a sort of sharp-edged, curved paddle in the other, striking the ripe heads down into the canoe, the ripe grain falling to the bottom. Many bushels are thus collected. They then make an enclosure on a square area of dry ground, by sticking branches of pine or cedar close together, to form a sort of hedge: in the centre of this place they drive in forked sticks, in a square of several feet, across which they lay others, and on this rude frame they extend mats of bass or cedar, for the manufacture of which the Indian women are renowned: they light a fire beneath this frame, and when reduced to hot, glowing coals, the rice is spread on the mats above the fire: the green enclosure is to keep the heat from escaping: the rice is kept stirred and turned with a wooden shovel or paddle, and, after it is dried, the husk is winnowed from it in large open baskets, shaken in the wind. This is the mere drying process of the green rice.

The parched Indian-rice is heated in pots over a slow fire, till it bursts and shows the white floury part within the dark skin. This sort is eaten by the Indians in soups and stews, and often dry, by handfuls, when on journeys, as the parched corn of the Israelites.

Indian rice is sold in the stores at 10s. a bushel: it affords a great quantity of food. The Indians sew it up in mats or coarse birch-bark baskets: it is dearer now than it used to be, as the Indians are indolent, or, possibly, employed in agricultural pursuits or household work.

In appearance this rice is not the least like the white rice of commerce, being long, narrow, and of an olive-green colour outside, but when cooked, is white within. The gathering of wild rice is a tedious process, and one rarely practised by the settlers, whose time can be more profitably employed on their farms; but I have nevertheless given this description of harvesting it, as it is not devoid of interest, and, should this book fall into the hands of any person, who by accident was reduced to having recourse to such expedients as the wild country afforded, for food to keep themselves from starving, they might be able to avail themselves of the knowledge.

Men who have gone up lumbering, on the shores of lonely lakes and rivers, far from the haunts of civilized men, have sometimes been reduced to worse shifts than gathering wild rice to supply their wants.

VINE CULTURE.

We have a native Vine which produces excellent and wholesome wine—and while tens of thousands of idle and thriftless landowners will stoutly deny the fact, the last Report of the Bureau of Agriculture, proves the complete success which has attended the experiment in the cases of Mr De Courtenay, who resides in the Eastern townships, and Mr. Henry Parker, who lives at Cookesville near Toronto. The country ought to feel deeply indebted to both these gentlemen. I quote the practical letter of Mr. Parker, on this subject:—

SIR,—Absence from home prevented my replying to your letter, dated Sept. 20.

It gives me the greatest pleasure to coincide with Mr. De Courtenay, in many respects, as regards the cultivation of vineyards. I cannot, of course, speak with certainty of the

Lower Province, but I consider it a matter of vital importance to Upper Canada.

I have proved, beyond a doubt, that immense crops of grapes can be raised without the necessity of either burying them, as in the Crimea, or pruning low, as recommended by Mr. De Courtenay.

Last year I cut several tons off a few acres, selling some ripe, turning some of the Green Grapes into Champagne, and also making some Red Champagne, as well as some Dry Sherry. I sold 100 gallons of Champagne to one person, who speaks highly of it, and I bottled a cask for home consumption, which is universally liked.

I am strongly of opinion that age will greatly improve the fabric, from the fact that a few bottles remaining from my first vintage are now far superior, and evidently still improving.

My plan of action is this: I strike any quantity of cuttings, a foot apart, and six inches in the rows; these remain two years, requiring little trouble to keep them free from weeds. In the meantime, I trench and underdrain the ground. This done, I take the two-year old plants and plant them out Spring or Autumn, encouraging their growth by frequent tillage, and the following year I receive a small return.

If large crops be required, it is necessary to be particular about the under-draining, and for the vineyard to be permanent to trench the ground, making use of whole bones, except the land be pure sand, when trenching may be dispensed with.

I have many vines growing over wire trellises, formed like the roof of a house, others simply tied to stakes. I have much larger crops from the wire trellises, but the expense of erection, and growth of grass and weeds under them, would prevent my making use of them on a larger scale. The spring frost has never injured my vines till this year, when that of the 4th June cut off my entire crop, leaving, however, the vines uninjured. The white frost in the autumn certainly improves the grapes; but I have proved that one, severe enough to cut off the leaves, injures the fruit.

I am of opinion that cuttings procured from abroad would certainly fail, from their requiring to be buried in the winter, thus causing a large amount of labour, and injuring the vineyard. On the other hand, the native grape, the Clinton, has stood the test of the hardest winters unharmed, while the Black Hamburg, Black Chester, Sweet Water, Isabella, Catawba, and Royal Muscadine have been all killed to the ground.

The Clinton, with sugar, makes a splendid wine. The resources of Canada can never be developed unless such men as Mr. De Courtenay meet with every encouragement. Canada covered with vines would be very different from Canada as it now is; and how many men have had grants of land, on which nothing has been done but felling the timber and planting potatoes!

I have tried everything in my power to encourage vine culture; but what can I do single-handed? I have given away plants, and tried to impress upon numbers the great advantage accruing to themselves and the country from Grape culture, but they will not incur the first necessary expense, and they also have a fear of the want of a market. Let the engine, however, be once set in motion, and there can be no doubt of the country being soon covered with a splendid article of commerce.

The interest I feel in the matter must be my apology for the length of this letter.

I am, Sir,
Your obedient Servant,
HENRY PARKER.

Cookesville, Toronto.
Sept. 30, 1860.

MEMORIES OF CHRISTMAS DAY IN THE BACKWOODS.

When I first came to Canada, I was much surprised at the cold indifference which most people showed in their observance of Christmas day. With the exception of the then few residing English families, the church was scantily attended. For in those days there was no dressing of the houses or churches with evergreens as is now so generally the custom, (long may it continue); and I missed the heartfelt cordiality that seems on that sacred day of Christian gladness to overflow all hearts, and break out into smiles of loving-kindness to the poorest and least-cared for of our fellow-creatures. There be many, who with a scoffing eye look upon the decoration of our hearths and altars on that day, and loudly condemn it as a rag of Romanism. But are we really better Christians for casting aside all those old customs, that tended to hold us in the bond of unity and Christian love? I cannot but think that this old custom had its origin in the palm branches, that were strewed in the way of our Lord when the multitudes cut down branches from the trees, and strewed them in the way, crying " Hosannah to the son of David !" Did Christ reprove the people for this simple sacrifice in honour of him?—Why then should our observance of this old custom draw down upon us the rebuke of our neighbours?

I remember the first Christmas day I passed in Canada being laughed at because I wandered out on to the plains near Peterboro', and brought in a leaf of the box-leaved trailing winter-green (which with its scarlet berries reminded me of the varnished holly with which we were wont to garnish the old house at home), and hanging it over the mantelpiece, and above the pictures of my host's parlour, in honour of the day. It seemed to me these green branches might be held as emblems to remind us that we should keep faith bright and green within our hearts.

But while the *nativity* of our Lord was little regarded, all its honour and glory was conferred on the New Year's day. This is with the Canadians the day of days. The world claims that which used to be given to Christ.

The increase of British settlers, however, has done something towards restoring a Christian feeling among us, and now our churches are duly dressed with evergreens, or hymns and anthems sung, and our friends and families meet together as of old.

I remember one Christmas day in the bush. It was the year after the memorable rebellion in Canada : my brother-in-law had been appointed to a company in the provincial battalion then stationed in Toronto; my sister, who had remained behind with her infant family, was alone, and we were anxious that she should spend this day with us; and that it might look more like an English Christmas day, I despatched Martin, the boy, and old Malachi, the hired man, to bring a sleigh-load of evergreens from the swamp, to dress the house with; but when all our green garlands were put up, we missed the bright-varnished holly and its gay, joy-inspiring red berries, and my English maid Hannah, who was greatly interested in all our decorations, remembered that there were high-bush cranberries at the lake shore, and winter greens in the swamp, but these last were deep beneath a covering of two or three feet of snow. With the red transparent berries of the cranberry we were obliged therefore to content ourselves, and little Katie brought her string of coral beads and bade me twist it among the green hemlock boughs, clapping her hands for joy when she saw it twined into the Christmas wreath.

Then we sent off the ox-sleigh for my sister, and her little ones, for be it known to you, my reader, that our settlement in those days was almost the *Ultima Thule* of civilization, and our roads were no roads, only wide openings chopped through the heart of the forest, along which no better vehicle than an ox-sleigh could make any progress without the continual chance of an overturn. We bush-settlers were brave folks then, and thankfully enjoyed every pleasure we could meet with, even though we had to seek it through means so humble as a ride in a rude vehicle like an ox-sleigh, through the wild woods, with the snow above, and the snow below, and in good truth many a pleasant ride have we enjoyed travelling through that dim forest, through bowers of snow-laden hemlocks and dark spruce, which shut us out from the cold wind, like a good fur-lined cloak.

Reposing on a bed of hay, covered with buffalo or bear skins, or good wool coverlets, and wrapped in plaids, with well-wadded hoods, we were not a whit less happy than if we had been rolling along in a gay carriage, drawn by splendid horses, instead of the rudest of all vehicles, and the most awkward and clumsy of all steeds. At night our lamps, the pale stars and the moon, walking in brightness in the frosty sky, casting quaint shadows of gigantic form across the snowy path, or wading through misty wrack or silvered-edged cloud.

A glorious goose, fattened on the rice-bed in our lake, was killed for the occasion: turkeys were only to be met with on old cleared farms in those days, and beef was rarely seen in the back-woods,—excepting when some old ox that was considered as superannuated was slaughtered to save it from dying a natural death. Remember this was sixteen years ago, and great changes have taken place since that time in the condition of all ranks of people in the province : now there are luxuries, where before necessaries were scarce. However there was no lack of Christmas cheer in the shape of a large plum-pudding, to which our little ones did ample justice. A merry day it was to them, for our boy Martin had made them a little sledge, and there was a famous snow-drift against the garden fence, which was hard packed and frozen smooth and glare. Up and down this frozen heap did James and Kate with their playmates glide and roll. It was a Christmas treat to watch those joyous faces, buoyant with mirth, and brightened by the keen air, through the frosty panes ; and often was the graver converse of the parents interrupted by the merry shout and gleesome voices of their little ones ; and if a sadder train of thought brought back the memory of former days, and home, country, and friends, from whom we were for ever parted, such sadness was not without its benefit, linking us in spirit to that home, and all that made it precious to our hearts ; for we knew on that day our vacant places would be eyed with tender regret, and " some kind voice would murmur,

" Ah, would they were here !"

That night, unwilling to part too soon, I accompanied my sister and her little ones home. Just as we were issuing forth for our moonlight drive through the woods, our ears were saluted by a merry peal of sleigh bells, and a loud hurrah greeted our homely turn-out, as a party of lively boys and girls, crammed into a smart painted cutter, rushed past at full speed. They were returning from a Christmas merry-making at a neighbour's house, where they too had been enjoying a happy Christmas ; and long the still woods echoed with the gay tones of their voices, and the clear jingle of their merry bells, as a bend in the river-road, brought them back on the night breeze to our ears. There then we were breaking the Sabbath stillness of the dark forest with the hum of joyous voices, and the wild burst of mirth that gushed forth from those glad children, who had as yet known little of the cares and regrets that later years bring with them as the inevitable consequence of a mature age. But soon over-

powered by excess of happiness, and lulled by the low
monotonous creaking of the runners of the sleigh, and heavy
footfall of the oxen, one by one, our happy companions dropped
off to sleep, and we were left in silence to enjoy the peculiar
beauties of that snow-clad scene, by the dreamy light that
stole down upon our narrow road through the snow-laden
branches above our heads.   And often in after years, when
far removed from those forest scenes, has that Christmas night
returned to my memory, and still I love to recall it, for it
brings with it the freshness of former days, and the array of
infant faces now grown up and fulfilling the state of life into
which they have been called by their heavenly Father.

C. P. T.

Christmas, 1853, Oaklands, Rice Lake.

A SONG FOR CHRISTMAS.

THE OLD HOLLY-TREE.

Oh! the old holly-tree is a beautiful sight,
With its dark glossy leaves, and its berries so bright;
It is gay in the winter, and green in the spring,
And the old holly-tree is a beautiful thing.

It gladdens the cottage, it brightens the hall,
For the gay holly-tree is beloved by us all:
It shadows the altar, it hallows the hearth—
An emblem of sacred and innocent mirth!

Spring blossoms are lovely, and summer flowers gay;
But the chill winds will wither and chase them away;
But the rude blasts of Autumn and Winter may rave
In vain round the holly, the holly so brave!

Though the " fine old English gentleman " no longer now is seen;
And customs old have passed away, as things that ne'er have been;
Though wassail shout is heard no more, nor mistletoe we see;
Yet they've left us yet the holly-green, the bonny holly-tree!

C. P. T.

Oaklands, Rice Lake.

INDIAN SUMMER.

This mysterious second summer comes for a brief season to quicken the vegetation of the new-sown grain, and to perfect the buds that contain the embryo leaves and blossoms of the future year, before the frost of winter shall have bound up the earth with its fetters of ice.

The misty warmth of the Indian summer steals drowsily upon our senses. We linger lovingly over each soft day that comes to us, folded in a hazy veil, and fear each one will be the last. They seem to us

> " Like joys that linger as they fall,
> Whose last are dearest."

We watch with anxious eye the sun go down in the smoky horizon, and wonder if we shall see another Indian-summer day arise on the morrow.

The earth is rendering up her increase on nature's great altar, giving back to us some of the teeming warmth that she had collected during the long hot days of July, August, and September.

It is natural to suppose that the mist that softens the atmosphere at this peculiar season arises from vegetable decomposition.

Or may be it has its origin in a remoter cause: the commencement of the polar winter. This subject has puzzled wiser heads than mine; therefore I will dismiss that part of my subject to the natural philosophers of this enlightened, reasoning age.

Among the peculiarities of this season, may be noticed frosty nights, followed by warm soft days: sometimes a hot stirring breeze comes on about noon, at other times a stillness almost sultry continues through the day. From notes made in my journal during a succession of years I have remarked that the Indian summer comes on directly after the rains which prevail during the equinox, and the first two weeks in October. From the 10th or 15th of October to the first week in November, I should fix as the usual period of Indian summer. Old settlers say that it comes earlier now than in former years. The date used to be as late as the 20th of November, but it is rarely so late now, whatever the cause.

The northern lights are frequently seen about the commencement of the Indian summer, often being visible for

many successive nights. The termination of this lovely serene
season is very generally accompanied with a tempest, a
hurricane, a violent rain, ending in snow and sharp frost.

Though so lovely to the senses, it is not always a season of
health : autumnal fevers and agues, with affections of the chest,
are common. Nevertheless, this Indian summer is hailed by
the Indian people with joy. It is, emphatically speaking,
indeed the INDIAN'S SUMMER—his own peculiar season—his
harvest in which he gathers in the winter-stores.

At this time the men forsake the villages and summer-lodges,
and go off to their far-off hunting-grounds, for venison and
furs. Now is their fishing-season; and it is in the month of
October, that the lakes swarm with myriads of wild-fowl.

The term *Indian Summer* always sounds to me as so expres-
sive of the wants, habits, and circumstances of the race. Their
summer is not our summer. Like the people, it is peculiar to
this continent.—*They* reap while *we* sow. While *they* collect,
we scatter abroad the seed for the future harvest.

It is by minute observation upon the objects with which he
is most familiar, that the Indian obtains his knowledge :—a
knowledge which has hitherto been sufficient for the supply
of his very limited wants. He knows by the thickness of the
down on the breasts of the wild-fowl, and the fur of his
peltries, whether the coming winter will be a severe one
or otherwise. By the number of small animals that congre-
gate in their several haunts, and the stores which they lay up,
whether the season will be of longer or shorter duration. By
the beavers repairing their dams; and the musk-rats building
their houses earlier than usual, that the cold will also set in
early.

In all these things the Indian trusts to the instinct of the
lower animals, which is a knowledge given from God above
—a great gift to help the weakest of his creatures.*

The unlettered Indian, in the simple faith of his heart,
believes that the Almighty Creator—whom he adores as the
GOOD SPIRIT—speaks to his creatures, tells them of his will,
and guides them how to act, and provides for the winter's cold,
be it little or be it much.

A great deal of the fruitfulness of the next year's harvest,
may depend upon the length or shortness of the Indian
summer.

It is during this season that the farmer stores his root-crops,

* " God's gift to the weak," as says Mrs. Southey.

and prepares his fallow lands. If, as it sometimes happens, the Indian summer is short, and early frosts stop the ploughing operations, the spring crops must suffer.

Therefore the thoughtful settler naturally regards the length of the Indian summer as a great blessing.

Nature has now exhausted her rich store of buds and blossoms. The rains and winds of October have scattered the last bright leaves upon the earth, The scarlet maple, the crimson oak and cherry, the dark purple of the black-ash, the lighter yellow of the birch and beech, lie withering at our feet—" the fading glories of the dying year."

Is there nothing but sadness and decay in those fallen leaves? In those gray, leafless branches, through which the wind is sighing a requiem over the faded flowers and foliage? In yon grey elder, those round knobs contain the embryo blossoms, closely packed like green seeds ; yet each tiny flower-cup is as perfect as it will be in the month of May :— it is only abiding its time ! Yes, truly, there is much of hope and promise, revealed to us at this season. There is a savour of death ;—but it is a death unto LIFE !

Look on those broad fields of emerald verdure, brightening into spring-like beauty, with the rays of the noonday sun. Do they not speak to us of the future harvest—of the fruits oi the coming year, which the harvestman is to reap.

He, too, must bide the time : first the blade ; then the ear ; then the ripened grain ; then, again, the seed cast upon the earth—the renewal of his toil and his trust. Thus, then, we perceive that the Fall of the year is the renewal of Hope. In its darkest gloom, there is ever a gleam of sunlight, pointing onward to future joys.

LIST OF THE TREES OF CANADA.

The following list of the trees of Canada is taken from Mr. Hutton's very useful pamphlet called "Canada."

I shall not attempt to give any 'generic' description of our giants of the forest; most of them are now pretty well known, at least by timber merchants Our Pine, Elm, Oak, Ash, &c., have been long known, and the more ornamental woods, such as the Black Walnut, Butternut, the Bird's-Eye, and Curled Maples, &c. are now rapidly becoming favourites for cabinet and ornamental work.

The *Oak.*—Of this we have several varieties, but the White Oak (Quercus alba) is the most valuable for general purposes; extensively used for ship-building and wheelwright's work. The wood of the others is not so valuable, but the bark is used for tanning.

The *Maple.*—Besides the two varieties named, the Curled and Bird's-Eye, we have the Sugar Maple (Acer saccharinum), yielding a sap from which delicious sugar is abundantly made. Its ashes are rich in alkali and furnish most of the potash made in the country. They all afford excellent fuel.

The *Walnut.*—Black and Butternut : the Black (Juglans nigra) attains the height of seventy or eighty feet, and three or four feet in diameter, and the wood is most beautifully grained, susceptible of a high polish, and highly prized for furniture, and gun-stocks. The nuts are very good, if kept for some time. The Butternut (Juglans Cinerea) is of infinitely less value, but the nuts are preferred to those of the former.

The *Hickory.*—This wood possesses great tenacity, and is much used for tool-handles, handspikes, &c., and its nuts are much esteemed.

The *Elm*—(Ulmus Americana)—grows to a prodigious height, and in size, perhaps, exceeds every other tree; but its wood is not much used. There is another variety (Ulmus Fulva), the Slippery or Red Elm, whose bark is used medicinally.

The *Pine.*—Of this we have two or three varieties, all growing to a vast height. The White Pine (Pinus strobus) attains a height of one hundred and sixty feet; but the wood of the Red Pine (Pinus resinosa) is far more valuable: the former is much used for masts, but it yields timber of larger size, which is adapted to a greater variety of purposes than any other tree.

The *Ash.*—Of this there are several kinds, but the most valuable is the White Ash (Fraxinus acuminata). This wood is greatly used for carriage-building, possessing great strength and elasticity.

The *Tulip Tree* (Liriodendron) is found in the south-western district, and attains the height of eighty or ninety feet. Its wood is useful.

The *Button-wood*, or Sycamore (Platanus occidentalis), called also Cotton Tree, is one of the largest of our forest trees, but its wood is of little value.

The *Birch.*—There are two or three varieties of this: one, the Canoe Birch (Betula papyracea), so called from its being made by the Indians into canoes: this tree is only found in the north; the wood of all is highly prized for fuel.

We have also the *Chestnut* (Castanea Americana), bearing an excellent fruit, and the wood producing good charcoal. The *Beech*, red and white (Fagus ferruginea and Americana), affording excellent fuel, and a very tough and compact wood. The *Ironwood* (Ostrya Virginica), called also Hop-Hornbeam, from its flowers resembling those of the hop: the wood of this is amazingly heavy, and used for the heads of mallets and other purposes. We have various *Willows* and *Spruces* (Abies). *Hemlocks* (Abies Canadensis), a beautiful tree attaining a height from sixty to eighty feet; wood not good, but the bark valuable for tanning. The *Black Spruces* (Abies nigra), equally large and extensively used in ship-building, and almost always for spars; from the young branches of which is made the spruce beer. The *Balsam Spruce* (Abies Balsamifera), from the trunk of which exudes a turpentine, vulgarly called "Balm of Gilead." The *Larch*, or *Hachmatak* (Laris microcarpa), attains one hundred feet in height: also used in ship-building. The *Cedar* (Cypressus'.—Of the white variety excellent charcoal is made, and the red is very durable; used for ship-building, and for posts and rails; the berry is used in the manufacture of gin. The *Sassafras* (Laurus Sassafras), a fine aromatic, and producing an alterative medicine. The *Wild* or *Bird Cherry* (Cerasus Virginiana) attains an enormous size; the fruit small, and only useful as an infusion; the wood highly prized for furniture. In the south-west, the *Safran* (Asimina triloba) is occasionally to be met with; it is a small tree, but produces a fruit which resembles the Banana in shape and flavour.

Shrubs and flowers of infinite variety and beauty grow in both provinces.

MODE OF ASCERTAINING THE QUALITY OF LAND IN THE BUSH.

The following chapter from Major Strickland's work is worth reproduction as the experience of an old settler :—

I shall now endeavour to give the emigrant some information to guide him in the selection of his land, and other matters connected with a settlement in the bush. In the first place the quality of the land is the greatest consideration, and to make a good choice requires a practical knowledge as to the nature of the soils, and the different kinds of timber growing thereon.

The best land is timbered with oak, ash, elm, beech, basswood, and sugar-maple. A fair mixture of this species of trees is best, with here and there a large pine, and a few Canadian balsams scattered among the hard-wood. Too great a proportion of beech indicates sand or light loam: a preponderance of rock-elm is a sign of gravel or limestone rock near the surface.

The timber should be lofty, clean in the bark and straight in the grain, and of quick growth. The woods should be open, free from evergreens, and with little under-brush. Generally speaking, the soil is of excellent quality, when timbered in the manner described.

It however, often happens, that the best land is full of boulders, which are both troublesome and expensive to remove. Two-thirds of these stones are not visible above the surface, and the remainder are so covered with moss and leaves, that they require a practised eye to detect them. I have no objection to a small quantity of stones, as they are useful to construct French drains, or to roll into the bottoms of the rail-fences.

When limestone-flag is near the surface, the stems of the

trees will be shorter, their heads more bushy, and the roots spreading along the top of the ground. Such land is apt to burn in hot weather, and soon becomes exhausted. White-pine, or hemlock ridges, are almost always sandy, and good for little —except the timber, which is valuable, if near enough to water. White-pine, mixed with hard-wood, generally indicates strong clay land, good for wheat; but the difficulty of clearing off such heavy timber, and the long time it takes to get rid of the stumps, render such a selection unprofitable, and add additional toil to the emigrant.

The best land for wheat should be gently undulating soil, rich loam, on a clay bottom. In the summer months you can judge the quality of the land by the freshly turned-up roots of trees, which have fallen by the wind.

In winter, when the surface of the ground is covered with snow, and frozen hard, the growth and quality of the timber, as before described, are your only mode of judging correctly.

A constant supply of water is absolutely necessary, in a country liable to such extreme heat in summer. Canada West, abounding, as it does, in small spring-creeks, rivers, and lakes, is, perhaps, as well watered as any country in the world; and, in almost every section of the country, even on the highest ridges, good water can be obtained by digging wells, which seldom require to be sunk more than twenty feet; and in many townships, not half that depth is required.

After the emigrant has selected a proper location, his next object is to choose the best situation to build his shanty, and chop his first fallow. Most settlers like to commence as near as possible to the concession-line or public road; but sometimes the vicinity of a stream of water or good spring is preferred. In fact, circumstances must, in some measure, guide them in their choice.

The best time of the year to commence operations is early in September. The weather is then moderately warm and pleasant, and there are no flies in the bush to annoy you.

A log shanty, twenty-four feet long by sixteen, is large enough to begin with, and should be roofed either with shingles or troughs. A small cellar should be dug near the fire-place, commodious enough to hold twenty or thirty bushels of potatoes, a barrel or two of pork, &c.

As soon as your shanty is completed, measure off as many acres as you intend to chop during the winter, and mark the boundaries by blazing the trees on each side.

G

The next operation is to cut down all the small trees and brush—this is called under-brushing. The rule is to cut everything close to the ground from the diameter of six inches downwards.

There are two modes of piling, either in heaps or in wind-rows. If your fallow is full of evergreens, such as hemlock, pine, balsam, cedar, and such description of timber, then I should say windrows are the best; but when the timber is deciduous, heaps are better.

The brush should be carefully piled and laid all one way, by which means it packs closer and burns better. The regular price for under-brushing hard-wood land, and cutting up all the old fallen timber—which is always considered a part of the under-brushing—is one dollar per acre, and board. Rough land and swamp vary from seven shillings and six-pence to ten shillings. Your under-brush should be all cut and piled by the end of November, before the snow falls to the depth of four inches, for after that it would be both difficult and tedious.

The chopping now begins, and may be followed without any interruption until the season for sugar-making com-mences. The heads of the trees should be thrown upon the heaps or windrows. A skilful chopper will scarcely ever miss a heap when felling the timber, besides it saves a great deal of labour in piling the limbs.

The trunks of the trees must be cut into lengths, from fourteen to sixteen feet, according to the size of the timber. Now and then a large maple or beech, when felled, may be left without cutting up, with the exception of the top, which is called a plan-heap, and is left to log against: this is only done when the tree is too large to be cut through easily with the axe.

All timber fit for making rails should be left in double and treble lengths, as it is less likely to burn.

A good axe-man should be able, with fair chopping, to cut an acre in eight days after the under-brushing is done. The regular price of chopping is five dollars per acre, with board, or six without.

The emigrant should endeavour to get as much chopping done as possible during the first three years, because after that time he has so many other things to attend to, such as increase of stock, barn and house-building, thrashing, plough-ing, &c., which, of course, give him every year less time for chopping, particularly if his family be small, in which case fifty or sixty acres are enough to clear at first, till his boys are old enough to give him assistance.

Clearing up too large a farm, when labour is so high, is not wise, for it will not answer to disburse much for hire, at the present prices. If, therefore, you are not able to cultivate what you have cleared properly, it will grow up again with raspberries, blackberries, small trees, and brush, and be nearly as bad to clear as it was at first. The size of the farm must, however, depend on the resources of the emigrant, the strength and number of his family, and the quantity of acres he may possess.

In the month of May the settler should spring-burn three or four acres, and log them up for his spring-crops, such as potatoes and Indian-corn. The Indian-corn should be planted with the hoe in rows, three feet apart and thirty inches in the row. A pumpkin-seed or two should be sown in every second or third hole in each third row. The corn must be earthed or hilled up by drawing the mould close round the roots, and five or six inches up the stalks, which should be done when the plants are fifteen or sixteen inches high. No further cultivation is necessary until the time of cutting, except breaking off some shoots from the roots, if too many are thrown out.

Potatoes on the new land are also planted with the hoe, and in hills of about five thousand to the acre. A hole is scraped with the hoe, in which four or five sets, or a whole potato is dropped. The earth is then heaped over them in the form of a mole-hill, but somewhat larger. After the plants have appeared above the surface, a little more mould is drawn round them. Very large crops of potatoes are raised in this manner. Two hundred and fifty bushels per acre are no uncommon crop. I have assisted in raising double that quantity; but of late years, since the disease has been prevalent, but poor crops have been realized.

Both white turnips and swedes do well, and grow to a large size, particularly on new land: the roots must be either pitted or put into a root-house, or cellar, as the winter is too severe for them to remain unhoused.

The remainder of the fallow should be burnt off and logged up in July, the rail-cuts split into quarters and drawn off to the site of the fences, ready for splitting into rails. After the log-heaps are burnt, you should either spread the ashes or rake them while hot into heaps, if you intend to make pot-

ash,* with which, by-the-by, I should advise the new-comer
to have nothing to do until he has made himself thoroughly
acquainted with the process.

As soon as the settler has cleared up fifteen or twenty acres,
his first care should be to erect a frame or log-barn; I should
strongly recommend the former, if boards can be obtained in
the neighbourhood, as it is undoubtedly the best and cheapest
in the long run. If I were commencing life again in the
woods, I would not build anything of logs except a shanty or
a pig-stay; for experience has plainly told me that log buildings are the dirtiest, most inconvenient, and the dearest
when everything is taken into consideration.

As soon as the settler is ready to build, let him put up a
good frame, roughcast, or stone-house, if he can possibly raise
the means, as stone, timber, and lime, cost nothing but the
labour of collecting and carrying the materials. When I say
that they " cost nothing," I mean that no cash is required
for these articles, as they can be prepared by the exertions of
the family.

With the addition of from a hundred to a hundred and
fifty pounds in money to the raw material, a good substantial
and comfortable dwelling can be completed. Two or three
years should be spent in preparing and collecting materials,
so that your timber may be perfectly seasoned before you
commence building.

Apple and plum orchards should be planted as soon as

* This article is very extensively made in nearly all the new settlements,
and may be considered one of the staples of the country. The process is
very simple; but great care must be taken in collecting the ashes clear of
sand or dirt of any description. If your ashes are well saved and from
good timber, ten acres should produce at least five barrels of potash, each
barrel containing five hundredweight. Several things should be considered before the emigrant attempts the manufacture of this article.
Firstly, his land should be well timbered with oak, elm, maple, and bass-
wood. Secondly, it must have a stream of water, near which he may erect
his works. And, lastly, it ought to be within reach of a market and a
remunerating price, which, to pay the manufacturer, should not be less
than twenty-five shillings, Halifax currency, per cwt.

The best situation to erect an ashery upon is the side of a bank, beside
a running stream; and if there should be fall enough in the creek to bring
a supply of water overhead into the leaches, a great deal of labour will
be saved. An ash-house, six or eight leach-tubs, a pot-ash kettle, and
three or four coolers are all the requisites necessary. Most persons use a
small portion of common salt and lime in the manufacture of pot-ash.
After the lye is run off it is boiled down into black salts, which are melted
into pot-ash, cooled off, and packed into air-tight barrels ready for market.

possible, and well fenced from the cattle and sheep. The best kind of grafted fruit-trees, from three to seven years old, can be obtained for a shilling a tree; ungrafted, at four shillings the dozen.

The apple-tree flourishes extremely well in this country, and grows to a large size. I gathered last year, out of my orchard, several Ribstone pippins, each of which weighed more than twelve ounces, and were of a very fine flavour. The native plums are not very good in their raw state, but they make an excellent preserve, and good wine.

PART THE SECOND.

PREFACE.

The Publisher avails himself, for this portion of the work, of various official documents in corroboration of the favourable views which, from many years, residence in Canada, and close attention to the subject matter of this little work, he has formed, and which fully justify him in recommending the class of emigrants for whose information this work is especially designed, to make Canada their home. The classes alluded to are farmers, with some little capital, farm-labourers, boys and girls from fourteen to eighteen, more or less acquainted with country life, and domestic servants.

The first authority used is the admirable pamphlet recently published for gratuitous information by the Government of Canada, and which gives an accurate " Outline of her Geographical Position, Climate, Capabilities, Minerals, Fisheries, Forests, &c."

The extracts made in this work are confined more especially to those portions which refer to agriculture, a subject of the deepest interest to the classes above alluded to.

The next authority quoted is the well-timed and statesman-like " Manifesto " of the able Finance Minister of Canada, the Hon. A. T. Galt, written with a view to refute and counteract the possible effects of some anonymous writer in Canada, who *somehow* found access to one or two British journals, by which these *ex parte* statements of a well-known political opponent were too easily admitted.

Mr. Galt's pamphlet has placed before the world, upon official authority, the true financial position of Canada, and the effect of this statement has been to strengthen and confirm the high opinion already entertained by capitalists of the judgment, honesty, and economy with which the fiscal arrangements of the country are administered, by means of which the national credit is upheld, and the smallest possible burden, in the way of direct taxation, placed upon the people.

Since the publication of Mr. Galt's pamphlet, he has taken the bold step of abolishing the tolls on the St. Lawrence and on the Canadian canals, and established free ports at the two extreme ends of the Province, Gaspe, and Saulte St. Marie, on Lake Superior.

The view taken by a writer in the United States on this point, so well and gracefully expressed, cannot be out of place here.

CANADA.

"The decision by 'the Government' of the Canadas that the canals of the provinces shall be, in effect, open to free navigation, is a bold and great step in the march of a nation. It indicates that there are statesmen in the administration of that valuable division of the British Empire. All Canada's relations towards home are changed within the last few years. The tenure of the provinces, that was weakening into a touch of recognition, has become a strong grasp, by the firmest of all bonds—confidence. The warmth of steam is in their international association. It is not now an affair of months before the voices of the Canadas are heard in the council at London. It is but a parenthesis of a few days, and only the fracture of a few strands of iron prevents it from being immediate. We deem our Pacific States firm links in the chain of the Republic; yet they are far more distant than are these provinces from Great Britain. Like affectionate mother and daughter, they have moved residence so as to be near neighbours.

"Our own people have been suggesting to themselves, that, let the Canadas labour ever so hard for commercial independence, it was, from the natural difficulties and impediments, at the best, 'an up-hill business,' and one which never could succeed. The discoveries of steam have thrust aside most up-hill embarrassments. We no longer realize practically that any deviation from the level is of our way—so rapidly are the wheels beneath us turning. Thus, one by one, the adverse circumstances of the Canadas are removed, or smoothed, or put aside. The best of railways, the widest and deepest of canals, bridges that face without falter the terrors of the frozen and of the fierce river, a wise and liberal policy towards the steam-moved vessel, a shore and coast brilliant with the warning watch-light, direct home intercourse, free institutions—all these have been suddenly developed in the Canadas. In the flight of Francis Bond Head, the fetters of the old system seemed to break, and the Crown to realize that no people are so likely to be loyal as those who are encouraged to prosperity.

"The St. Lawrence river, like the den of the wild beast in the fable, has its tracks all one way. From the day that the white man first saw and wondered at the canoe's course down the rapids, through the successive voyaging of Jesuit, and priest, and missionary, and poet, tourist, and traveller and raftsman and steamboat—a long history of delicate and dangerous navigation—the thin and fragile bark almost cut in two by the sharp crag that divided the bubbling current—the great Canada and America, vessels built for the waves and storms of Ontario—in the keel-

boat of the moving army, the batteau of warbling Tom Moore—under all
these passages of the great river, the journey has been—downwards. Not
even the stalwart Indian of Caughnawaga, who, with his three assistants,
still astonishes the tourist, can pilot *up* the Lachine; nor could Robert
Hoe himself construct engines that could *ascend* the fighting, foaming
torrent of the lost channel.   The tide itself waits beneath the piers of the
Victoria Bridge, and rests from its journey.

"These English people may be somewhat of one idea more than ourselves ; but they combine a vast strength in that one idea.   If they work
only with one purpose, that purpose is wrought out to the end.   The
Government many years since determined to overcome the dangers of the
rapids.   They did *not*, believe, with the drowsy power of Spain, that
Heaven intended us to be bound by the line of the rivers.   They realized
the great truth of Christian civilization, that Art is the agency of Nature.
It was not to be allowed that everything in Canada should go down.   To
go up—to go back—to return—to begin again, was an attribute of a living
enterprise ; so, under one name and another, to meet the nomenclature of
form, these canals were built—for military purposes, for provincial improvement—out of the military chest—this or that way, till they were
completed; and as the one vessel rushed frantically down the rapids, the
other, almost by its side, went peaceably through the canal in another
direction.

"The great step is now taken of declaring these canals free —changing
them into a river—and opening wide the way from lake to ocean.   It is a
lesson of some significance to the Republic, and most of all to the State of
New York."

The next official document quoted is the very valuable and
encouraging one published under the authority of the Bureau
of Agriculture, the contents of which deserve extensive circulation and careful perusal.

The crops of 1859 exceeded by 16 per cent. the general
average of the past twenty years, *and those of* 1860, *as far as
hitherto known, exceed those of* 1859 !

The free-grant system, directly and collaterally, has been
very successful, and from 4,000 acres of land cropped in 1859,
there was a result, for sale, equal to 140,000 dollars.

A most interesting report upon emigration has been published, and the evidence taken before the committee has
suggested many valuable recommendations.   Several of these,
however, have been anticipated by the Government, such as
the establishment of agents in Norway and Germany, (from
whence a valuable and increasing class of emigrants has
reached the Province,) and in Liverpool.   The Government
map, recommended by the committee, was in course of distribution before the report appeared, and is eagerly sought
after by parties interested in Canada.

The able and unanswerable "Remarks upon Mr. Caird's
Pamphlet on Prairie Farming in America," deserve and will

repay an attentive perusal. The high personal character of
Mr. Hutton, his thorough knowledge and long practical
experience in Canadian farming, entitle his opinion to much
weight; and hundreds returning now from the Western
States to Canada, and hundreds more who once contemplated
going thither, have reason to bless the voice which warned
them against a district unfitted for the production of European
crops, a climate unsuited to European constitutions, and where
under a foreign rule and flag, there is an absence of "British
feeling, British tone of morality, and a British social atmosphere."

The list of rivers, all of which afford splendid salmon and
salmon-trout fishing, will be interesting to sportsmen. The
best months for the sport are the latter end of June, the
whole of July, and part of August. The flora and fauna of
Saguenay afford an ample and almost unexplored field for the
naturalist. The map published herein is official.

THE CLIMATE OF CANADA.

THE most erroneous opinions have prevailed abroad respecting the climate of Canada. The so-called rigour of Canadian winters is often advanced as a serious objection to the country by many who have not the courage to encounter them, who prefer sleet and fog to brilliant skies and bracing cold, and who have yet to learn the value and extent of the blessings conferred upon Canada by her world-renowned "snows."

It will scarcely be believed by many who shudder at the idea of the thermometer falling to zero, that the gradual annual diminution in the fall of snow, in certain localities, is a subject of lamentation to the farmer in Western Canada. Their desire is for the old-fashioned winters, with sleighing for four months, and spring bursting upon them with marvellous beauty at the beginning of April. A bountiful fall of snow, with hard frost, is equivalent to the construction of the best macadamized roads all over the country. The absence of a sufficient quantity of snow in winter for sleighing, is a calamity as much to be feared and deplored as the want of rain in spring. Happily neither of these deprivations is of frequent occurrence.

The climate of Canada is in some measure exceptional, especially, that of the Peninsular portion. The influence of the great Lakes is very strikingly felt in the elevation of winter temperatures and in the reduction of summer heats. East and West of Canada, beyond the influence of the Lakes, as in the middle of the states of New York and Iowa, the greatest extremes prevail,—intense cold in winter, intense heat in summer, and to these features may be added their usual attendant, drought.*

* Professor Hurlburt says: Britain lies between the 50th and 59th degrees of North latitude, and Illinois between the 37th and 42nd. Emigrants from the South of England to the North of Illinois, pass South

Perhaps the popular standard of the adaptation of climate to the purposes of agriculture is more suitable for the present

over eight degrees of latitude, those from the North of Britain to the South of Illinois over 22 degrees, and those from the central counties of Great Britain and Ireland or from the Northern States of Germany to the central parts of Illinois must go fifteen degrees further South than their native land. This is a change in climate equivalent to going from the British Channel to Algeria in Africa, or to Palestine and Persia in Asia. The Southern nations of Europe are not identical in climate with corresponding latitudes in the meridian of Illinois in America, because the South and South-west of Europe are washed by the Atlantic and Mediterranean, the cool breezes and moist air of which mitigate the burning rays of the sun; but Illinois is situated in the central parts of the continent with a dry hot atmosphere such as is never experienced in Southern Europe. As the winds almost uniformly in summer are from the West and S. W., between 30° and 50° North latitude on this continent, Illinois does not receive any of the moist cool breezes of the great lakes. Hence the arid and parched plains in mid-summer of all the regions from Illinois West; these summer droughts often extending into Ohio.

The summer temperature of Glasgow (lat. 55° 51min.) is 56; that of Edinburgh 57; of London (lat. 51°) 61; of Liverpool (lat. 53°) 57; of Berlin in Prussia (lat. 52°) 64; but in lat. 88° 40 min. in Illinois it is 78°. This gives a very imperfect idea of the heat of the day, which from 10 a. m. to 3 p. m. in June, July and August, is often as high as 90 to 100 *in the shade* in Illinois, (if there be any shade where there are no trees) and 120 under the burning sun.

The effect of such tremendous changes of temperature ought to be well weighed by emigrants from the high cool latitudes of Europe.

Secondly. The emigrant from the British Isles, Norway, Sweden, or from any of the States of Germany, must change almost his entire system of agriculture in going to Illinois. He there gets too far South for the profitable culture of the European grains—the wheat, barley, oats, peas and rye; he gets beyond the region of green pastures and fertile meadows, beyond the land of the dairy. I do not mean that there are no meadows and no pastures in Illinois; but I do mean that South of 39° (and the Southern part of Illinois is in Latitude 37°) the European grasses (the grasses which make our green pastures), as a general rule will not grow, and the prairie grasses, most of them without *seeds*, cannot be reproduced, after being once destroyed. Hence the absence, throughout the South, of the green pastures so beautiful and so profitable in the North. In a wild, untilled state, the pastures are abundant, but not so when the country shall have been brought under culture. The dairy, with all its rich benefits, will be unknown.

Professor Norton, in his Appendix to Stephen's Farmers' Guide, says, that in many of the Eastern States, where wheat was once largely grown, its culture has greatly decreased, and in some districts scarcely any is to be found, except an occasional small patch of spring wheat. It is common to ascribe this to the Hessian fly, to the prevalence of rust, &c., but after we have made all due allowances for these causes of uncertain produce, the principal reason, in my judgment, is to be found in the deterioration of the land.

The climatic adaptation of the Western Province to certain forage and occasion than a reference to monthly and annual means of temperature. Much information is conveyed in the simple narration of facts bearing upon fruit culture. From the head of Lake Ontario, round by the Niagara frontier, and all along the Canadian shores of Lake Erie, the grape and peach grow with luxuriance, and ripen to perfection in the open air, without the slightest artificial aid. The island of Montreal is distinguished everywhere for the fine quality of its apples, and the island of Orleans, below Quebec, is equally celebrated for its plums. Over the whole of Canada the melon and tomato acquire large dimensions, and ripen fully in the open air, the seeds being planted in the soil towards the latter end of April, and the fruit gathered in September. Pumpkins and squashes attain gigantic dimensions; they have exceeded 300 pounds in weight in the neighbourhood of Toronto. Indian corn, hops, and tobacco, are common crops, and yield fair returns. Hemp and flax are indigenous plants, and can be cultivated to any extent in many parts of the province. With a proper expenditure of capital, England could be made quite independent of Russia, or any other country, for her supply of these valuable products.

The most striking illustration of the influence of the great Lakes in ameliorating the climate of Canada, especially of the western peninsula, is to be found in the natural limits to which certain trees are restricted by climate. That valuable wood, the black walnut, for which Canada is so celebrated, ceases to grow north of latitude 41° on the Atlantic coast, but under the influence of the comparatively mild Lake climate of Peninsular Canada it is found in the greatest profusion, and of the largest dimensions, as far north as latitude 43°.

---

root crops, is well deserving of notice. When ordinary care and attention are devoted to the cultivation, in the way of mere surface draining, and the application of farm-yard manure, gypsum, or lime, they grow with remarkable luxuriance. White clover springs up wherever the virgin soil is stirred with the plough, or even exposed to the sun's rays, after the process of clearing the land of its forest growth. The red clover flourishes year after year, without diminution in yield, if sparingly top-dressed with gypsum or leached wood ashes. Certain varieties of beans (not the common horse bean), such as the dwarf, French, and kidney beans, come to maturity with remarkable rapidity, and are at the same time very prolific. Some of the dwarf varieties are especially adapted for forage crops, or even food, as in Germany and France. They may be sown in this country broadcast as late as the middle of July: they produce most abundantly and are well adapted to serve as green manure, on light soils deficient in vegetable matter.

TABLE of Mean Monthly and Annual Temperature at Toronto, Canada West, from 1840 to 1859, taken from the Records of the Provincial Magnetic Observatory, by Professor Kingston.

	MONTHS.												Mean Annual.
	Jan.	Feb.	March.	April.	May.	June.	July.	August.	Sept.	October.	Nov.	Dec.	
1840 } 1859 }	°23·72	°22·83	°30 07	°41·00	°51·38	°61·27	°67·06	°66·12	°57·98	°45·27	°36·65	°25·97	°44·11

Mean Monthly and Annual Fall of Rain at Toronto, from 1840 to 1859.

	MONTHS.												Mean Annual.
	Jan.	Feb.	March.	April.	May.	June.	July.	August.	Sept.	October.	Nov.	Dec.	
	In.	In.	In.	In.	In.	In.	In.	In.	In.	In.	In.	In.	In.
1840 } 1859 }	1·480	1·043	1·553	2·492	3·305	3·198	3·490	2·927	4·099	2·557	3·109	1·606	30·859

Dr. Lillie, in his Essay on Canada, remarks, that "Professor Hind holds the climate of Canada West to be superior to those portions of the United States lying north of the 41st parallel of latitude, in mildness—in adaptation to the growth of cereals—in the uniformity of the distribution of rain over the agricultural months—in the humidity of the atmosphere—in comparative indemnity from spring frosts and summer droughts—in a very favourable distribution of clear and cloudy days for the purposes of agriculture—and in the distribution of rain over many days—as, also, in its salubrity. In the following points he regards it as differing favourably from that of Great Britain and Ireland, viz.—in high summer means of temperature—in its comparative dryness—and in the serenity of the sky."

AGRICULTURAL CAPABILITIES OF THE SOIL.

A reference to the display of cereals and other agricultural productions made by Canada at the Exhibitions of London and Paris, might be considered sufficient to illustrate the remarkable adaptation of the soil to their growth and cultivation ; but so limited a notice would leave the question of permanent fertility still unanswered. When, however, it is known that the area in which the astonishing crops of wheat are raised, for which Upper Canada is so distinguished, extends over three-fourths of the present inhabited parts of the country, and that the prevailing soils consist of rich clays of great depth, the question of permanent fertility resolves itself into that of husbandry.

In the valleys of some of the larger rivers of Upper Canada, wheat has been grown after wheat for 20 years; the first crops yielded an average of forty bushels to the acre, but under the thoughtless system of husbandry then pursued, the yield diminished to twelve bushels to the acre, and compelled a change of system, which soon had the effect of restoring the land to its original fertility. This system of exhaustion has effected its own cure, and led to the introduction of a more rational method of cultivating the soil. Years ago, when roads were bad, and facilities for communicating with markets few and far between, wheat was the only saleable produce of the farm, so that no effort was spared to cultivate that cereal to the utmost extent. Now, since railroads, macadamized roads, and plank roads have opened up the country, and Agricultural Societies have succeeded in disseminating much useful instruction and information, husbandry has improved in all directions, and the natural fertility of the soil of the old settlements is in great part restored.

The average yield of wheat in some townships exceeds twenty-two bushels to the acre, and where an approach to good farming prevails the yield rises to thirty and often forty bushels to the acre. On new land fifty bushels is not very uncommon ; and it must not be forgotten that Canadian wheat, grown near the city of Toronto, won a first prize at the Paris Exhibition. It may truly be said that the soil of what may be termed the agricultural portion of Canada, which comprises four-fifths of the inhabited portion, and a vast area still in the hands of the Government, and now open to settlement, is unexceptionable ; and when deterioration takes place, it is the fault of the farmer and not of the soil. In Canada the yield of wheat in 1859 considerably exceeded 25,000,000 bushels; and the quality of Canadian wheat is so superior, that the American millers buy it, for the purpose of mixing with grain grown in the United States, in order to improve the quality of their flour, and in some instances to render it fit for exportation.

VALUE OF LAND.

Australia excepted, no country can furnish such singular instances of the rise in value of surveyed lands, as the last seven years have witnessed in Canada. The cause, too, is so obvious, now that it is understood, that men wonder why the event had not been foreseen years before its occurrence. The reason is fully conveyed in the assertion that the country was not prepared for it. Eighteen hundred and fifty-two saw Canada without a railway; eighteen hundred and sixty sees her with 1876 miles completed, and many more in process of construction. The rise in the value of land is thus easily explained. Means of communication, of the highest order, have opened up the country, made available a vast amount of inert wealth, stimulated industry, and effected a complete revolution in farming economy within twenty miles on either side of the course they pursue.

The lines of railways are nothing more than a series of accessible markets for the country they serve. The natural consequence is, that every portable product of the farm has acquired a certain money value, although, before the construction of the railway, it may have been absolutely valueless, and perhaps even an incumbrance. This suddenly increased rate of interest, obtained for the same outlay of labour, has necessarily enhanced the value of the capital. Hence, land in old settlements, remote from lake ports, has doubled itself in value in seven years; while wild lands in new settlements, near to which a railway passes, have been trebled, and in some instances quadrupled in value during the same period.

Land adapted for farming purposes can seldom be obtained from land companies, speculators, or private individuals, under twenty shillings an acre. The Canadian Government being desirous of preventing the acquisition of large tracts of lands by private companies, or private individuals, for the purpose of speculation, have coupled the sale of the Government lands with such conditions as to prevent undue or improper advantage being taken of their liberality in offering farming land at a low rate. Every purchaser must become an actual settler. This simple condition drives out of the field a host of speculators who hitherto enriched themselves at the expense of the country, retarding its progress, and leaving its resources undeveloped.

FREE GRANTS.

The Provincial Government have recently opened seven great lines of road in Upper Canada, and five in Lower Canada, and laid out for settlement the lands through which these roads pass.

The roads in Upper Canada are styled:—

1st. *The Ottawa and Opeongo Road.*—This road runs East and West, and will eventually be 171 miles in length, and connect the Ottawa River with Lake Huron ; about 62 miles are now finished, and 235 settlers already located thereon. Resident Agent, T. P. FRENCH, Mount St. Patrick, near Renfrew.

2nd. *The Addington Road,* running North and South, 61 miles long, and starting from the settlements in the county of Addington, until it intersects the Opeongo Road; the number of settlers on this road is 178. Resident Agent, E. PERRY, Tamworth.

3rd. *The Hastings Road,* running nearly parallel to the Addington Road, 68 miles long, and connecting the county of Hastings with the Ottawa and Opeongo Road : there are 306 settlers on this road. Resident Agent, M. P. HAYES, Village of Hastings.

4th. *The Bobcaygeon Road,* running from Bobcaygeon, between the counties of Peterborough and Victoria, north, and intended to be continued to Lake Nipissing; 36 miles are already completed, and there are 168 settlers on the line ; the number of the family of each settler, on the above roads, averages about four. Resident Agent, R. HUGHES, Bobcaygeon.

5th. *The Frontenac and Madawaska Road,* of which 33 miles. are completed. Resident Agent, J. SPIKE, Hinchinbrooke.

6th. *The Muskoka Road,* of which 21 miles are completed : this road runs from the head of the navigation of Lake Couchiching to the Grand Falls of Muskoka, where it will intersect the road called Peterson's Line, which will eventually meet the Ottawa and Opeongo Road, now gradually opening westwardly, and by it the intending settler, arriving at Toronto, can, in one day's journey from that city, reach the very centre of the country. Resident Agent, J. ALEXANDER, Barrie.

7th. *The Sault Ste. Marie Road*, intended to run from Sault Ste. Marie to Goulais Bay, and of which 4 miles are already completed.

The five roads in Lower Canada are :—

The Elgin Road, in the county of l'Islet, about 35 miles long, from St. Jean, Port Joly, to the Provincial line. Resident Agent, S. DRAPEAU, St. Jean, Port Joly.

The Matane and Cap Chat.

The Tache Road, from Buckland, in the county of Bellechasse, to Kempt Road, in Rimouski—about 200 miles.

The Temiscouata Road, from River du Loup to Lake Temiscouata ;—and

The Kempt Road, from Metis to Restigouche.

In order to facilitate the settlement of these parts of Canada, the Government has authorised FREE GRANTS of land along these roads, not exceeding, in each case, 100 acres, and obtainable upon the following conditions :—

1st. That the settler be eighteen years of age ;—2nd. That he take possession of the land allotted to him within one month ;—3rd. That he put into a state of cultivation 12 acres of land in the course of four years ;—4th. That he build a log-house, 20 by 18 feet, and reside on the lot until the foregoing conditions are fulfilled.

Families may reside on a single lot, and the several members having land allotted to them will be exempt from building and residence upon each individual lot. The non-fulfilment of those conditions will cause the immediate loss of the land, which will be sold or given to another. The lands thus opened up, and gratuitously offered by the Government for settlement, are chiefly of excellent quality, and well adapted in respect of soil and climate, to all the purposes of husbandry.

The reports of the resident agents on these roads for the past year convey the most favorable accounts of the prosperity of the settlers thereon, and of the large amount of produce they have raised on the newly-cleared lands.

In addition to the Free Grants along the lines of road which are before described, the Government have at their disposal several million acres, which may be purchased by persons intending to become actual settlers, at prices varying from one shilling to five shillings per acre.—(10d. to 4s. sterling.)—It may also be stated here, that other lines of road, have been made, or are in course of construction, in different parts of the province :—

H

In the Eastern townships :—

There remains a large tract, nearly 2,000,000 of acres of land, yet for sale. It is intended to open it up, and render it available to settlers, by Colonization Roads. This district is well-known for its agricultural capabilities of all kinds, and especially as a grazing and dairy country; it is also abundantly provided with water-power for manufacturing purposes. The population consists, more than any other portion of equal extent in Lower Canada, of English, Scotch, and Irish—and a large and thriving settlement of Norwegians has recently been formed therein. The mineral riches of the townships, especially in copper, are well ascertained, and several mines are now being profitably worked.

The whole district is accessible, all the year round, by railway or steam-boat accommodation, and has ready communication with the markets of Quebec, Montreal, Portland, Boston, and New York.

FISHERIES.

The fisheries belonging to the province are attracting much attention, and will no doubt prove a productive source of wealth. They are inexhaustible, and are now subjected to a regular system of licensing. Inspectors have been recently appointed, and every endeavour is being made to preserve them, and encourage their increase. They are, but as yet, in their infancy, and a brief statement of them is here given, showing their extent and their value even in the very limited use of them now made.

FISHERIES, LOWER CANADA

Lower Canada possesses, in the river and gulf of St. Lawrence, an extent of coast of 1000 miles, where the cod, herring, mackerel, salmon ,and other fisheries are carried on successfully.

Whale fishing is also carried on by vessels fitted out from the port of Gaspé. Average season value of whale oil has been about 27,000 dollars.

The cod fishing is carried on along the whole shore of Canada. The herring fishing principally at the Magdalen Islands, in the Bay of Chaleur, and on the coast of Labrador. The mackerel fishing at the Magdalen Islands, along the coast of Gaspé, and in the lower part of the river St. Lawrence.

Square and manufactured timber is exported in large quantities from the different ports of the coast of Gaspé. There is also found an abundance of wood of the best quality for ship-building purposes. The lands in the District of Gaspé are composed of a light but fertile soil, producing all kinds of grain and vegetables. There are millions of acres of those lands which are still in the wild state and covered by beautiful forests.

The population of the district of Gaspé and of the north coast of the river and gulf of St. Lawrence is 32,000 souls.

The district of Gaspé alone could contain and support a population of more than 100,000. By a recent enactment Gaspé has been made a free port, which will add immensely to its value and importance.

The inland lakes and rivers abound in fish.

FISHERIES, UPPER CANADA.

The merchantable fish products derived from the lakes and rivers of Upper Canada consist chiefly of white fish, salmon, salmon-trout, herring, lake-trout, speckled-trout, sturgeon, pickerel, bass, mascalonge, &c. Inferior kinds also abound in the smaller lakes, tributaries and streams.

The extensive area, great depth, clear cold waters, abundant feeding banks, shoals and spawning grounds, of the principal Upper Canadian lakes, render the fish found therein numerous, of good quality and large size.

The annual take of the different species of fish is carefully estimated at 380,000 dollars value.

This produce is variously disposed of, by export, fresh and cured, to the neighbouring United States, and for domestic sale and consumption.

Ready markets are found, both at home and abroad, for any seasonable catch.

Tracts of arable land, bordering on the great lakes, are still at the disposal of the Government for sale and settlement.

TRADE AND REVENUE.

The general revenue of the province is derived from customs, Government land sales, revenue from public works, and minor sources of income ; Government or Provincial taxation never reaches the Canadian in a direct manner, and if he choose to limit his wants to the simple necessaries of life, and clothe himself, as tens of thousands do, in home-spun—the stamp of domestic industry and frugality—indirect taxation will only meet him in the articles of tea or coffee, each of which cost about one-half as much as they do in Britain. The only taxes he is called upon to pay he has the opportunity of voting for or against; his opinion, in other words, is taken as to whether the tax is just or necessary. Such taxes are for school purposes, road-making and bridge-building in the township in which he lives, and by which he benefits to a degree often one hundred-fold greater than the amount of money or labour he is required to contribute.

The commerce of a producing country like Canada, drawing its wealth from its agriculture, forests, mines and seas, is fairly represented by statistical tables of exports and imports. The following tables, compiled from official returns, will show the direction in which the industry of the province exerts itself. The exports for 1858 and 1859 are thus classified :—

	1858. Currency.	1859. Currency.
Agricultural products	£1,976,100	1,834,949
Produce of the forest	2,361,932	2,415,990
Animals and their products	615,691	947,376
Manufactures	81,344	121,808
Produce of the sea	179,574	204,356
Produce of the mine	78,706	117,128
Other articles	28,134	27,683
	£5,225,781	5,670,203
Estimated short returns from inland ports . .	360,761	416,151
In addition to these items, we have the value of ships built at Quebec, amounting to . . .	185,910	105,391
Giving a grand total of Exports of	£5,772,452	6,191,745

The tonnage employed in the transatlantic commerce of Canada, and with the sister provinces, amounted, in 1855, to 419,553 tons; and in 1859, to 641,652, inwards; and in 1855, to 451,241 tons; and in 1859, to 640,561 tons, outwards.

The following statement shows the number and tonnage of Canadian and American vessels, distinguishing steamers from sailing craft, employed in the carrying trade, and passing through the canals of the province :—

	No.	Tons.	No.	Tons.
Canadian sail	633	66,903	751	74,715
Canadian steam	88	7,812		
American sail	553	98,753	588	106,844
American steam	35	8,091		
Total			1,339	181,559

The following is a comparative statistical view of the

commerce of Canada, exhibiting the value of exports to, and imports from, Great Britain, her Colonies, and Foreign Countries, during the years 1858 and 1859 :—

	Value of Exports.		Value of Imports.	
	1858.	1859.	1858.	1859.
Great Britain	£2,224,653	1,994,189	3,073,872	3,696,521
North American Colonies	240,107	210,119	103,844	95,439
British West Indies . . .	. .	1,756	. .	133
United States of America	2,982,523	3,483,579	3,908,895	4,398,229
Other Foreign Countries	60,108	88,952	183,021	198,468
Total	£5,507,391	5,778,095	7,269,632	8,388,790

There are above seventy salmon fishery rivers in Lower Canada, which the Government are now fostering, with a view to enhance the commerce in this valuable fish. The latest annual catch is 3,750 barrels. The Bay of Chaleurs alone formerly exported 10,000 barrels.

The number of boats belonging to Canada, fishing on the Canadian shores, is from 1,200 to 1,500.

Nearly 100 Canadian vessels are employed in the fisheries of Canada.

The number of fishing vessels from Nova Scotia and the other lower provinces, fishing on our shores, is from 250 to 300.

The number of fishing vessels, from the United States, frequenting our shores, principally for the cod and mackerel fishing, is from 200 to 300.

Quantity of dried and smoked fish yearly exported from Canada	846,567 Quintals.
Quantity of pickled fish exported from Canada . . .	118,257 Barrels.
Consumed in Canada, above kinds	75,000 'Quintals.
Quantity of fish oil exported from Canada	100,218 Gallons.
Number of seal-skins do. do.	12,000
Quantity of salmon taken in the rivers of Canada, .	3,750 Barrels.
Quantity of trout and halibut taken in Canada, . .	900 Barrels.

Total fish productions, valued at 942,528 dollars.

NOTE.—The take by vessels, other than Canadian, is not computed in this table. _____

The Emigrant Agents at Quebec, Montreal, Ottawa, Toronto and Hamilton, will furnish immigrants with the best information as to routes, distances, rates of conveyance, crown and other lands for sale; and also point out those localities which offer the best prospect of employment.

EXPLANATION OF THE REMARKS IN THE TARIFF.

G. T. R.—Grand Trunk Railway; Quebec.
O. S. & H. R.—Ontario, Simcoe, and Huron Railway; Toronto.
G. W. R.—Great Western Railway; Toronto.
C. & P. R.—Cobourg and Peterborough Railway; Cobourg.
P. H. & L. R.—Port Hope and Lindsay Railway; Port Hope.
P. & O. R —Prescott and Ottawa Railway; Prescott.
E. T.—Eastern Townships; Lower Canada.

———

Through Tickets can be obtained on application at this Office.

A. C. BUCHANAN,

H.M. Chief Emigration Officer.

GOVERNMENT EMIGRATION OFFICE.
Quebec, March, 1860.

———

VALUE OF ENGLISH COIN THROUGHOUT CANADA.

1 Sovereign	£1	4	4	$4.85
1 Crown	0	6	1	1.20
1 Shilling	0	1	3	0.24

———

PROTECTION TO EMIGRANTS.

The Imperial and Provincial Passengers' Acts provide, as far as possible, against frauds and imposition, any instance of which should at once be made known to the nearest Emigrant Agent. "The Colonization Circular," published, yearly, by Authority, at Park-street, Westminster, contains the regulations, dietary scales, &c., required by the Imperial Passengers' Act.

The Provincial Passengers' Act provides that Emigrants may remain and keep their baggage on board 48 hours after the vessel's arrival in harbour, and imposes a penalty on the master who compels passengers to leave before—that they shall be landed free of expense, and at proper hours—that no person, without a licence, shall influence passengers in favour of any particular steamboat, railroad, or tavern—that tavern-keepers shall have posted, in some conspicuous place, a list of prices to be charged for board, lodging, &c., and they will not be allowed to have any lien upon the effects of a passenger, for board and lodging, beyond five dollars—about one pound sterling.

The personal effects of emigrants are not liable to duty.

NOTICE TO EMIGRANTS—PRICE OF LANDS, &c.

Emigrants desirous of purchasing any of the Crown Lands in Upper or Lower Canada may obtain the fullest information as to the price and quality of the lands for sale, in their respective counties, by applying to the undermentioned Agents.

Prices of lands range from Twenty cents to One dollar per acre, subject to the following regulations :—

One-fifth of the purchase money to be paid down, and the remainder in four equal annual instalments, with interest ; no patent, in any case (even though the land be paid for in full at the time of purchase), shall issue for any such land to any person who shall not by himself, or the person or persons under whom he claims, have taken possession of such land within six months from the time of sale, and shall from that time continuously have been a *bond fide* occupant of, and resident on, the land for at least two years, and have cleared and rendered fit for cultivation and had under crop, within four years at farthest from the time of sale of the land, a quantity thereof, in the proportion of at least ten acres to every one hundred acres, and have erected thereon a house, habitable, and of the dimensions at least of sixteen by twenty feet. No timber to be cut or removed, unless under licence, except for agricultural purposes.

All emigrants requiring information as to the best routes and cheapest rates of conveyance, to any of the above districts, should apply to the undermentioned agents, who will also direct those in want of employment to places where they would be most likely to obtain it. The agents will also give settlers information as to the best and safest mode of remitting money to their relations or friends residing in any part of Great Britain or Ireland.

Quebec, - - - A. C. BUCHANAN, Chief Agent.
Montreal, - - - J. H. DALEY.
Ottawa, - - - FRANCIS CLEMOW.
Toronto, - - - A. B. HAWKE, Chief Agent for C. W.
Hamilton, - - - T. C. DIXON.
Kingston, - - - JAMES MCPHERSON.

NOTICE.—Emigrants arriving at Quebec, holding through tickets for their inland transport, and desiring to obtain information, may delay their journey for that purpose, as the railway or steamboat company to whom they are addressed will take charge of their luggage until they are ready to proceed.

Government Emigration Office,   A. C. BUCHANAN,
    Quebec, May, 1860.   CHIEF AGENT.

Average Wages in Canada, in Sterling, prepared to 1st June, 1860.

CALLING.	Eastern Lower Canada.		Western Upper Canada.		REMARKS
	Per Day. Without Board.	Per Month. With Board.	Per Day. Without Board.	Per Month. With Board.	
Bookbinders and Printers	4s.	..	4s. 6d.	..	Compositors most commonly engaged by piece-work.
Blacksmiths	4s.	..	5s. to 5s. 6d.	40s. to 60s.	Generally engaged by the year, at the rate per month.
Bread and Biscuit Makers	4s.	40s. to 60s.	4s. to 6s. 3d.	40s. to 60s.	
Butchers	4s.	40s. to 60s.	4s. to 4s. 6d.	40s. to 60s.	Generally by contract per 1000.
Brickmakers	3s.	..	3s. 6d. to 5s.	..	
Bricklayers and Masons	4s. 6d. to 5s. 6d.	..	6s.	..	
Carpenters and Joiners	4s. to 4s. 6d.	..	6s.	..	Cabinetmakers, though requiring more skill than carpenters, are not generally paid higher wages, because of the lesser demand for them.
Cabinetmakers	4s. to 4s. 6d.	..	6s.	..	
Coopers	3s.	..	5s.	..	
Carters, with Horse and Cart	7s. 6d. to 8s.	..	10s.	..	
Coachmen and Grooms	..	30s. to 45s.	..	50s. to 60s.	
Cooks (Women)	..	15s. to 20s.	..	20s. to 25s.	
Dairy Women	..	12s. to 15s.	..	15s. to 17s. 6d.	
Dressmakers and Milliners	1s. 6d. with Board.	16s. to 17s. 6d.	2s. 6d. to 3s.	..	
Farm Labourers	..	40s. to 60s.	..	32s. to 60s.	Only employed by the day on pressing occasions, when high wages prevail.
Common ditto	2s. to 4s.	..	2s. 6d. to 4s.	..	

AVERAGE WAGES in CANADA—continued.

CALLING.	EASTERN LOWER CANADA.		WESTERN UPPER CANADA.		REMARKS.
	Per Day Without Board.	Per Month With Board.	Per Day Without Board.	Per Month With Board.	
Gardeners	..	40s. to 50s.	4s. to 5s.	60s. to 90s.	Commonly remunerated with share of profits.
Millwrights and Machinists	6s.	60s. to 80s.	5s. to 6s. 3d.		
Millers			5s.		
Painters and Glaziers	4s. 6d. to 5s. 6d.		5s. to 6s.		
Plasterers	4s. 6d. to 5s. 6d.		5s. to 6s. 6d.		
Plumbers	5s. to 6s.		5s. to 6s.		
Quarrymen	3s. to 4s.		2s. 6d. to 3s. 6d.		
Ropemakers	3s. 9d. to 4s. 6d.		4s.		
Shoemakers	3s. 9d. to 4s. 6d.		4s. to 5s.		Commonly employed on piece-work.
Sawyers	4s.		4s. to 5s.		Very little employment
Shipwrights and Boatbuilders	3s. 6d. to 4s. 6d.		5s. to 6s.		
Stone Cutters	5s. 6d.				
Saddlers and Harnessmakers					
Sailmakers	4s.		4s. to 5s.		Very little employment,
Servants, Male	..	35s. to 45s.	4s. 6d. to 5s. 6d.	35s. to 45s.	
„ Female		12s. 6d. to 16s.	3s. 6d. to 5s.	12s. 6d. to 17s. 6d.	
Slaters and Shinglers	4s. 6d. to 5s. 6d.		3s. 6d. to 4s. 6d.		
Tanners and Curriers	3s. 6d. to 5s.		4s. to 5s.		
Tailors	3s. 6d. to 4s.		4s. to 5s.		
Tinsmiths, Braziers, &c.	5s. 6d.		5s. to 5s. 6d.		Very few employed.
Wheelwrights	3s. 6d. to 4s.				
Whitesmiths	5s. to 5s. 6d.				

CROWN LAND AGENTS IN UPPER (WESTERN) CANADA.

AGENTS.	RESIDENCES.	COUNTIES.	TOWNSHIPS.	Acres at disposal.	Price per Acre.
					Seventy cents cash—or, one dollar, if paid by instalments as above.
William Harris	Admaston, near Renfrew.	Part of Renfrew	Admaston, Bagot, Blithfield, Bromley, Brougham, Canonto, Griffith, Stafford, Wilberforce.	250,000	
James P. Moffat	Pembroke	Parts of Renfrew and District of Nipissing.	Alice, Buchanan, Fraser, Head, Maria, McKay, Petewuwa, Rolph.	214,000	
Thomas P. French	Sebastopol	Parts of Renfrew and District of Nipissing.	Algona, Brudenel, Grattan, Sebastopol.	182,000	
James Macpherson	Kingston	Lennox and Parts of Frontenac and Addington.	Kennebec, Olden, Oso, Palmerston, Bedford, Hinchinbrooke.	190,000	
Ebenezer Perry	Tamworth	Parts of Frontenac, Addington and District of Nipissing.	Abinger, Anglesea, Barrie, Denbigh, Kaladar, Sheffield.	220,000	
Martin P. Hayes	Madoc	North part of Hastings.	Dungannon, Faraday, Lake, Herschel, Monteagle, Limerick, McClure, Tudor, Wicklow, Wollaston.	200,000	
Richard Hughes	Bobcaygeon	Parts of Peterborough and Victoria.	Galaway, Snowdon, Minden, Somerville.	150,000	
G. M. Roche	Lindsay	Part of Victoria.	Carden, Draper, Laxton, Macauley.	100,000	
John Alexander	Barrie	Simcoe	Muskoka	25,000	
Joseph Wilson	Sault St. Marie	District of Algoma	Awenge, Awéres, Korah, St. Mary, Tarentorus.	50,000	

CROWN LAND AGENTS IN LOWER (EASTERN) CANADA.

AGENTS.	RESIDENCES.	COUNTIES.	TOWNSHIPS.	Acres at disposal.	Price per Acre, except in cases of special valuation.
			South of the River St. Lawrence.		
John Felton	Sherbrooke	Samstead, Sherbrooke, Richmond, and parts of Wolfe and Compton.	Marston, Auckland, Hereford, Weedon, Hampden.	160,000	60 cents.
F. H. Pratte	Stanfold	Part of Arthabaska	Maddington, Blandford, Stanfold, Bulstrode.	100,000	do.
			North of the River Ottawa.		
Wm. Thompson	Fitzalen—Arundel	Part of Argenteuil	Harrington, Montcalm, Arundel, De Salabery.	101,000	30 cents.
G. W. Cameron	Thurso	Part of Ottawa	Hartwell, Ripon	35,000	60 cents.
E. W. Murray	Buckingham	Part of Ottawa	Portland, Derry, Villeneuve, Bowman, Templeton, Buckingham.	160 000	do.
Robert Farley	Wakefield	Part of Ottawa	Wakefield, Low, Masham, Hincks, Aylwin.	185,000	do.
Michael McBean	Northfield	Part of Ottawa	Cameron, Bouchette, Northfield, Kensington, Aumond, Wright, Egan.	190,000	do.
G. M. Judgson	Clarendon	Part of Pontiac	Aldfield, Thorne, Cawood, Leslie, Onslow.	180,000	do.
Thomas Barron	Lachute	Part of Argenteuil	Wentworth	30,000	30 cents.
John Lynch	Allumette	Part of Pontiac	Allumette, Waltham, Sheen, Chichester.	60,000	do.

CROWN LAND AGENTS IN LOWER (EASTERN) CANADA—continued.

AGENTS.	RESIDENCES.	COUNTIES.	TOWNSHIPS.	Acres at disposal.	Price per Acre.
			North of the River St. Lawrence.		
A. B. Lavallée	St. Jerome	Terrebonne	Abercromby, Morin, Beresford, Chilton, Wexford, Chertsey,	35,000	30 cents.
Alex. Duly	Rawdon	Montcalm	Kilkenny, Rawdon.	121,000	do.
Jules Bourgeois	Kildare	Joliette and Berthier	Cathcart, Kildare, Joliette, Brandon.	49,000	do.
A. Dubord	Three Rivers	St. Maurice and Maskinongé.	Peterborough, Caxton, Shaw-enegan.	40,000	do.
A. Bochet	St. Anne de la Pérade	Champlain	Radnor, Alton, Montauban	25,000	do.
J. P. Dery	St. Raymond	Portneuf	Gosford, Colbert, Roquemont	28,000	do.
Vincent Martin	Chicoutimi	Chicoutimi	Bagot, Chicoutimi, Laterrière, Jonquière, Mesy, Tremblay, Charlevoix, Metabetchouan, Kenogami.	132,000	20 cents.
Vincent Martin	Chicoutimi	Chicoutimi	Labarre, Caron, Signay, Simard, Harvey, St. Johns.	118,000	do.
			South of the River St. Lawrence.		
J. T. LeBel	Wotton	Parts of Wolfe and Compton.	Wotton, Ham and augmentation, Wolfstown, Garthby, Strafford, Whitton, Winslow.	290,000	60 cents.
J. O. C. Arcand	St. Joseph Beauce	Part of Megantic	Broughton, Thetford	44,000	40 cents.
L. C. Blanchet	St. François, Beauce	Beauce	Price, Adstock, Tring, Lambton, Forsyth, Aylmer, Gaylurst.	130,000	do.

CROWN LAND AGENTS IN LOWER (EASTERN) CANADA—continued.

AGENTS.	RESIDENCES.	COUNTIES.	TOWNSHIPS.	Acres at disposal.	Price per Acre.
Andrew Ross	Frampton	Dorchester, and part of Beauce.	Shenley, Jersey, Marlow, Risborough, Ditchfield, Linière, Watford, Cranbourne, Frampton, Buckland, Standon, Ware.	200,000	30 cents.
S. V. Larue	St. Charles, Riv. Boyer.	Bellechasse	Mailloux	20,000	do.
Frs. Têtu	St. Thomas	Montmagny, and part of L'Islet.	Montmagny, Ashburton, Bourdages, Panton Arago.	120,000	do.
Jos. Jolivet	St. Gervais	Bellechasse	Roux, Bellechasse, part Buckland, Daaquam, Armagh	92,000	do.
Stanislas Drapeau	St. Jean, Port Joly	L'Islet and Elgin Road.	Fournier, Ashford, Garneau, Casgrain, Lafontaine, Dionne.	93,000	do.
F. DeGuise	St. Anne La Pocatière	Kamouraska	Ixworth, Chapais, Woodbridge, Painchaud, Parke, Bungay, Chabot, Pohenegamook.	285,000	do.
L. N. Gauvreau	Isle Verte	Temiscouata	Whitworth, Viger, Demers, Denonville, Begon, Rodot.	135,000	do.
J. Bte. Lepage	Rimouski	Rimouski	Duquesne, Macpes, Neigette, Cabot, Fleurian, Macnider, Matane and augmentation.	300,000	do.
J. A. LeBel	New Carlisle	Bonaventure	St. Dennis, Cap Chat, Romieu, D'Alabert, Cherbourg Metapediac, Restigouche, Mann, Nouvelle, Carleton, Maria, New Richmond, Hamilton, Cox, Hope, Port Daniel.	180,000	20 cents.
John Eden	Gaspé Basin	Gaspé	Newport, Percé, Malbaie, Douglas, York, South Gaspé Bay, North Gaspé Bay, Fox, Sydenham.	120,000	do.

1 8 5 9.

ROUTES, DISTANCES, and RATES of PASSAGES by RAILWAY and STEAMER, from Quebec to all parts of Canada, by Grand Trunk Railway, daily, from Point Levi, or by the Mail Steamer during summer, transhipping at Montreal to through line of Steamers to all Ports on the St. Lawrence and Lake Ontario.

PLACES. CANADA.	Miles from Quebec.	FARE BY G. T. RAILWAY OR STEAMER.		REMARKS.
		Sterling.	$ Cts.	
Barrie	565	26s. 8d.	6 50	By O. S. and H. R. from Toronto
Belleville	388	14s. 4d.	3 50	„ G. T. R. do. do.
Brockville	293	12s. 4d.¹	3 00	„ do. or steamer.
Brighton	410	16s. 6d.¹	4 00	„ do. do.
Brampton	522	22s. 6d.	5 50	„ do. from Toronto.
Berlin	562	25d.	6 25	„ do. do.
Bradford	544	24s.	6 00	„ Railway do.
Bowmanville or Darlington	457	18s.	4 50	„ G. T. R.
Chatham	679	28s.	7 00	„ G. W. R. from Hamilton.
COBOURG	431	18s.	4 50	„ G. T. R. or steamer.
COLLINGWOOD	593	28s.	7 00	„ O. S. and H. R. from Toronto.
Cornwall	236	10s.	2 50	„ G. T. R.
Colborne	417	17s.	4 25	„ do.
Gananoque	323	14s.	3 50	„ G. T. R. or steamer.
Guelph	550	24s.	6 00	„ -do. - do.
Galt	570	23s.	5 75	From Hamilton by G. W. R., via Harrisburg.
HAMILTON	539	20s.	5 00	By steamer or G. T. R.
Hamburg	576	26s.	6 50	„ G. T. R. from Toronto.
KINGSTON	340	15s.	3 75	„ G. T. R. or steamer.
LONDON	615	27s.	6 75	„ G. W. R. from Hamilton.
Lennoxville, E. T.	123	11s. 3d.	2 75	„ G. T. R. via Richmond, E. T.
MONTREAL	168	4s. 2d.	1 00	„ do. do.
Niagara	537	22s.	5 50	From Toronto by steamer.
Napanee	367	16s.	4 00	By G. T. R.
Newmarket	542	24s.	6 00	„ O. S. and H. R. from Toronto.
OTTAWA CITY, (Byt.)	335	14s.	3 50	„ P. and O. R. from Prescott.
Oshawa	467	18s.	4 50	„ G. T. R. or steamer.
Owen Sound	630	29s.	7 25	„ O. S. and H. R. from Toronto
Oakville	518	20s.	5 00	„ Steamer or G. T. R.
Prescott	281	12s.	3 00	„ do. do.
Paris	565	23s.	5 75	„ G. W. from Hamilton.
Perth	386	13s.	3 25	„ Brockville and Ottawa, R. R.
PORT HOPE	437	18s.	4 50	„ G. T. R. or steamer.
Peterborough	459	22s.	5 50	„ C. and P. R. from Cobourg, or P. H. and L. R. from Port Hope.
Richmond, E. T.	96	4s.	1 00	„ G. T. R.
Sherbrooke	120	8s.	2 00	„ do.
St. Catharine's	560	22s.	5 50	From Hamilton by G. W. R.
Stratford	589	26s.	6 50	By G. T. R. from Toronto.
TORONTO	500	20s.	5 00	„ G. T. R. or steamer.
Trenton	400	15s.	3 75	„ G. T. R.
Whitby	471	19s.	4 75	„ G. T. R. or steamer.
Woodstock	587	26s.	6 38	„ G. W. R. from Hamilton.
Williamsburg	260	11s.	2 75	„ G. T. R. or steamer.
Windsor	631	28s. 6d.	7 12¼	„ G. W. R. from Hamilton.
St. Andrews, N. Brunswick	629	36s.	9 00	⎰ G. T. R. to Portland, and thence
St. Johns, New Brunswick	676	40s.	10 00	⎱ by steamer.

Letter Postage to and from England.

Two ocean steamers carrying mails for Canada leave Liverpool in each week.

A Canadian packet sails direct for Quebec every week during the summer months, and every alternate week for Portland during the winter months, by which the postage rate is 6d. sterling per ½ oz., and a British Cunard packet on every Saturday, landing mails alternately at Boston and New York, by which the postage rate to Canada is 8d. sterling per ½ oz.

The British Post Office forwards letters to Canada by the first of these packets sailing after the letters are posted,—unless the letters bear a special direction " *By Canadian,*" or " *By British Packet,*"—and in that case, the letters are kept over for the packet designated. Therefore to pass for the 6d. sterling rate, a letter for Canada must be posted so as to arrive at Liverpool in time for Wednesday's Canadian steamer, carrying letters at the 6d. rate, or it must be directed " *By Canadian Packet.*"

When a letter not especially directed " *By Canadian Packet,*" reaches Liverpool between Wednesday and Saturday, it will be forwarded by the Saturday British packet at the 8d. rate, and if only prepaid 6d., there will be 5 cents additional charged on the letter, and payable on delivery in Canada.

In like manner as regards letters going from Canada to the United Kingdom,—in order to pass at the 6d. rate,—they must be posted on the proper days for the Canadian packet mails, or bear the words " *By Canadian Packet.*"

All letters to or from the United Kingdom should be prepaid. Letters posted unpaid will be forwarded, but they will be chargeable on delivery with a fine of 6d. sterling (12½ cents) each, *in addition to the postage.*

Newspapers to and from Canada.

Publishers of newspapers at home, as well as individuals, should remember that in *all* cases a newspaper for Canada must have a penny stamp affixed—but if sent " By Canadian steamer," there is no further charge on the recipient there ; whereas when sent by the Cunard Line, each paper costs the recipient there one penny, which *goes into the United States treasury !*

All newspapers sent from Canada to England must have a cent stamp affixed, but if directed " By Canadian Steamer," they are delivered free at home, whereas every newspaper sent from hence by the Cunard Line costs the recipient in in Great Britain one penny!

N.B. The proprietors of British newspapers should memorialize the Governor General to allow newspapers *from the place of publication* to "Exchange Papers," in Canada to go free, as they do in every part of British North America and the United States. This arrangement would be mutually advantageous, and the courtesy would be cheerfully reciprocated by publishers of Canadian papers.

Equivalent Value of Currency and Cents, from One Copper to One Dollar.

Currency.		Cents.	Currency.		Cents.	Currency.		Cents.
d.			s. d.			s. d.		
½	equal to	5-6	8	equal to	13⅓	1 5	equal to	28⅓
3-5	„	1	8 2-5	„	14	1 5 2-5	„	29
1	„	1⅔	8½	„	14 1-6	1 6	„	30
1 1-5	„	2	9	„	15	1 6 3-5	„	31
1½	„	2½	9½	„	15 5-6	1 7	„	31⅔
1 4-5	„	3	9 3-5	„	16	1 7 1-5	„	32
2	„	3⅓	10	„	16⅔	1 7½	„	32½
2 2-5	„	4	10 1-5	„	17	1 7 4-5	„	33
2½	„	4 1-6	10½	„	17½	1 8	„	33⅓
3	„	5	10 4-5	„	18	1 8 2-5	„	34
3½	„	5 5-6	11	„	18⅓	1 9	„	35
3 3-5	„	6	11 2-5	„	19	1 9 3-5	„	36
4	„	6⅔	11½	„	19 1-6	1 10	„	36⅔
4 1-5	„	7	1 0	„	20	1 10 1-5	„	37
4½	„	7½	1 0 3-5	„	21	1 10½	„	37½
4 4-5	„	8	1 1	„	21⅔	1 10 4-5	„	38
5	„	8⅓	1 1 1-5	„	22	1 11	„	38⅓
5 2-5	„	9	1 1 4-5	„	23	1 11 2-5	„	39
5½	„	9 1-6	1 2	„	23⅓	2 0	„	40
6	„	10	1 2 2-5	„	24	2 3	„	45
6½	„	10 5-6	1 3	„	25	2 6	„	50
6 3-5	„	11	1 3 3-5	„	26	3 0	„	60
7	„	11⅔	1 4	„	26⅔	3 6	„	70
7 1-5	„	12	1 4 1-5	„	27	4 0	„	80
7½	„	12½	1 4½	„	27½	4 6	„	90
7 4-5	„	13	1 4 4-5	„	28	5 0	„	100

Table for Calculating the Difference between Sterling Money and Currency.

One Pound Sterling equal to One Pound Four Shillings and Four Pence Currency.

Pence.

Stg. *d.*		Currency £	*s.*	*d.*
1	..	0	0	1¼
2	..	0	0	2½
3	..	0	0	3¾
4	..	0	0	5
5	..	0	0	6¼
6	..	0	0	7½
7	..	0	0	9
8	..	0	0	10
9	..	0	0	11¼
10	..	0	1	0¼
11	..	0	1	1½
12	..	0	1	3

Shillings.

s.		£	*s.*	*d*
1	..	0	1	2¾
2	..	0	2	5¼
3	..	0	3	8¼
4	..	0	4	10½
5	..	0	6	1
6	..	0	7	3¾
7	..	0	8	6½
8	..	0	9	9
9	..	0	10	11¾
10	..	0	12	2
11	..	0	13	4¾
12	..	0	14	7½
13	..	0	15	10¼
14	..	0	17	1
15	..	0	18	3
16	..	0	19	5¾
17	..	1	0	8½
18	..	1	1	11½
19	..	1	3	1½
20	..	1	4	4

Pounds.

Stg. £		Currency £	*s.*	*d.*
1	..	1	4	4
2	..	2	8	8
3	..	3	13	0
4	..	4	17	4
5	..	6	1	8
6	..	7	6	0
7	..	8	10	4
8	..	9	14	8
9	..	10	19	0
10	..	12	3	4
11	..	13	7	8
12	..	14	12	0
13	..	15	16	4
14	..	17	0	8
15	..	18	5	0
16	..	19	9	4
17	..	20	13	8
18	..	21	18	0
19	..	23	2	4
20	..	24	6	8
21	..	25	11	0
22	..	26	15	4
23	..	27	19	8
24	..	29	4	0
25	..	30	8	4
26	..	31	12	8
27	..	32	17	0
28	..	34	1	4
29	..	35	5	8
30	..	36	10	0
31	..	37	14	4
32	..	38	18	8
33	..	40	3	0
34	..	41	7	4
35	..	42	11	8
36	..	43	16	0
37	..	45	0	4

Pounds.

Stg. £		Currency £	*s.*	*d.*
38	..	46	4	8
39	..	47	9	0
40	..	48	13	4
41	..	49	17	8
42	..	51	2	0
43	..	52	6	4
44	..	53	10	8
45	..	54	15	0
46	..	55	19	4
47	..	57	3	8
48	..	58	8	0
49	..	59	12	4
50	..	60	16	8
51	..	62	1	0
52	..	63	5	4
53	..	64	9	8
54	..	65	14	0
55	..	66	18	4
56	..	68	2	8
57	..	69	7	0
58	..	70	11	4
59	..	71	15	8
60	..	73	0	0
61	..	74	4	4
62	..	75	8	8
63	..	76	13	0
64	..	77	17	4
65	..	69	1	8
66	..	80	6	0
67	..	81	10	4
68	..	82	14	8
69	..	83	19	0
70	..	85	3	4
71	..	86	7	8
72	..	87	12	0
73	..	88	16	4
74	..	90	0	8

Pounds.

Stg. £	Currency £	*s.*	*d.*
75	91	5	0
76	92	9	4
77	93	13	8
78	94	18	0
79	96	2	4
80	97	6	8
81	98	11	0
82	99	15	4
83	100	19	8
84	102	4	0
85	103	8	4
86	104	12	8
87	105	17	0
88	107	1	4
89	108	5	8
90	109	10	0
91	110	14	4
92	111	18	8
93	113	3	0
94	114	7	4
95	115	11	8
96	116	16	0
97	118	0	4
98	119	4	8
99	120	9	0
100	121	13	4
200	243	6	3
300	365	0	0
400	486	13	4
500	608	6	8
600	730	0	0
700	851	13	4
800	973	6	8
900	1095	0	0
1000	1216	13	4

CANADIAN MINERALS.

With the exception of the drift, or those most recent deposits which constitute the soils of the country, the rocks of Canada are either so old as to be without indications of organic remains, or to show only the most ancient forms of created beings. As a geologist would say, they are either *Azoic* or *Palæozoic*. The former constitute all the northern part of the country, from Labrador to Pigeon river on Lake Superior, and afford a somewhat mountainous region, giving the products that render Canada celebrated for her timber. The latter compose the southern and flatter part, from Gaspé to lake St. Clair and Sault Ste. Marie, and include vast areas that cannot be surpassed for soils and agricultural capabilities. The geological formations of this part are Silurian, Devonian, and carboniferous, a large portion of the rocks being calcareous. The western peninsula of Canada is Devonian and upper Silurian. The country from this to Memphramagog lake and Quebec is lower Silurian, and the remaining part comprehends Silurian, Devonian, and carboniferous, the lower Silurian being near the St. Lawrence, the upper Silurian in a line from Memphramagog lake to Gaspé, with the Devonian southward of it, occupying the interior part, and the carboniferous composing a narrow strip on the north coast of the bay Chaleur, where it constitutes a part of the margin of the great coal-field of New Brunswick, the workable coal seams of which do not extend beyond the south side of the same bay.

The prolongation into Canada of the Green Mountains (a part of the Apalachian chain), constitutes a mineral region of much importance. It is of the Silurian age, and extends from the boundary of the province east of Lake Champlain to the extremity of Gaspé. This region abounds in excellent roofing-slates, which are beginning to be worked, and have been carried for use to the westward as far as Chicago. Large intrusive masses of white granite afford a material for the purposes of construction equal to that of Devonshire and Cornwall, or of Aberdeen. A range of serpentine, like that of the Lizard of Cornwall, traced for nearly 300 miles, and beds of calcareous rocks, will yield a great diversity of variegated marbles. Thick beds of soapstone, potstone, and whetstone exist abundantly in this region. In some parts, the strata present important masses of magnesite or carbonate of magnesia, the only known substance yielding a cement capable of resisting the decomposing action of sea-water, and at present manufactured in France from the sea for this application, at a cost of thirty dollars the ton.

Indications of the ores of copper mark the region in a great number of places. In Megantic county, these are so abundant as to have induced the formation of an English company, with a capital sufficient thoroughly to test the ground in Leeds, and their mining operations have been continued for two years with a fair prospect of success. Their operations have proved that valuable deposits of the ores here occur in beds, as they do in the copper slates of Germany, and this has been confirmed by the recent discovery, at Acton, of a most remarkable mass of the vitreous variegated and pyritous sulphurets of copper, constituting apparently the paste of a conglomerate with limestone pebbles, subordinate to the stratification. In nine weeks after mining operations commenced last year, 300 tons of ore, containing about 30 per cent. of pure copper, were obtained, and the work still continues with much the same results. This discovery naturally enhances the importance with which smaller indications are regarded in other parts. Highly argentiferous lead ore has been met with in some parts of the region, but not in large quantities. Gold is widely spread over the region in the drift, but apparently too thin to be made profitably available. Chromic iron, one of the minerals usually accompanying gold, occurs in beds of some promise.

Among the minerals of the region above described, are the magnetic and specular oxides of iron, occurring in beds of some importance, often accompanied by titanium; but the great iron-bearing rocks of Canada, of the same age as those of Sweden, are associated with the Laurentian mountains, which occupy the north side of the St. Lawrence and Ottawa, and extending from Labrador to Lake Superior, have been alluded to as the azoic series. In many parts of this range, beds of iron ore, of from 10 to 500 feet in thickness, containing from 60 to 70 per cent. of pure iron. Several of these have been worked in furnaces established at Marmora and Madoc, and from mines to the eastward of Kingston. 15,000 tons of the ore have been exported within two years to Pittsburgh, in the United States, where it is in great demand. It has lately been announced as a discovery by Mr. Mushet, an English metallurgist of some authority, that the excellence of the Swedish iron, for the manufacture of steel, is due to a small proportion of titanium which they contain, and it is asked where titanium is to be obtained to improve by mixture the character of the iron of other places. It occurs in abundance in some of the Laurentian iron ores, as well as those of the eastern townships. In certain bands of crystalline limestone belonging to the Laurentian range, veins of lead ore exist, often apparently of workable character, and the same limestones yield variegated marbles and rock masses of rensselærite, a mineral about as hard as limestone but resembling soap-stone, and applicable to the same and some other useful purposes. In the same calcareous bands, occur graphite or plumbago and mica, with phosphate of lime in workable quantities, and traces of corundum or emery have been met with.

An important copper region exists on the shores of Lakes Huron and Superior, which, though somewhat removed from the present centres of population, cannot fail in time to be a great means of support to native industry. That part of the region which is in Canada has a length exceeding 500 miles; its breadth is not yet fully ascertained, but one of twelve miles would give it a superficies ten times that of the mineral region of Cornwall and Devonshire. Ores of lead, zinc, nickel, and silver are associated with those of copper in this region, and the copper occurs subordinate to both lodes and beds. In the Lake Huron part of the region, a considerable quantity of copper ore has been obtained at the Bruce mines and Wellington mines, and the Copper Bay mines have more recently come into productive operation. The ores have been exported to Baltimore, Boston, and Swansea.

Various parts of the country, not included in what may be more especially considered mineral regions, abound in bog iron ore, excellent building stone, sandstone for glass making, white and red brick clays, extensive areas of peat, with occasional deposits of fresh-water shell-marl. Petroleum springs exist in the western district, from which large quantities of illuminating and lubricating oils are produced. Others are known to occur in Gaspé, which have not yet been turned to account, and shales occur in many places, containing from four to eleven per cent. of bitumen.

It would occupy too much space to continue a special mention of these and various other mineral products with which the province abounds, and most of which are included in the following catalogue :—

Metals and their Ores.

Magnetic iron ore ; specular iron ore ; bog iron ore ; titaniferous iron ore ; sulphuret of lead (galena) ; sulphuret of zinc (blende); native copper; pyritous, variegated, and vitreous sulphurets of copper; argentiferous and auriferous sulphurets of copper; sulphuret of nickel; hydrated oxide of nickel; native silver with native copper; sulphuret of silver with galena; gold.

Minerals requiring special chemical treatment to fit them for use.

Uranium; chromium; cobalt; molybdenite; bog manganese (wad); iron pyrites; dolomite; magnesite.

Mineral Paints.

Barytes; iron ochre; phosphate of iron; ferruginous clay.

Minerals applicable to Jewellery and the Arts.

Agates; jasper; Labradorite; peristorite; perthite (sunstone); zircon (hyacinth); ruby; sapphire; amethyst; ribbon chert; lithographic stone; statuary marble.

Refractory Minerals, and Minerals for Glass-making.

Soapstone; potstone; rensselærite; asbestus; graphite (plumbago); sandstone; pure white silicious sandstone; pitchstone; basalt and allied rocks.

Mineral Manures.

Gypsum; phosphate of lime (apatite); fresh-water shell-marl.

Grinding and polishing Minerals.

Buhr stone and other millstones; grindstone; whetstones and honestones; corundum (emery); Canadian tripoli; garnet rock.

Minerals for Building, Paving, &c.

White granite; red syenite; free silicious sandstone; calcareous sandstone; limestone; magnesian limestone; hydraulic limestone; magnesia stone; brick clay; flagstones; roofing-slates; variegated marbles; serpentine; porphyry

Miscellaneous Minerals.

Fuller's earth; moulding sand; peat; petroleum; asphalt.

CANADA, 1849 to 1859.

By the Honourable A. T. Galt, Finance Minister of Canada.

Certain persons in Canada having, *somehow*, obtained access to one or two English newspapers, conveyed through them such ungenerous and untruthful views of the financial and commercial condition of Canada, that Mr. Galt found it desirable, under the sanction of his name and position, to answer them in a pamphlet, which has completely silenced the anonymous authors of the articles above referred to; and also given, what was much needed, a succinct history of Canada during an eventful period of her young national history—a statement calculated not only to give confidence in her present position, but to encourage not only intending emigrants, to make a land thus " green with hopeful promises," their future home, but to assure capitalists that Canada and Canadians, are capable of affording as many and as safe investments as can be found in any part of the world; and offers a boundless field for British skill, capital, and enterprise.

The pamphlet on " Canada," (recently published under the authority of the Government, for gratuitous circulation, and professing to be " a brief outline of her geographical position, climate, capabilities, productions, fisheries, and railroads, &c.)," enters into various details of interest to be found in future pages.

The following extracts from Mr. Galt's pamphlet touch upon some points not included in the above-named work :—

There have been two questions which, more than any others, have agitated the public mind in Canada, and produced the greatest bitterness and animosity. Each was peculiar to its own section of the Province. In Upper Canada, the Clergy Reserves; and in Lower Canada, the Feudal or Seignorial Tenure. The former has indeed been regarded by many as the prominent cause of the outbreak in 1837, while the latter has been an incubus of the most fatal character upon the industry and intelligence of Lower Canada.

THE CLERGY RESERVES IN UPPER CANADA

were an appropriation of one-seventh of the land of Upper Canada, made by the Imperial Legislature for the support of a Protestant clergy. They were claimed, and possessed originally, by the Church of England; but, simultaneously, the other churches asserted their rights, and a never-ending agitation was kept up on the subject. It raised the question of a connection between Church and State, as well as of an Established Church, both being obnoxious to a large class of the inhabitants of the Province; and it proved the fruitful cause of evil of every kind. Many unsuccessful attempts had been made, both by the Imperial Legislature and by the Colony, to compromise the question; but in every case the agitation was renewed with increased bitterness; and it was not until 1854, that a final settlement could be arrived at. The Legislature, acting under the authority of an Imperial Act, decreed the complete separation of the State from all connection with any Church, and provided that a commutation equivalent to the value of existing stipends should be paid to the incumbents, and, after provision for widows and orphans of clergy, divided the remaining land and funds amongst the municipalities of Upper Canada, according to their respective population. This measure has been fully carried out, and the Province has at length found a solution for an evil that had convulsed it since its earliest settlement.

THE FEUDAL TENURE IN LOWER CANADA.

In Lower Canada the disastrous effect of the Feudal Tenure upon the progress of the people can scarcely be understood now by the people of England : to the student of history, however, it is familiar, through its effects in Europe, where its extinction in every country has been the result of long-protracted struggles. Civil insurrection, bloodshed and crime have marked the progress of Europe in casting off this burden; and though stripped of many of its worst features in Canada, yet the system remained, repressive of the industry of the

120   FEUDAL TENURE.

people, degrading them in character, and effectually preclud-
ing Lower Canada from sharing in the flow of population
and wealth, which was so steadily setting in to every other
part of North America. The French Canadians had grown
up under this system for years; but the progress around them
had awakened their intelligence, and produced that strong
movement in the masses which betokened a steady persistent
effort, at all hazards, to free themselves from every trace of
serfdom. No more difficult problem could be offered for solution to a Legislature, than the settlement of a question which
had its roots in the very fundamental laws of property, and
which could not be approached without endangering the destruction of the whole social edifice; and the difficulty was not
decreased by the fact that the body which had to deal with it
consisted, to the extent of one-half, of representatives from
Upper Canada, who might not unnaturally suppose they had
no immediate interest in it. This problem has, however,
been solved; and by the Acts of 1854, and of last Session, the
Feudal Tenure has been completely extinguished in Canada,
and lands are now held by freehold tenure equally in both
sections of the Province. The rights of property have been
respected; no confiscation has taken place, but, with the con-,
sent of all interested, the obnoxious tenure has been abolished,
on payment of a certain amount by each tenant, and by a con-
tribution of about 650,000l. from the Province generally. A
social revolution has thus been quietly, and without excitement, effected, at a most trivial cost to the country, which
will be repaid a hundredfold by the increased progress of the
Lower Province; and yet this very measure is that which,
more than any other, has been charged against the Government of Canada, as a lavish and wasteful outlay of public
money. One single week of disturbance of the public peace
would have cost the Province vastly more than the indemnity
given to those whose rights of property were required to be
surrendered for the public good. If there be one point in the
whole working of constitutional Government which should
encourage its fr'ends, it is the fact that the people of Canada
have been them elves able to approach and deal with such a
question as this without excitement, disturbance, or individual
wrong.

Mr. Galt then briefly alludes to the educational establishments of the two Provinces—the settlement of the country—
the construction of macadamized roads—the fisheries of the

St. Lawrence, heretofore unaccountably neglected—the institutions for the care of lunatics and criminals—reformatory schools—the encouragement given to science—the valuable contributions to astronomical and meteorological science given by the Toronto Observatory—as affording evidence that the progress of the country is not confined wholly to material objects, and Mr. Galt, with honest pride, asks whether that system can be intrinsically bad, or administered by vicious instruments, which has produced within ten years,—

The care of lunatics;
The management of criminals;
The establishment of reformatory prisons and supervision of gaols;
The promotion of science;
The reform of the criminal code;
The simplification of the civil laws;
The consolidation of the statute law, and
The codification of the French law;
A thorough reform of the Legislature;
An extension of the franchise, and registration of votes;
A complete system of municipal self-government;
A perfect system of elementary and superior education;
The separation of Church and State; and
The settlement of the Clergy Reserve question;
The abolition of the Feudal Tenure;
Provision for emigration and the settlement of the country.

THE NATIONAL DEBT OF CANADA

It cannot but be matter for surprise and congratulation, that, considering the vast extent of Canada, which is 350,000 square miles, which is nearly three times as large as Great Britain, one third larger than France, and three times as large as Prussia, and whose public works must therefore have extended over an enormous space, to find that,—

The direct debt of Canada, including advances to railways, is only 9,677,672*l.*, and after deducting the sinking fund for the redemption of the Imperial Guaranteed Loan, amounts to 8,884,672*l.*, and the payments on account of the public works of the Province, without reckoning interest, have been as follows:

Canals, lighthouses and other works connected
with the development of the navigation of
the St. Lawrence, represent £3,962,900
Railway advances 4,161,150
Roads and bridges, and improvement of rivers . 738,350
                                          ———————
                                          £8,862,400

The public of England can now judge how far the expenditure of Canada has been reckless and unwise; or, whether it has not been incurred for objects in which the prosperity of the country was wholly bound up, and which fully justified the sacrifices that have been made to attain them.

Before quitting the subject of the present debt of Canada, it is proper I should advert to the outstanding Municipal Loan Fund Bonds, amounting, on 1st December, 1859, to 1,920,160*l.*

These bonds are issued upon the security of a fund constituted by the municipalities, who have become borrowers to this amount. The object was to secure on their united credit loans on better terms than they could obtain as individual borrowers. The Province is in no way guarantee for the fund, but acts as trustee, and has never pledged the general revenue for the payment of either principal or interest. Owing, however, to the commercial crisis in 1857, and the bad harvest of that and the following year, the Province has made large advances to enable the fund to meet the interest due to the bondholders, with whom faith has thus been kept by the several municipalities. But the plan having been thus found to work badly, and to entail unexpected charges upon the general revenue, the Act was repealed last session, so far as related to further loans, and the Government authorized to redeem the outstanding debentures, and to hold them against the indebted municipalities.

Measures are now being taken for the redemption of this debt, which will be the more easily effected, as the Government already hold large amounts of these bonds in trust for the special educational, Indian, and other trust funds.

It now only remains for me to state the commercial policy, and the position of the trade and finances of the Province of Canada; and I am the more desirous of doing so, as great misapprehension prevails in England on these points, and the steps called for by the imperative dictates of honour and good faith are represented as based upon a return to an unsound commercial policy, and fraught with injustice to our fellow-subjects in Great Britain.

Canadian statesmen of all parties have invariably adhered to the faithful and punctual discharge of the obligations of their country; they have never swerved from the principle, that whatever may be the faults or follies of their Government or Legislature, the public creditor should not suffer; and, supported by the unanimous voice of the country, Parliament has never hesitated to provide by taxation for the necessities of the State.

INCREASED TAXATION.

The increase of taxation is never a popular step, and it may well be believed that no Government would adopt it without the strongest conviction that good faith demanded it. It is unpleasant enough to be exposed to attack in Canada for an unavoidable increase of duties; but it is certainly ungenerous to be reproached by England, when the obligations which have caused the bulk of the indebtedness of Canada, have been either incurred in compliance with the former policy of Great Britain, or more recently assumed to protect from loss those parties in England who had invested their means in our railways and municipal bonds.

The indirect public debt of Canada, including railway advances, in 1858, was 6,271,762l., bearing 6 per cent. interest, which, prior to 1857, had not been a charge upon the revenue. In that year, as has been already stated, owing to the commercial crisis, it became necessary to make large payments upon it, and in 1858, almost the whole amount had to be met from the general revenue. In addition to the commercial depression, the harvest of 1857 was below an average, and that of 1858 was nearly a total failure. It became manifest that the indirect debt must for many years be a charge upon the country, and Parliament was required to make provision for it. The interest on the public debt, direct and indirect, thus required, in 1858, 636,667l.; and without flagrant breach of faith it could neither be postponed nor repudiated. The pressure had come suddenly and heavily upon the people of Canada; but neither the Government nor the Legislature hesitated in making such provision as in their judgment would meet the exigencies. The Customs Act of 1858 was therefore passed, and subsequently, with the same objects in view, and others which will be hereafter explained, the Customs Act of 1859 was also passed.

After subjecting the engagements of the Province to the

strictest possible scrutiny, the Government were of opinion
that it was possible to reduce the annual outlay on many items
of expenditure, and their best efforts were therefore directed
towards economy; the ordinary expenditure in 1858 having
been 1,837,606*l.*, and the estimate for corresponding service in
1859 being 1,540,490*l.*   But after making every possible
reduction, it was manifest that unless an increase of revenue
could be obtained, a serious deficiency must occur in 1859.

The Customs Act of 1859 is evidently believed in England
to have imposed very large additional taxation on imported
goods, whereas in reality such was neither the intention nor
the fact.   The new tariff was designed certainly with the
intention of obtaining an increased revenue of about 100,000*l.*
on the estimated importations of 1859, but the real increase
was looked for from a revival of trade; the main object was to
re-adjust the duties so as to make them press more equally
upon the community, by extending the *ad valorem* principle to
all importation, and thereby also encouraging and developing
the direct trade between Canada and all foreign countries by
sea, and so far benefiting the shipping interests of Great
Britain—an object which is partly attained through the duties
being taken upon the value in the market where last bought.
The levy of specific duties, for several years, had completely
diverted the trade of Canada in teas, sugars, &c., to the American markets, and had destroyed a very valuable trade which
formerly existed from the St. Lawrence to the lower provinces
and West Indies.

By this statement, it is shown that the increased rate of
duty as compared with the tariff of 1858, as given previously,
has only been from 12½ to 13½ per cent., which can scarcely
be deemed excessive; while so far from the apprehensions
entertained of a diminution of imports and consequent loss of
revenue being verified, in both cases the estimates of the
Government are borne out as nearly as could be expected,
considering the state of the country and its gradual recovery
from depression.   Until the close of the year, the comparison
cannot fairly be made, inasmuch as we are only now beginning to benefit from our late good harvest; but as an indication
of the result, it may be stated, that in the case of cotton goods,
which were raised from 15 to 20 per cent., the importations for
the first nine months of 1857-8 and 9, were as follows:

$$1857 \quad . \quad . \quad . \quad . \quad . \quad . \quad . \quad . \quad . \quad £89,993$$
$$1858 \quad . \quad . \quad . \quad . \quad . \quad . \quad . \quad . \quad . \quad 58,823$$
$$1859 \quad . \quad . \quad . \quad . \quad . \quad . \quad . \quad . \quad . \quad 88,844$$

I can also point with satisfaction to the fact, that the proportion which free goods bear to the whole importation, is exactly that of 1858, and of the average for the four previous years, viz. : 29 per cent. of the imports; indicating that the new tariff has not produced any disturbance of trade, nor checked importations: for it is remarkable that where so large an increase has taken place in the imports, as from 4,520,993*l.*, in the first nine months of 1858, to 5,403,393*l* 5*s.*, in the corresponding period of 1859, the proportion of free goods to the whole remains the same."

The foregoing extracts are sufficient to show how completely Mr. Galt has vindicated his financial policy from the charges made against it by parties ill-informed and influenced by political prejudice: that policy was dictated by a due regard to national honour; and in carrying it into successful effect, the smallest possible burden was placed upon those classes, least able to bear any new fiscal impost.

The harvest of 1859, according to official returns from both sections of the Province, was highly satisfactory, being the best with which the Province has been blessed for twenty years.

The accounts of the harvest prospects for 1860 are extremely cheering, and those on the Free Grant Roads, where the lands have not been exhausted by repeated crops of the same description of grain, are described as really splendid.

Providence has again looked graciously upon the land, blessed the labours of the husbandman, cheered the statesman in his anxious efforts for his country's good, and given to Canada the promise and earnest of future prosperity.

APPENDIX.

STATEMENT of the Value of the Goods Imported into Canada, with the Amount of Duty collected thereon, from the Year 1841 to 30th September, 1859, inclusive; also the Value of Free Goods Imported during the same time.

YEAR.	IMPORTS.			DUTY.			FREE GOODS.		
	£	s.	d.	£	s.	d.	£	s.	d.
1841	2,694,160	14	6	225,834	7	10	146,268	17	8
1842	2,588,632	13	2	278,930	7	4	85,944	2	4
1843	2,421,306	16	4	241,572	9	0	13,526	18	0
1844	4,331,050	17	4	441,331	15	2	83,666	10	4
1845	4,191,325	16	6	449,960	1	7	59,061	17	4
1846	4,515,821	1	11	422,215	16	8	61,300	10	8
1847	3,609,692	14	11	414,633	5	6	Estimated 77,139	5	4
1848	3,191,328	5	10	334,029	8	9	92,978	0	0
	27,543,319	0	6	2,808,507	11	10	619,886	1	8
1849	3,002,891	18	3	444,547	5	1	269,200	7	9
1850	4,245,517	3	6	615,694	13	8	294,133	7	2
1851	5,358,697	12	7	737,439	0	2	425,671	5	9
1852	5,071,623	3	11	739,263	12	9	311,962	17	4
1853	7,995,359	1	1	1,028,676	15	7	443,977	18	1
1854	10,132,331	6	9	1,224,751	4	8	703,435	17	1
	35,806,420	6	1	4,790,372	11	11	2,448,381	13	2
1855	9,021.542	7	3	881,445	12	6	2,596,383	13	8
1856	10,896,096	16	2	1,127 220	10	5	2,997,941	14	9
1857	9,857,649	11	9	981,262	15	11	3,101,976	1	7
1858	7,269,631	15	0	845,347	7	7	2,093,403	10	0
	37,044,920	10	2	3,835,276	6	5	10,789,705	0	0
1859 to 30th September	6,574,128	5	0	888,946	15	4	1,915,603	0	0

Quebec, 22nd October, 1859.

Inspector-General's Office,
Customs Department.

N.B.—In the foregoing pages, the above figures have been reduced to their equivalent in sterling money.

STATEMENT of the Value of Goods Imported into Canada, and the Duties collected thereon, for nine months to 30th September, 1859; showing the relative per-centage which the values and the duties at the different rates of duty bear to the whole importations, and the whole amount of duties.

RATE OF DUTY	VALUES.		DUTY.	
	Amount.	Percentage.	Amount.	Percentage.
	Dollars.		Dollars. Cents.	
5 and 10 per cent. . . .	1,680,311	$6\frac{48}{100}$	160,626 80	$4\frac{53}{100}$
15 per cent.	1,722,735	$6\frac{55}{100}$	258,293 27	$7\frac{26}{100}$
20 ditto	10,784,512	41	2,157,205 76	$60\frac{67}{100}$
25 ditto	216,917	$\frac{83}{100}$	54,049 25	$1\frac{53}{100}$
Tea, Sugar, and Molasses } Specific, and over 25 per {	3,142,974	$11\frac{95}{100}$	579,921 04	$16\frac{31}{100}$
Other articles } cent. {	1,087,372	$4\frac{13}{100}$	345,707 60	$9\frac{73}{100}$
Free goods	7,662,412	$29\frac{71}{100}$	. .	. .
Total . .	26,296,513	100	3,555,803 72	100

Quebec, 22nd October, 1859.

Inspector-General's Office,
Customs Department.

N.B.—The above figures have been reduced to sterling money.

SALMON AND SEA-TROUT FISHERIES OF LOWER CANADA.

The following list includes the principal SALMON RIVERS and SEA-TROUT STREAMS which discharge into the St. Lawrence and Saguenay Rivers, along the north-east, or Labrador coast, between the Province boundary eastwards (Blanc Sablon), and the River Jacques Cartier, above Quebec; also those emptying upon the south or eastern shore of the St. Lawrence, and others flowing easterly into the Bay of Chaleurs—emphasising the Crown Rivers now open to public sale, and so mentioned in the accompanying advertisement.

In addition there are many other bay, cove, and inlet stations along these extensive coasts, but which are disposable chiefly as sedentary NET-FISHINGS for Salmon and Trout.

The immediate expiry of the lease of that vast territory, commonly known as " The King's Posts," opens up to public competition numerous valuable COAST FISHERIES (such as Tadousac, Seven Islands, &c.), besides many famous SALMON RIVERS and SEA-TROUT STREAMS, and renders disposable certain COMMODIOUS BUILDING ESTABLISHMENTS long occupied as FUR TRADING POSTS, by the Honourable Hudson's Bay Company, at the mouths of the most important of these fine rivers.

Locality.	Names of Rivers.	Remarks.
ST. PAUL'S.	ESQUIMAUX . .	Fine Salmon river. Formerly yielding 52,500 Salmon each season.
	CORKEWETPEECHE	Neighbouring stream. Contains steady run of Salmon.
	STE. AUGUSTINE	Well supplied with Salmon.
	SHEEP BAY . .	Considerable size. Good Salmon-fishery station.
	LITTLE MECCATINA	Discharges large body of water by several channels. Fine Salmon river.
	NETAGAMU . .	Large, deep stream. High Falls inside. Swarms of Trout. Salmon ascending it only to the Falls.
	NAPETETEEPE .	Empties into spacious bay. Abounds with Salmon.
	ETAMAMU . .	Celebrated for its Salmon-fishery.
	COACOACHO . .	Discharges into fine basin. Good Salmon river.
	ROMAINE . .	Large, but shoal stream. Salmon abound. Is remarkable for a rare, beautiful, and flavorous quality of white or silver Trout.
	Musquarro . .	Bold, rapid river. Affords fine Salmon-fishing with fly. Good net-fishery station.
	KEGASHKA . .	Salmon abundant—steep rapids impeding their ascent. Fishery in bay.
	Gt. Natashquan .	Famous stream Salmon of finest kind and numerous.
	AGWANISH . .	Large stream. Good Salmon-fishery location. (N. E. bound of " Lordship of Mingan.")

North Shore. — *Discharge into River St. Lawrence.*

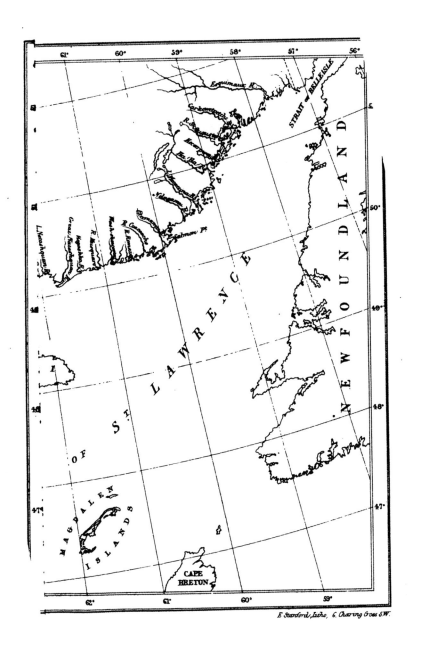

Locality.	Names of Rivers.	Remarks.
ST. PAUL'S.	PASHASHEEBOO .	Tolerable size. Fair fishery.
	MINGAN . . .	Excellent net and fly fishing for Salmon. Pools · always hold a heavy run of large fish.
	MANITOU . .	Branch of the Mingan, equally good and well-known.
	SAINT JOHN . .	Very large stream. Splendid Salmon-fishery.
	MAGPIE . .	Tolerably good fishery for Salmon. Rapid little river.
	SAW BILL . .	Considerable stream. Chiefly net-fishery.
	MANITOU . .	Large—obstructed by perpendicular fall. At its mouth both Salmon and Trout resort.
	Moisic . . .	Noted for numbers of weighty Salmon. Extensive and lucrative net-fishery. Fine fly-fishing.
	Ste. Margeurite (en bas)	Excellent river for Salmon and Trout.
	Pentecost . .	Full, swift stream, much frequented by Salmon. Stationary fisheries at the mouth.
	Trinity (BAY) .	Favourite river. Salmon and Trout fishing, for net and rod.
	Goodbout . .	Fine Salmon river, widely known as such. The net-fishery in its tide-water and adjacent bay is very productive.
	English . . .	Empties into deep cove. Salmon-fishery. Plenty of Trout.
	Bersimis . .	Immense stream, and has many tributaries. Scenery interesting. Abounds with largest-sized Salmon. They do not affect the fly except on the waters of its branches.
	NIPIMEWECAW'NAN	Tributary of Bersimis. Fairy-like stream. Falls nine miles inside. Exquisite fly-fishing.
	Jeremie . .	Small. Trout only. Fur trading-post chiefly.
	Colombier . .	Good Salmon-fishery.
	Plover . . .	Ditto.
	Blanche . . .	Ditto.
	Laval . . .	Picturesque and wild river, alternating with gentle rapids and deep narrow pools. Besides valuable net-fishery, it affords abundant Salmon and Trout-fishing.
	Sault de Cochon .	Steep falls, hinder ascent of Salmon. Famous for Trout-fishing along the estuary border.
	PORTNEUF . .	Pleasant stream to fish with fly. Up to the first falls swarms with Trout. For several miles higher up is frequented by Salmon. Net-fishery station along the tide-way
	Grand Escoumain	Once famous for Salmon. Mill dam has now an artificial fishway. Fine net-fishery for Salmon in bay.
	G. Bergeronne .	Good Trout stream.
	L. Bergeronne .	Fair Salmon and Trout river. (Both the Bergeronne Rivers are within a few miles of Saguenay and Tadousac.)

K

Left margin labels: Seigniory Mingan. — Within Frontage Limits of "King's Posts," now renuming by the Canadian Government. — North Shore. — Discharge into River St. Laurence.

Locality.	Names of Rivers.	Remarks.
ST. PAUL'S. *Within Frontage, &c.:—continued.* North Shore. *Into Saguenay.*	St. Margaret (*en haut*)	Large tributary of river Saguenay. Fine Salmon-fishing for both net and fly. Trout abundant.
	L. Saguenay . .	Considerable stream, affording tolerable rod and good net-fishing. Mill-dam inside, not in use.
	St. John's (*en haut*)	Ditto.
Into River St. Laurence.	Black, or Salmon .	Formerly good fishery.
	MURRAY . .	Flows down beautiful valley. Yields Salmon.
	DU GOUFFRE .	Much deteriorated.
	STE. ANNE . .	Pretty river, and latterly has afforded fair Salmon-fishing just below the chute.
	MONTMORENCI .	Cataract at mouth. The upper water swarms with (river) Trout.
	JACQUES CARTIER	Excellent Salmon stream.
	DU SUD . .	Promises to become again a good Salmon river. Mill-dam and fishway.
	OUELLE . .	Well-stocked with Salmon. Mill-dam broken up.
	G. MITIS . .	Large stream. Has dam.
	MATANNE . .	Fine Salmon river. Dam, and Salmon-pass in course of erection.
	ST. ANN . .	Formerly good. Now few Salmon taken. Mill-dam across.
	MOUNT LEWIS .	Important stream. More noted of recent seasons for Sea-Trout than Salmon.
	MAGDELAINE .	Salmon river, clear.
	DARTMOUTH . .	First-class stream, flowing into Gaspé basin Abounds with Salmon.
	YORK . . .	Ditto Ditto Ditto.
	ST. JOHN'S, (*du sud*)	Ditto Ditto Ditto.
	GRAND . . .	Fine Salmon-fishery. Mill above.
South Coast. *Flow into B. Chaleurs.*	G. PABOS . .	Salmon-fishery. Superior station.
	G. BONAVENTURE .	Large and valuable stream. Many tributaries. Abounding with Salmon.
	CASCAPEDIACS .	Both the little and great Cascapediac yields high numbers of Salmon.
	NOUVELLE . .	Good Salmon-fishery in bay.
	METAPEDIAC . .	Considerable magnitude, and abounds with Salmon.
	RESTIGOUCHE . .	Noble river. Has fine tributary streams. Salmon frequent it in large numbers, and of heavy weight. Head of Bay Chaleurs.
	PATAPEDIAC . .	Branch of Restigouche. Salmon ascend it about forty miles.
	MISTOUCHE . .	Feeder of Restigouche. Salmon river.

Addenda.

Nearly all|of the rivers described in the foregoing schedule are tidal streams, and most of them have stationary Salmon and Trout fisheries within the embouchure, and at bays, coves, and inlets on either sides. Those upon the north shore of the St. Lawrence descend out of wild, rocky, and mountainous country.

Most of these streams, with their numerous tributaries, and, the large lakes at the head of each branch, present every variety of river and lake adapted to the breeding and feeding of fish.

Where there are mill-dams it is specially so noted. None elsewhere.

The names of certain rivers at present advertised for sale are printed in italics.

The true Salmon (*Salmo Salar*), and the Tide Trout (*Salmo Trutta Marina*), are herein mentioned.

The Grand Trunk Railway, now in operation at St. Thomas, will be opened next autumn to River du Loup, 110 miles below Quebec. Passenger steamboats ply between Quebec and the Saguenay.

Synopsis of the Laws and By-Laws now in force in Lower Canada, having especial reference to the Preservation and Regulation of Salmon and Trout Fisheries.—Act 22nd Vic., cap. 86.

SECTION 4. The Governor in Council to grant special Fishing Leases and Licenses; and make all needful or expedient regulations for management and disposal of Fisheries.

    5. A General Superintendent and Local Overseers to be appointed, and paid by the Government, for each Province.

    8. The Government may set apart any waters for natural or artificial propagation of Salmon and Trout.

    24. The open season for Salmon-fishery limited betwixt 1st March and 1st August. Fly surface-fishing extended to 1st September. Exception in procuring spawn_for scientific purposes.

    25. Spawning-pools of Salmon protected against all fishing.

    26. Nets and fishing apparatus shall not obstruct the main channel or course of any river; and such channel or course shall be at least one-third of the whole breadth of a river.

    27. Owners of dams must attach fishways thereto.

    28. All parties concerned in breach of 24th Section, become liable to fine or imprisonment.

    29. The meshes of Salmon-nets must measure five inches in extension from knot to knot.

    31. Trout-fishing illegal oetween 20th October and 1st February.

    33. Netting for Trout, in any lake or stream, prohibited, except upon the River St. Lawrence.

    36. Purchase, sale, or possession, during prohibited seasons, of any Salmon or Trout, made a punishable offence.

Regulations under Order in Council.

BY-LAW A.—Parties forbidden to occupy Salmon or Sea-Trout fishery-stations without Lease or License from the Crown.

B.—The use of nets confined to the brackish waters within the estuary tide-way; and forbidden upon the fresh-water stream above confluence of tide.

C.—All nets, &c., to be set no less than 200 yards apart.

E.—No other fishing whatever allowed over limits covered by exclusive Leases or Licenses from the Crown, except by express consent of lessees or licentiates.

F.—Prohibits capture of Salmon or Sea-Trout by torchlight, and with leister or spear.

H.—The receipt, gift, purchase, sale and possession of speared Salmon or Trout declared illegal.

J.—No mill-rubbish to be drifted awaste in any Salmon or Sea-Trout river.

Appropriate penalties of fine or imprisonment, with forfeiture of materials and fish, are provided by law for the contravention of the several preceding Sections and By-Laws.

Also effective and summary modes of proceeding are laid down for recovery of the same.

CROWN LANDS DEPARTMENT,
　　(*Fisheries,*)
Toronto, December, 1858.

AGRICULTURAL REPORT OF UPPER CANADA FOR 1859.

In analyzing the seventy-two returns received from Upper Canada, it appears

There are six counties out of the twenty-four from which there is only one return each; four from which there are only two returns each; and five from which there are three returns each: five counties give four returns each, and the rest have five or six—none exceeding the latter number. The highest is Carleton. Winter Wheat, 28¼ bushels to the acre; Spring Wheat, 22¾. The next highest is Northumberland;— 27½ for Winter, and 19 for Spring Wheat. The next is Simcoe;—26¼ for Winter, 23¾ for Spring. York gives, Winter Wheat, 27, and Spring Wheat, 20; but there is only one return. Bruce gives, Winter Wheat, 25, Spring Wheat, 20. Leeds,— Winter Wheat, 25, Spring Wheat, 16½. Peel gives, 24¾ Winter Wheat, 18¾ Spring Wheat. Ontario gives, Winter Wheat, 22½, Spring Wheat, 23½. The total average is 21 bushels for Winter Wheat, and 18¾ for Spring Wheat; and this appears reliable. There is great reason for rejoicing that the averages are so far beyond those of last year, which were for Winter Wheat, 11¼ bushels, and for Spring Wheat, 13½; being an improvement on last year's growth of about 76 per cent. on one, and about 46 per cent. on the other, and being about 16 per cent. above the general average of the last twenty years.

As to damage done to the Wheat crop by midge and rust, forty-two report that no mischief was done to Winter Wheat in 1859. Eighteen report that very slight damage was done; eight report serious and extensive injury—say from 10 to 25 per cent., and three report a loss of 50 per cent.—one from the county of Welland; one from Haldimand; and one from Wentworth. Six returns further report serious injury by heavy frost on the 5th June.

The remedy for the midge universally given, is to sow early kinds of Winter Wheat, very early, and the Fife Spring Wheat either very early, or not till after the 20th May. The Souler, White, Flint, and blue Stem, and also the White Kentucky. are mentioned in very many of the returns as the earliest and best Winter Wheat, and the Fife as the best Spring Wheat. Good draining and good cultivation are much recommended ; and, in fact, good drainage is the grand essential of successful husbandry. Without it there cannot be early and luxuriant crops, except on very peculiar soils. In five or six cases, however, it occurred that the earliest wheat was the most injured by the June frost; but this frost was exceptional, never having occurred in Canada, except once before, since wheat began to be cultivated in Upper Canada, and but for this early frost, this wheat would have been of the very finest.

The Hon. Mr. French, in what is said to be one of the completest essays ever published on the subject of drainage, thus sums up the loss to undrained land which the excessive evaporation from its surface entails upon it :—

1st. The drained land comes into condition for working a week or ten days earlier in the Spring than other lands.

2nd. The growth of the crops is quickened all through the summer by an increase of several degrees in the temperature of the soil. And,

3rdly. The injurious effects of frost are kept off several days later in the Fall.

In Lower Canada there is very little progress in this important branch of agriculture. Only seven report that a little drainage is done ; all the rest report that none is done. Its value is evidently very little understood. If premiums were offered by societies for the greatest extent of underdraining, the benefit would soon be manifest, and the present averages of grain crops greatly increased.

As to the proportion which Winter Wheat bears to Spring Wheat, thirty-one returns state that the growth of Spring Wheat greatly predominates, being double that of Winter Wheat: the whole crop consisting of two-thirds of Spring to one-third of Winter Wheat. Thirteen state that the growth of both is about equal,—and fifteen state that the growth of Winter Wheat predominates over that of Spring, to the extent of one-third. From comparing the returns it may be estimated that the number of acres under Wheat, is about one-third of Winter Wheat, and two-thirds of Spring. Five years ago there was not one acre of Spring Wheat in Upper Canada for every ten of Winter Wheat. This certainly is an extraordinary change, brought about chiefly by the fearful invasions of the Wheat Midge, but will probably be temporary, and will continue only until draining and high cultivation shall have rendered the insect innocuous here, as it has been already rendered in Great Britain by what is called "high farming." The general average of the Wheat crop in Great Britain is 28 bushels (three-quarters and a half), and the average weight 60 lbs. per bushel. There seems no good reason why the average of Upper Canada should not in a few years equal that of Great Britain, by attention to drainage and high cultivation. Soil and climate are naturally well adapted for the growth of Wheat.

OATS.

The total average of Oats, in Upper Canada, is 34½ bushels per acre.

Two counties report 50 bushels per acre.
Three   ,,   ,,   45 ,,   ,,
Nineteen ,,   ,,   40 ,,   ,,
Thirteen ,,   ,,   35 ,,   ,,
Twenty-two   ,,   30 ,,   ,,
Seven   ,,   ,,   25 ,,   ,,
Two   ,,   ,,   20 ,,   ,,

Simcoe, Ontario, Kent, and Wentworth, give the highest returns, Lanark and Renfrew the lowest: the common black oats are the most recommended: the average of 1858 was 32 bushels per acre, so that there is an improvement of about 8 per cent. on the crop of last year.

Considering that the statute bushel of oats here is only 34 lbs. and that the average of Great Britain is 60 bushels per acre, of 40 lbs. per bushel, there is great room for improvement in the cultivation of this crop. There does not appear anything in the soil or climate of Upper Canada detrimental to the growth of this grain, and it may be inferred that the difficulty arises from inferior cultivation. The importation of new varieties of seed has taken place to a considerable extent, and it is to be hoped that the improvement will continue progressing, till we approximate somewhat nearer to British averages.

In Lower Canada the returns show an average of 22½ bushels per acre. Megantic returns 30, and Pontiac 25 bushels.

BARLEY.

The average return of this grain in Upper Canada is 27½ bushels per acre; sixteen returns report but little grown— there are fifty-six returns. In Lower Canada the average is 23 bushels per acre; Chicoutimi, Bellechasse, Megantic, Nicolet, and Pontiac, give 30 bushels. The growth of this species of grain is very much on the increase in Lower Canada; there are only three reports out of the thirty which state that very little is grown. Winter Barley is coming into use, and is a prolific and valuable cereal. Some idea may be formed of the extensive growth of Barley, when it is stated that in the city of Albany, about 600,000 bushels were imported from Lower Canada in the Fall of 1859. Some very fine crops of Winter Barley are reported to the Bureau. A Mr. Haven, near St. Catharines, states that he grew 150 bushels on three acres. A Mr. Mc Carty, near Niagara, reaped a field on the 12th July. He says:—" I sow 3 bushels per acre, and my yield has been in fallow 60 bushels—and on corn-land 40 bushels per acre. The corn-land was equally good as the fallow: what made the difference in the yield in my opinion was, that the latter was sown on the 20th September, and the former on the 1st of that month." He adds:—" I believe under any circumstances it will yield double the quantity of Spring Barley; it is ripe on the 1st July before the midge can strike it—we sell it at 1 dollar per bushel.

FLAX AND HEMP.

Forty returns from Upper Canada state that neither of these is grown; twenty-two state that very little flax is grown, and that chiefly for the seed; one states that the growth of flax is on the increase, and one from the county of Lincoln states that hemp has been tried there this year. It may be satisfactory, however, to know that the transactions of the Board of Agriculture for December, report that the Messrs. Perine had 400 acres under this crop in the township of Woolwich, in the county of Waterloo, this last season, (1859,) and that it proved very remunerative, producing twelve bushels per acre of flax—seed weighing 56 lbs. per bushel, and 325 lbs. of fibre per acre, which Messrs. Perine consider a pretty fair yield, for dew-rotting; they prepare the fibre for cloth thread, and twine, but complain that they have no market in Canada West. This latter evil will soon be remedied, for if farmers will only produce the article of good quality, moveable scutching mills will soon be forthcoming. There is a great demand for flax in Great Britain at remunerating prices. At the present time flax is selling at from 6d. to 8½d., sterling, per lb. in the North of Ireland, and the acre of flax is worth from 12l. to 20l. sterling.

In Canada the soil and climate are both suited for this crop, and there is abundance of water to allow of it being water-rotted, which is much superior to dew-rotting, and produces much better quality of flax. Full particulars of method of cultivation and process of steeping were furnished to the Board of Agriculture in Toronto by this department, and are to be found in the "Canadian Agriculturist" of February and March, 1860.

The returns in Lower Canada all report that the cultivation of this crop is not on the increase. A very little is grown by many, and manufactured entirely by the hand for domestic use.. There is no machinery for scutching or dressing: one returns the produce as 200 lbs. of flax, and 600 lbs. of seed per acre; another gives 125 lbs. of prepared flax, and 12 bushels per acre of seed; another gives 150 lbs. of flax, and 9 bushels of seed per acre. This crop would be a very profitable one if machinery was available for scutching and preparing; and it would be well for agricultural societies to offer a handsome premium for the introduction of a moveable machine for rendering the crop marketable.

It is stated that sixty tons of flax were prepared this last season in the county of Waterloo, and about 6,000 bushels of flax seed produced there. The value has not yet been fully ascertained; but flax is now worth, in England, from 300 to 350 dollars per ton. Mr. Hespeler, it is said, is about to erect a mill in this county. A portion of a letter addressed to the "Free Press," by Mr. Godfrey of Delaware, is subjoined. He says:—

"Had I been sure of obtaining a sufficient quantity of flax for the English market, I, as well as other agents in the colony, could have obtained orders to some thousands of tons. The price is now from 60l. to 70l. sterling, per ton, in England. I have seen some specimens of growing flax, unfortunately in but small patches, equal to that grown in Ireland or on the Continent. I intend to forward samples of the lint to my mercantile friends in England, and would invite growers to send some specimens to me—P. O. Lambeth, late Junction, Westminster, near London, Canada West."

HAY.

This crop was exceedingly deficient in Upper Canada; three only out of seventy-two return the produce at two tons per acre; twenty-six return one ton and a half per acre; fifteen return one ton per acre, and twenty-eight return from one-fourth to three-fourths of a ton. Forty-eight use gypsum or plaster as top-dressing, and ten use barn-yard manure occasionally.

In Lower Canada this crop was very far superior to that of the Upper Province.

The averages are nearly two tons per acre, and there has been a considerable export of it to the Upper Province. In this article of produce Lower Canada generally surpasses Upper Canada.

TURNIPS.

Sixty-nine of the returns from Upper Canada report that the cultivation of turnips is on the increase, and that they are grown very successfully: one report 1,000 bushels; one 900; six report 800; fifteen report from 500 to 700 bushels, and eighteen report from 300 to 500. This shows a great increase on former years, and it is a very favourable sign, as there cannot be successful cultivation of grain crops unless there be also that of green crops. In fact the extensive and proper culture of green crops is the very foundation of good farming. Last year the returns of green crops cultivated were so inconsiderable, that they were not included in the report of this Department, but it is now becoming an important item in the production of the country.

In Lower Canada nineteen of the returns state that this crop is on the increase; sixteen have reported the growth of from 400 to 1000 bushels; one reports 1000 bushels; one 700; six 600; and two 500.

SHEEP.

The whole seventy-two reports from Upper Canada are unanimous in stating that the numbers of sheep kept is very much increased, and that both fleeces and carcasses are heavier than in 1851, and, with ten exceptions, approving of the Cotswolds; four are in favour of Southdowns, and two in favour of Merinos and Cheviots. All recommend the Leicester sheep as being very profitable. The actual weight of carcass is given per quarter as 17 lbs., and that of fleece 4 lbs. 8 oz. The number kept on each 100 acres varies from twenty to forty—one only stating the number at sixteen, and one making it seventy. The average (not including these) is twenty-six for every hundred acres, which must be understood to refer to old and long-cultivated farms, and the queries having been sent to the most prominent farmers in each county. According to the census of 1852, there were ten sheep to every 100 acres of occupied land in Upper Canada, and the weight of fleece was only 2 lbs. 18 oz. ; so that the improvement in the number and quality of sheep must be very considerable. Taking the number of sheep to bear the same proportion to the population that they did in 1852, viz. : nine sheep for every ten inhabitants, and calculating the average weight of fleece at 3½ lbs. for all Canada, we would have 2,592,000 sheep, and 9,072,000 lbs. of wool, as the produce of this last year, a very important item in raw material for Canadian manufacturers, if it were retained in the colony. But the trade returns of 1858 show an export to the United States of 1,545,412 lbs. at 22½ cents per lb., against an import of 224,664 lbs. at 20½ cents ; and the returns of 1859 show an export of 1,630,531 lbs. against an import of 121,830 lbs. In round numbers our net export of wool was 1,500,000 lbs., whilst the export of the United States was only 951,938 lbs., showing how much more extensive must be their home manufacture of this important staple. The official returns of the United States, taken from the journal of the Society of Arts, show that the whole Union possessed, in 1859, 30,000,000 of sheep and 75,000,000 lbs. of wood, making the average 2½ lbs. per fleece,—very many of their sheep being Merinos, will account for this low estimate of the weight of fleece.

Several new woollen factories have been established in Canada within the last year, and the home manufacture of woollen goods will, without doubt, continue to increase to a great extent. The average price of wool given in the returns is 24 cents per lb., and it may be of importance to know that the supply is so large as to induce others to embark in the manufacture of woollen fabrics. Upper and Lower Canada are both specially adapted to the growth of wool. The climate is very similar to that of Switzerland, where large flocks of sheep are successfully kept with fair remuneration.

In Lower Canada the returns show a very great improvement, both in the quality of sheep and weight of fleece, and also in the number kept on each occupied 100 acres. Five farmers report as many as thirty ; one, twenty-seven ; four report twenty-five, and the rest from eleven to twenty ; and the weight of fleece is given from 2 to 7 lbs., averaging on all the returns the large weight of 4 lbs. to the fleece. I have, however, taken 3½ lbs. as the general average.

LOWER CANADA RETURNS.

SPRING WHEAT.

Twenty-three report the growth of some Spring Wheat—one from Terrebone states the average to be about 20 bushels ; one from Pontiac, and one from Megantic, give 18 ; one from Grantham 17 ; one from Leeds 16½ ; three from Pontiac and Lotbiniére 15 ; one from Megantic 14 ; one from Ottawa 13 ; three from Bellechasse, Bagot, and Lotbiniére give 11 : one from Chicoutimi and Montmagny give 11 ; and six others state the average to be 9 bushels. The total average of Spring Wheat in Lower Canada, is 13 bushels per acre.

Ten of the returns state that very considerable injury has been done to Spring Wheat by the wheat midge :—Chicoutimi, Iberville, Bagot, Joliette, and Timiscouata, report from 25 to 50 per cent. ; seventeen report that the damage done has been very little, if any, this year. The remedy suggested is, to sow very early or very late, and by one to run a rope steeped with turpentine over the heads of the wheat when in blossom. The Black Sea wheat is the most recommended. The Fife is mentioned only by five parties in Lower Canada, although universally esteemed in Upper Canada.

REMARKS

ON

MR. CAIRD'S PAMPHLET,

ENTITLED

"PRAIRIE FARMING IN AMERICA, WITH NOTES BY THE WAY, ON CANADA AND THE UNITED STATES."

Mr. Editor,

Goethe has said, "It is not by attacks on the false, but by the calm exposition of the true, that good is to be done." Taking the above as an excellent rule of action, I have given Mr. Caird's pamphlet, entitled "Pairie Farming in America," a very attentive perusal; and I think Mr. Caird deserves much credit for the candid way in which he has treated the subject of the British settlers' prospects in Illinois, in very many points of vital importance. The inferences, however, which may be fairly drawn from the facts and figures he has given us, are in many instances, calculated to produce widely different results from those which he appears to have anticipated, and no doubt expects his reader to arrive at. Without dwelling upon the report that Mr. Caird is personally and largely interested in the Illinois Central Railroad Company, and their lands, I proceed to examine the merits of his pamphlet.

The prevalence of ague, to which Mr. Caird has alluded in pages 11, 12, 28, 29, 40, 59, 64, 75, 95 and 96, New York edition, especially in pages 95 and 96, where he gives the experience of a leading physican of twenty years' practice, cannot fail to be very apalling to intending emigrants who carefully peruse his work, especially as this physician plainly states that in his opinion "old people ought not to come (to Illinois) at all, as the ague is very fatal to them;" and adds, by way of solace, that, "Chicago (being an older settlement) was now almost free from ague, that typhus had taken its place in a greatly modified extent, and that pneumonia and

rheumatism were the only other diseases that were severe."
Candid and explicit as these warnings are, it may be fairly
added, that the very great prevalence of ague, and the total
prostration with which it is accompanied, often extending
even to weeks and months together on these prairie lands,
is not sufficiently portrayed. It not unfrequently happens
that whole families are so prostrated, that it is with
difficulty any one member of it can be found able to alleviate
the sufferings of the rest; and in remote situations it is often
extremely difficult to procure aid from other families. The
effects of this prostration are often very seriously felt in the
delay and even non-performance of the necessary farm-work,
the neglect of cattle, and often the partial loss of a season's
crops. For this reason, if farmers *are determined* to settle on
prairie land, they should make arrangement for three or four
or more families to settle together, and, in charity, Mr. Caird
should have suggested this; but it is my purpose to show that
settlers in the bush of Canada have much better prospects
in every way than in the prairies of Illinois, not only as
regards the comparative freedom from ague, but for acquiring
actual prosperity and speedy independence. In endeavouring
to show this I will take Mr. Caird's own representations as the
basis; although very great errors have crept into his work,
seriously affecting the general character of Canadian soils
and Canadian farming. The quotation of a few passages
will serve to show how hurried must have been his ride
through the country, how very erroneous the ideas which he
formed. At page 20 he says, "From Prescott to Kingston,
and thence to Coburg, the country is but partially cleared;
very often the train shoots for many miles together through
the primeval forest, a path having been cut in the woods for
the railway track, and the felled trees and branches still
lying where thrown, on both sides of the line." This latter
assertion may be *literally* true, but Mr. Caird himself, as well
as his readers, will be surprised to learn, that at least seven-
eighths of this very route is through a remarkably fine agricultural country; through lands held by the very best and
and most successful farmers, having very large clearances,
comfortable dwellings, and out-houses, and good orchards.
The counties from Prescott to Coburg, through which Mr.
Caird's route lay, contain 240,000 inhabitants. For twenty
years there have been fine herds of Ayrshire and Durham
cattle little inferior to the best cattle in England, and even
40 miles back of the frontier, may be seen farms of from 200

to 400 acres, well cultivated, heavy crops, excellent horses, cattle and sheep. The railway track passes through the rear part of their farms, purposely reserved " a primeval forest," for firewood; three-fourths, more probably, of their large farms being under cultivation. The railway company purchased the land *in rear* because the farmers did not wish their farms to be intersected by railroads, and they sold the land in the rear cheaper than they would have sold any other part of their farms. The quotation above given, shows the great danger of judging a country merely by a railroad ride; and the danger of *publishing* the impressions thus erroneously acquired, especially by so well known a man as Mr. Caird, is greater still. This may be further illustrated by extracts from pages 26, 27, 28, and 29 ; and it is certainly much to be regretted that Mr. Caird remained so short a time in Canada, and took such a very cursory glance of the colony. Many of his remarks are truthful and valuable, but no individual, travelling as Mr. Caird did, *could* form a correct opinion of the agricultural status and prospects of Canada. At page 26, &c., he says, " the country from Hamilton to Paris is undulating, and seems an easier and more fertile soil ; very little of it is wholly cleared ; certainly more than half is still an unbroken forest, but the trees are immensely tall, and show the rapid growth which only a fertile soil could produce. Though this district is quite within the limit profitable of the culture of Indian Corn, a small proportion only of the land seems to be occupied by that crop. Its great value is everywhere admitted, but on this description of soil its cultivation demands too much labour. The last grain crop can hardly have been great, for in very few instances indeed are ricks to be seen outside the barns, and they are not capacious enough to contain large crops," &c.

Had Mr. Caird journeyed through this country in any other way than by railway, he would have formed a much more correct opinion of the extent under cultivation : this he has very much underrated. Fully three-fourths of this whole district of country is cleared and enclosed, and a large portion of it highly cultivated. If there was little Indian Corn in 1858, it was because other crops promised to pay better, and the spring of 1858 was peculiarly wet and cold ; but there is a very large extent of it this year, and although a little late it will prove an abundant crop. The absence of ricks outside the barn, as alluded to by Mr. Caird, is owing to the great abundance of timber, and the great facility with which Canadians construct large barns, quite sufficient to hold even very luxuriant crops. Every good Canadian farmer provides substantial covering for his whole crops, instead of having recourse to ricks with their temporary covering of straw. The material, except nails, they have within themselves, and most of them can help to build them. The work of building a barn 60 feet by 30, and 18 feet post, can be done for 40*l.* sterling: and most farmers have two if not three of these large barns, besides long sheds in which to store hay, &c.; so that the absence of ricks is no criterion of deficiency; but, on the contrary, their presence is rather a sign that the farmer is a new settler, and as yet unable to put up the permanent covering for his produce, which old and successful farmers universally provide. As to Mr. Caird's assertion that on this "easier and more fertile soil" the cultivation of Indian corn demands too much labour, it may be safely urged that labour is cheaper in Canada than in Illinois, and that the corn crop is nearly as productive in the district he alludes to as it is in Illinois, and being of a much superior quality sells at a much higher price. The fact is, that wheat in this district has been hitherto so fine, and selling at such high prices, that the growth of Indian Corn has been neglected too much for the welfare of the farmer. This very part of Canada which Mr. Caird describes in the above quotation is noted for producing the very finest samples of wheat, weighing 62 lbs. and even 63 lbs., to the Winchester bushel, and has for years carried off the Canada Company's prize of 100 dollars; and it was in this district that the prize wheat exhibited at the Crystal Palace in England, was grown. There are often from 50 to 150 acres of wheat on one farm in this section. The great inducement to sow wheat has hitherto caused many farmers to trespass too much, perhaps, upon the properties of the soil required for this crop; but if Mr. Caird were this year to visit this part of the country, and view it (not from a railway car window) he would find more extensive fields of his favourite crop, and likely to pay a higher *acreable* profit than the Illinois prairie land, because the prices in Canada are almost double those of Central Illinois, where the corn is of a coarser description. This perseverance in the growth of wheat is an evil that time will remedy; especially as the growth of other grain, and also sheep and dairy farming, are more certainly remunerating. Another extract from page 28 gives a remarkable instance of misguided judgment and grievous misrepresentation, the first clause, however, of the extract being perfectly true.

Mr. Caird says, "a light sandy loam of good quality, only half cleared, is still valued at from 7*l.* to 8*l.* an acre, (sterling no doubt, as all his pounds are sterling throughout the pamphlet). It is this comparatively high price of land in addition to the cost of clearing off the timber, that forces the emigrant westwards to a country where better soil with equal facilities of transport, can be bought for less than the mere cost of clearing this of its timber."

Taking the word "westwards" to mean Central Illinois, which seems to be the summit of Mr. Caird's American predi- lections, it may be most safely asserted that the soil there is *not better*, that the facilities of transport are *not equal*, and that even supposing land in Illinois could be bought for less than the mere cost of clearing in Canada (say 3*l.* 10*s.* sterling per acre), Mr. Caird has omitted to state the value of the timber cleared off. He will be surprised to be told that many pine trees on these very farms are and were worth from 6*s.* to 15*s.* each. It is not unusual for one tree to produce five saw logs of twelve feet long each, worth 4*s.* to 5*s.* sterling each log. The timber alone, of well-grown cedar swamps in all the settled districts of Canada West, is worth 4*l.* to 5*l.* per acre on the spot; and even if the hard wood is all burnt to ashes, the ashes of three acres will, with very little outlay of capital or labour, produce a barrel of potash worth 6*l.* sterling. The value of the timber on our wild lands in good situations, where saw-mills, or rivers to float saw-logs, are accessible, is very considerable. Our forests, instead of being a bugbear to the intelligent emi- grant, are a very great source of wealth, and enable him to pay for his land, and erect the required buildings, and supply fence rails, and fuel, sugar, &c., which the settler on the prairie has to purchase, and sometimes at very high rates. That the soil is not better in Illinois than in Canada West can be easily proved. Which gives the largest crops of wheat per acre of the best quality? Decidedly Canada West. The probable average of Illinois is stated by Mr. Caird, at pages 55 and 89, as twenty bushels per acre, but at page 54 he gives the *probable* yield at eighteen to twenty, and the *real* yield "nothing but shrivelled husk;" and again at page 52, as nearly a total failure, and six hundred acres killed by frost, and at pages 75 and 76, he gives the yield of 1857 as little more than six bushels per acre; and ac- cording to the United States Census of 1850-1, Illinois did not yield ten bushels per acre, whereas the average of all Canada West that year was 16, 14-60; and of the counties to which Mr. Caird alludes to in the above extract, the average was twenty-one bushels. Then as to *quality of wheat*, that of Central Illinois is notoriously inferior. Merchants in Toronto import large quantities of it at about half the price of Canada wheat for distillery purposes, not being fit for making flour, except what is denominated by the Americans "stump-tail flour," being of a third or fourth rate quality, and this is the general character of the prairie wheat in Central Illinois. Then as to price, Mr. Caird quotes it in several places at 3s. sterling, (75 cents). At the very time Mr. Caird quotes this as being the price in the Illinois markets, Canada wheat was selling in Toronto and Hamilton and all our frontier markets, at exactly double that amount, 6s. sterling, (1½ dollar); and at this date Upper Canada wheat is selling in our markets at double the price of Illinois wheat in Illinois markets.

Let old-country farmers remember this, that even supposing the yield of bushels per acre to be the same, the price in Canada is double, and of course the value per acre double, and giving Mr. Caird's own averages, 20 bushels per acre, and his own prices, 3s. sterling per bushel, the Canadian farmer would pocket 3l. sterling per acre more than the prairie farmer in Illinois; and this 3l., be it remembered, is good interest for 50l. on every acre of land sown in wheat, say one-sixth of the whole arable land, or 8l. 6s. 8d. per acre on all the wheat-producing land on the farm.

As far, therefore, as the culture of *wheat* is concerned, the settler in Canada West has a vast advantage over the settler in the Illinois prairie, the yield, the quality, and the price, being all superior in Canada West. The peninsula of Upper Canada consists of soils similar to those of the Genesee valley, in the State of New York, distinguished for the finest quality of wheat, which the American miller eagerly buys to mix with the coarser wheats of the western states. Canadian wheat makes the very finest flour, whilst western wheat makes only second and third rate qualities. The area of the fine wheat-growing lands on this continent is very limited, and Upper Canada occupies a large portion of it.

But, says Mr. Caird, "Indian corn is a great staple in Illinois." Let us take him at his own showing, and let us see the result. The average produce he gives in two places is 50 bushels per acre, and at another 40. The price at page 61 is 8d. per bushel; at page 74, 10d.; and at another place, page 51, one farthing per pound, or 1s. 3d. per bushel; at pages 87 and 89, 1s. 8d. per bushel. Taking the price at 1s. 3d sterling on the spot, and the produce per acre at 50 bushels (which is far too high an average, 40 being much more like the truth), we have 3l. 2s. 6d. per acre the produce of a good average corn crop in Illinois. The cost of twice ploughing, planting, horse-hoeing, &c., is at least 2l. 2s. 6d. per acre, and the prairie farmer has 1l. per acre at this show-ing for himself for interest on his purchase money, fencing, buildings, &c. Mr. Caird has truly and admirably said (page 54):—" If a man buys 600 acres and has not the means of cultivating more than sixty, the 540 acres are a dead loss to him. He has to pay either the price or the interest of the price of this large, unproductive extent of land. The produce of the sixty acres is called upon to bear not only its own burden, but that of the nine-tenths which are idle.—The lean kine thus eat up the one fat one." Probably four-fifths of the settlers buy what is called one quarter section (being 160 acres), and are not able for two or three years to cultivate more than the fourth of it; thus, the forty or eighty acres under cultivation or whatever it may be, have to pay the whole interest on the purchase money of the 160 acres, and buildings erected. The rent or interest of course will vary, but taking the price at 3l. sterling, and the fencing at 16s. per acre, and the build-ings, &c., at 100l., the rent of forty acres cropped, with house built, would be about 42l. 10s.,—thus:

First cost of land, at £3 per acre	£480	0	0
Cost of fencing 160 acres, at 16s. per acre, being 640 rods, at 4s. sterling	128	0	0
Buildings, Well, &c. &c	100	0	0
	£708	0	0

This 708l. at six per cent. would be about 42l. 10s., or 21s. 3d. sterling per acre, leaving the farmer minus 1s. 3d. per acre on the actual cost, giving him barely labourer's wages, and no interest for his working-cattle, implements, &c., &c. The fencing of 160 acres requires 640 rods of fence, which, at a very low calculation, is worth 1 dollar per rod, or 4s. sterling. Mr. Caird makes the expense of fencing 60l. per mile (see page 55); but considering that price too high, I have taken 40l. per mile. If a whole section is purchased (a mile square), the outside fence on all sides would be four miles, and the acreable cost of enclosing would be much less than where

only a quarter section is purchased ; but every prairie farmer
as well as every other farmer requires subdivisions of his
farm, and 16s. sterling per acre is a very low estimate of the
cost of fencing on any farm.   So that Mr. Caird's representation, at pages 89 and 90, where he says, " The third year
begins by the prairie farmer finding himself the unencumbered
owner of his land, all fenced and improved, with a stock of
horses and implements, and the whole of his original capital
in his pocket," is a monstrous delusion, calculated to do
immense injury to his readers, who may be thereby tempted
to settle on the aguish, treeless, shelterless, and arid prairies
of Illinois.   The idea, too, expressed at page 90, that, " he
may continue to crop his farm with Indian corn from which
he will reap very large returns on his capital," is, to say the
least of it, a much too glowing and sanguine view of the
prairie farmer's prospects.   At page 60 he gives the opinion
of a Mr. Brown, an old farmer in the country, " that more
money has been made, and may be made in this state by *stock*
farming than by corn growing ;" and adds (page 61), " but he
has not found short-horned stock so successful on the natural
prairie grass, of which, on his own lands, he has no longer
any."

To give us an idea of *stock* farming, Mr. Caird tells us
(page 71) that " Oxen of three years old, large, and in what
we should reckon fair condition for stall feeding, are valued·
here, i. e., Central Illinois, at not more than 4l. !"   And again,
at page 69, he quotes the price of beef at 2d. per lb. ; and at
page 72, a Kentucky farmer admits that two acres of his best
blue grass land in Illinois were needed to fatten a three-year
old short-horned ox.   At these prices stock farming cannot be
profitable at all, and if *better* than corn growing, what inference
may we draw ?   The story of the ox and two hogs eating a
hundred bushels of Indian corn (page 74), and then being sold
at 2d. per lb., is not calculated to give very favourable views
of prairie farming.   It is well Mr. Caird has so frankly represented these facts to enable British farmers to judge for themselves.   It may be well to state here that cattle, sheep, beef,
mutton, pork and grain of all kinds in Canada, are fully
double the prices quoted by Mr. Caird as being the prices in
Central Illinois ; and intelligent British farmers will no doubt
govern themselves accordingly, especially as all other crops,
except Indian corn, are more productive in Canada West, and
labour quite as cheap.   These high prices may be supposed
to militate against mechanics and manufacturers, but where

agricultural products are high, mechanics find more employment and better wages than when they are low. The farmers being more prosperous, are better able to carry on improvements of all kinds. Mr. Caird, at page 50, quotes the wages of a journeyman carpenter at 4s. per day, with his board; these wages are rather lower than in Canada, but the colony has suffered so severely by the late exceptional reverses, that there is little employment for tradesmen at present at high wages. If we have a good harvest and an average crop, times will improve rapidly; but it may be safely stated that it is not probable that either Illinois or Canada will ever again reach that state of inflated prosperity, caused by the late expenditure of millions of dollars in the purchase and formation of railway routes. The benefit of the colony will be permanent and substantial, but the first pioneers of the benefit will probably be severe sufferers. Mr. Caird has well said, and it appears true with regard to Canada also, that, "the development of railway accommodation has been too rapid, and has for the present outrun the immediate requirements of Illinois."

I have alluded to the fact that wheat and all other grain, except Indian corn, are more productive in Canada West than in Central Illinois. The circumstances of climate are, perhaps, the chief cause of the superiority of Canada West. The great wheat-producing countries of Europe lie between the 50th and 59th degrees of north latitude, where the summer temperature is from 55° to 65°; but in Central Illinois, where the latitude is about 38°, the summer heat is 78°, and often as high in the shade as from 90° to 100° in June, July, and August. This climate is too hot for the profitable culture of European grains or grasses: they grow there, it is true, but are generally of a very inferior description. The wheat this year (1859) is fortunately a very tolerable sample, and the yield a fair average; much of it was harvested the first week of July: one very large field, I was told by a farming friend who witnessed the operation, was cut with a "heading machine," i. e. the heads of the wheat were cut off immediately below the ear, and dropped into a box which was emptied into waggons accompanying the machine. The straw, being of little value, was left standing.

As far as regards the wheat crop, this year is an improvement upon several of the past years; but as to other crops, barley, oats, rye and peas, there does not appear to be much change for the better. With the exception of Indian corn, they are not by any means extensively or successfully cultivated.

By the last census of Canada, taken in 1851-52, her population was about 1-13th of that of the Union, her occupied acres about 1-17th ; yet her growth of wheat was very nearly one-sixth of that of the whole Union, of barley it was more than one fourth, and of oats one seventh.   Of all grain, exclusive of Indian corn, Canada produced *one-sixth of that of the whole Union, territories included.*

These are important facts for the consideration of British emigrants, who, instead of settling on the bleak prairies of the United States, may wish to enjoy a climate not very different from their own, and decidedly healthful ; and who may wish to cultivate the same species and description of grain that they have been used to, or to continue their dairies, or to indulge in their beef and mutton producing tendencies, with a fair hope of remuneration.

The prospect of having but little fruit in Central Illinois, is another very important consideration.   The land where trees do not naturally grow, can scarcely be expected to be very congenial to fruit trees.   It is only too true that, in many parts of Illinois, fruit trees will not thrive.

Another extract from Mr. Caird (page 29) is worthy of comment, as it portrays a great want of knowledge of facts with regard to the relative increase of population in Canada and Illinois, and is calculated to mislead his readers.   Mr. C. says, "Canada West is richer than Canada East, and is more populous ; but there is a richer territory still farther west, where labour is yet more productive, and, though in the present state of the country the risk of health is greater, it is ten times more populous, for men push on to the land in which they can most quickly and easily earn an independence."

What will Mr. Caird himself say, when he is told that Canada West has increased in population in a much greater ratio than his favourite State of Illinois !

By the United States Census of 1850, it appears that the three states of Ohio, Michigan, and Illinois, contained in 1830, 1,126,851, and in 1850, 3,505,000; a little over 320 per cent. in twenty years.   Canada West contained in 1830, 210,437; in 1850, 791,000, which is over 375 per cent. for the same period of twenty years ; so that the increase in these choice states was fifty-five per cent. less than that of Canada West during the same time.   Some of our counties in Canada West, viz., Huron, Perth, and Bruce, have increased 571 per cent. in ten years.

Comparing the last decade of Canada West with that of the United States, we find that the increase during the ten years from 1840 to 1850, was 35·27 per cent., whilst that of Upper Canada was 104·58 per cent.

We have had no census in Canada since 1851-52 ; but there is every reason to believe that the ratio of increase, not including immigration, has continued very much the same, and there is a *certainty* that Mr. Caird's representation as to comparative increase of population in Illinois is entirely *erroneous*. Immigration to the United States has fallen off quite as much in proportion as that into Canada. The statement that an independence can be more quickly and easily earned in Illinois than in Canada West, is simply a delusion, and has been frequently proved by the return of settlers, who, like Mr. Caird, were attracted by the more inviting appearance of prairies to old-country eyes. But as Mr. Caird has given a Dr. and Cr. for Illinois, at page 89, I will give a similar one for Canada. Let old-country capitalists who can command the required sum (say 750*l.* sterling), diligently compare the two, and keep in mind the permanent difference in the quality and prices of produce, and the healthfulness of Canada, and the choice between the two will be no difficult matter to decide, even in the matter of dollars and cents, without alluding to our British Constitution, our British feeling, British tone of morality, our British social atmosphere, &c., which Britons always appreciate more highly after a short residence in the United States.

Mr. Caird thus gives the probable Dr. and Cr. of 100 acres of land for two years in Central Illinois.

Dr.

Cash price of 100 acres, sterling	£200	0	0
Contract price of fencing, breaking, sowing with wheat, reaping and threshing, and building a labourer's cottage, and stable and shed	250	0	0
Capital invested in the purchase of four horses, implements, and harness	110	0	0
	£560	0	0
2nd year, wages of 2 men, horse-keep, taxes and accounts	200	0	0
	£760	0	0

Cr.

1st crop wheat, 2000 bushels at 3*s.* 6*d.*, 350*l.*; 2nd crop Indian corn, 5000 bushels, at 1*s.* 8*d.*, 416*l.*	£766	0	0
Surplus after 2nd crop, besides the value of land and stock	£ 6	0	0

In Canada West the Dr. and Cr. are on the same basis. Taking 100 acres brought into cultivation, they would stand thus : Capitalists can bring 100 acres into cultivation in Canada, as well as in the United States, although such is seldom or never done that I am aware of.

Dr.

Cash price of 100 acres of land, at 3*s.* 3*d.*	£16	5	0
Contract price of clearing, fencing, and seeding, at 3*l.* 10*s.* per acre	350	0	0
Contract price of building a small house or shed	50	0	0
Capital invested in oxen, (two yoke) chains, &c	34	0	0
Capital invested in potash kettle	10	0	0
Capital invested in labour making potash and barrels	40	0	0
Second year, board and wages of 3 men and 5 in harvest, ox keep, &c.	180	0	0
	£680	5	0

Cr.

Potash, 20 barrels, at 6*l.*	£120	0	0	
Pine timber, say 100 trees, at 6*s.*	30	0	0	
(Where the timber is good for making potash there is not much pine, for this reason I have set down a small sum)				
First crop of wheat, 2000 bushels, at 5*s.*	500	0	0	
Second crop, barley, rye, oats, peas, and potatoes, at 3*l.* per acre, average.	300	0	0	
			950	0	0

Surplus after the second crop, besides land, &c £269 15 0

This comparison, which is justly and fairly given, shows that the Canadian capitalist has the advantage over the prairie capitalist of 269*l.* 15*s.* sterling in two years ; and to show that these representations are by no means overdrawn, I give below the *official* published returns by our Government Agent, on the Ottawa, of the total produce of 800 acres of newly cleared land, for the year 1858, with the prices which he has attached, and which are not, as may be deemed, exceptional.

Mr. French says :—"Upon these 800 acres there were raised :—

" 5726 bushels of wheat, at 1 dollar per bushel	$	5726	00
2916 „ oats, at 40 cents per bushel . .		1166	40
149 „ barley, at 50 cents per bushel .		74	50
168 „ Indian corn, at 1 dollar per bushel		168	00
16799 „ potatoes, at 40 cents per bushel,		6718	80
6350 „ turnips at 10 cents per bushel		635	00
87 tons of hay, at 5 dollars per ton		435	00
260 tons of straw, at 4 dollars per ton . . .		1040	00
4012 lbs. of sugar, at 10 cents per lb		401	20
108 barrels of potash, at 24 dollars per barrel		2522	00
9159 bushels of ashes, at 8 cents per bushel .		739	92
Making a total of . . .	$	19695	82

and showing the average value of each acre to be something over twenty-four dollars sixty cents, or 5l. sterling for one year," an amount far above Mr. Caird's representation of the Illinois prairies. For *three* of the above articles, viz., potatoes, hay, and straw, a market could not be found on a prairie farm; and three other articles, potash, ashes, and sugar, could not be produced. Mr. French has omitted to give credit for the timber used in their houses and sheds, or sold to timber merchants.

Let old-country farmers carefully compare these two statements, and remember also that they are likely to have good health in Canada, good water, and plenty of it, and no necessity of Artesian wells 127 feet deep; good apples and pears and small fruit, and vegetables of every kind in abundance, good markets for everything they grow, good timber for their houses and fences and fires, and a good Government that provides handsomely for the education of their families —even much better than in the United States; and if they will be guided by the honest opinion of a man of twenty-five years' experience in Canada as an agriculturalist, they will pause before they prefer the prairies of Central Illinois to the woods of Canada. The woods modify the heat of summer and cold of winter, whilst the prairies of Illinois are subject to terrific winds and storms and snow in winter, and often most dreadful and devastating fires—and the ever-falling leaves of our woods are ever depositing a rich compost, far superior to that of the long thin prairie grass. There is still another very important consideration regarding these level prairie lands, that is, that many of them cannot be settled on till drained of the sour and unwholesome surface water; and, from the nature of the country, draining is a very expensive operation, and not unfrequently entirely impracticable. Deep permanent springs are often very difficult to find, and there is much suffering both by man and beast for want of really good pure water.

To corroborate what I have said, with regard to the deficiency of the yield of wheat, and other crops in the United States, I give below a quotation from a very late and very clever publication by John Jay, being "A Statistical View of American Agriculture, its Home Resources and Foreign Markets, &c., in an Address delivered at New York before the American Geographical and Statistical Society, on the Organization of the Agricultural Section," New York, 1859. "The average number of bushels of wheat to the acre in Alabama and

154 REMARKS ON MR. CAIRD'S PAMPHLET.

Georgia is five; in North Carolina, Virginia, and Tennessee, seven; ranging upwards in the other States until it reaches twelve in New York, Ohio, and Indiana; thirteen in Maryland and Vermont; fourteen in Iowa and Wisconsin; fifteen in Florida, Pennsylvania, and Texas; and sixteen (the highest average) in Massachusetts. Oats range from ten bushels to the acre through various intermediate gradations, to thirty-five and thirty-six bushels, which is the highest." The Journal of the Highland Society of Scotland thus observes: "If the above statement, as given by Mr. Jay, be correct, the state of farming in many parts of America must be indeed in a wretched condition—the American maximum corresponds to our minimum;" adding however the following, which appears to be only too true with regard to late years; but reports of this year's crop indicate that the evil is not progressing. "We believe," says the 'Journal,' "that the wheat crop has recently suffered much from the increased ravages of insects, and from various diseases to which it seems to be becoming more and more subject."

Since the above was written, the prospects of the wheat crop in the United States this year appear to be more promising than usual, and in Canada there is every prospect of a very handsome return. From all quarters of Canada West, reports have been sent to this office of expected large crops of wheat, say from thirty to forty bushels per acre; and of spring grain most abundant supplies, including that of Indian corn: and corroborative of what I have stated, with regard to the yield of this grain in Illinois not exceeding forty bushels per acre, I again quote Mr. Jay's statement, as given by the same journal:—"Commencing," he says, "at eleven bushels per acre, the returns of produce of Indian corn range through various gradations in the different States, up to thirty-two in Vermont and Iowa; thirty-three in Missouri; thirty-six in Ohio, and forty in Connecticut." This last is the highest return given.

I am, Sir,
   Yours, with respect,
     WILLIAM HUTTON,
      Secretary to Bureau of Agriculture.

Toronto, July 22, 1859.

THE PRINCIPAL KINDS OF TIMBER EXPORTED FROM CANADA are White and Yellow Pine, Oak, Ash, Bass-wood, Tamarac, Birch, Walnut, Butternut, and Maple. Besides the large quantities of the above descriptions of timber exported in their hewed state, large quantities of deals, planks, boards, scantling, lath-wood, and staves, are also exported. The principal timber territories are the *Ottawa*, upper and lower, watered by the river Ottawa and its tributaries, from which the White Pine Red Pine, and Ash, exported, chiefly come. The Ottawa and its tributaries drain an area of about 75,000 square miles. The *St. Maurice*, watered by the river St. Maurice and its tributaries, which contains large quantities of White, Yellow, and Red Pine, besides Spruce, Birch, Maple, and Elm. The St. Maurice river and tributaries drain an area of about 22,000 square miles. The *Saguenay*, watered by the river Saguenay and its tributaries, which contains large quantities of White and Red Pine, Spruce, Birch, and Tamarac, are found in this territory. Its timber resources have as yet only been partially explored. The Saguenay river and its tributaries drain an area of about 21,000 square miles. The *Madawaska* (Lower Canada), watered by the river Madawaska and the eastern head-waters of the river St. John, contains still considerable quantities of White Pine. The Madawaska river and its tributaries drain an area of about 1,000 square miles.

The territory *north and east of the shore of Lake Huron*, watered by the rivers Severn, Muskoka, Au Sables, Maganetewan, French, Spanish, Serpent, Mississaga, and Garden, contains large quantities of White and Red Pine, Spruce, Cedar, Birch, and Maple. Very little timber has yet been manufactured in this territory. Its proximity to the Chicago and other markets will, however, make the timber very valuable in a few years. The peninsula of Canada West contains considerable quantities of Oak, Walnut, and Elm of superior quality. Nearly all the staves and walnuts exported come from this territory. The Ontario territory, situated north of Lake Ontario, contains considerable quantities of White Pine and Elm : large quantities of plank, boards, and saw-logs come from this territory.

P. M. PARTRIDGE,

Woods and Forests Branch.

PART THE THIRD.

LETTERS FROM CANADA.

No. I.

"Toronto, C. W.
" My dear Wyndham,   August, 1854.

" I am very glad to hear that my answers to your
various questions for the guidance of the parties about to
leave your noble relative's estates have been useful. Be
assured that upon their arrival here they shall have the best
advice and assistance I can render them, in locating them
near those who have preceded them, and almost all of whom,
I am happy to say, are progressing favourably, and many of
them have had great success, and have already, from small
land-renters and cottagers, become landowners to the extent
of many hundreds of acres—say nothing of having arrived at
the dignity of squires, town-councillors, reeves, and, in more
than one case, the privilege of writing J. P. after their names.

" Among the names of those which will be most familiar to
you are those of   *   *   *   *   *
All of them desire to be kindly, and some of them 'grate-
fully,' remembered to you and to him ; an expression which
nine years ago would not have fallen from their lips. The
very step which, at that time, seemed harsh to those who
cling to the ' auld roof-tree,' however humble that home may
be, has turned out a blessing to them, and raised them to a position which, in the old country, they never could have reached.

" ' The old country,' and ' home !' It is truly cheering
to see and hear how fondly and frequently these words are
uttered here. It has made my old heart stir within me, to
hear them in the Viceroy's speech, the Provincial Parliament,
the drawing-room of the colonial aristocrat, and the shanty of
the settler, far, far away in the backwoods, where tidings of
' home ' seldom come. There are in these words endearing

associations, which time and distance cannot diminish or obliterate. Here they have a magic and a force which I cannot describe. It is a word that conjures up memories of the past on which the heart loves to linger—the memory of prayers uttered on bended knees at the feet of departed parents, who blessed our early, and guided our advancing years, when the passions of youth were unsubdued, and the principles of manhood unconfirmed. It recals the abode of distant, most loved, and loving friends, and brings back scenes on which the eye has not rested for many a year of anxious struggle and final success. I must tell you a little anecdote on this point which moved me exceedingly. 1 called one day while in the bush at the house of a venerable old man of eighty—a soldier and a gentleman—who had been here forty years, and seldom got any tidings from home. I happened to have in my pocket-book a primrose which dearest —— sent me in a letter, and I placed it on the old man's knee, and said, 'Did you ever see a flower like that?' The old man took it up, and when he recognised it, he kissed the pale flower over and over again, and, bending his aged head, he wept like a child, so long and so violently that I was alarmed. Who can tell what thoughts this little flower awakened in the old man's mind? The thoughts of some shady lane, perchance, near the unforgotten home of his childhood—

'The first love-beat of his youthful heart,'—

a mother's gentle look—a father's word of approbation or sign of reproof—a sister's gentle love—a brother's fond regard—handfuls of flowers plucked in green and quiet meadows—bird's-nests admired, but not touched—the Sabbath call to prayer and praise. It was too sacred a sight for a stranger's eye. I don't *think* he could have spoken; I am *sure* I could not. So I wrote in pencil a few words promising to see him again, and, if we should be both spared, that he should next spring have a pale memorial of spring and home from the same green lane as the one which had, much to his honour, elicited ' a soldier's tear.' * * *

" All the favourable impressions of Canada which I named to you before have been fully confirmed upon a more accurate inquiry into her *wonderful* resources and capabilities; if there be any country which deserves to be known at home, that country is Canada. We seem never to have realized what Canada really is, and have always thought of her as a desolate and chilly place, the abode of anthropophagi and

mosquitoes, from whence we got ice and pine timber; instead
of which, it is a country about four times the size of the
British Possessions in Europe, producing almost everything
which can minister to the comforts and luxuries of life, and
where, within the space of less than fifty years, millions of
acres of land have been converted from forest and swamps
into fruitful and well-cultivated farms, supplying not only the
wants of its own rapidly-increasing population, but enabling
us to export produce to the States and England to the value of
many millions sterling every year.

" I am not surprised that the despatch for Lord Elgin has
been read with surprise and interest, and it must have been a
proud day for him when the temporal condition and prospects
of the country enabled him to dictate and sign that document.   It is well for Canada that she has as ruler a man of
enlightened mind and onward views ; and his name will be
remembered with gratitude when passion, and prejudice, and
politics enable another generation to estimate his talents more
calmly than can be done just now.

" The progress of Upper Canada has been really wonderful,
especially when it is borne in mind, that during the brief
period of our national history, not yet sixty years, she has
had to contend against the disadvantages of a war in 1812
and a rebellion in 1837.   At present, the information I convey
to you is confined to Upper Canada.   I do not know much
yet of the Lower Province, but quite enough to make me
desirous of knowing more of the country and of the people.
They are not one whit behind Upper Canada in loyal devotion to our good Queen; and if within the last sixty years they
have not progressed quite as much as the Upper Province,
some of this shortcoming must be attributed to a climate less
favourable to the production of wheat—our great staple—and
also to the operation of the Seignorial Tenure Bill, which,
within five years, I hope to see abolished.

" Canada has a fruitful soil· and a fine climate—she has
before her a glorious prospect, and her sons and daughters a
lofty mission—she is a land of kindling energies, and of untold
and undeveloped resources, which will give her soon a place
and a name among the nations of the earth—she entertains a
warm and affectionate regard for the ' old house at home,' and a
deep feeling of loyalty towards her Sovereign, and it would have
delighted that distinguished personage could she have seen
the way in which her last birthday was celebrated on this
side of the Atlantic.

" I speak advisedly when I say that Canada can offer to the

capitalists of England as good security for any monies they may invest here, and for which 8 per cent. is cheerfully given, as can be offered in that great old-world institution—that 'beautiful simplicity'—your 3 per Cent. Consolidated Annuities. The kind of securities I more particularly allude to are the Government, County, Township, and Municipal Bonds, all of which are secured, directly or indirectly, upon the 340,000 square miles of freehold land,* of which

THIRTY MILLIONS OF ACRES

are owned, occupied, and cultivated by 200,000 industrious, contented, and loyal landowners. These lands, which form a very, very small proportion of those equally capable of successful cultivation, are assessed at a clear annual value of 60,000,000l. sterling; while the whole national debt does not amount to the private fortune of many individuals in Great Britain.

"Bonds of one hundred pounds each and upwards are to be had, the interest on which at six per cent. can be paid in London as regularly as they can get it at home. Six per cent. is the legal rate of interest, but there is no penalty, by a recent law, for taking more. The banking system here rests upon a most solid foundation. No new bank can be established which has not first deposited with the Government an amount of Provincial Bonds equal to its intended circulation of notes, and these notes must be countersigned by the Inspector-General, or some one appointed by him. The Government permits these bonds to be issued, and *guarantees the repayment of principal and interest at six per cent. to the lender.* The whole sum is paid off in the course of twenty-four years, and care is taken that the sum borrowed shall only bear a certain proportion to the assessed value of the county or township. No security can be better than this.

"The Township Bonds are issued for similar purposes, and afford equal security, the only difference being that the County Bonds are a mortgage upon the whole county, and the Township Bonds upon the lands of the township only. They, too, are prohibited from raising beyond a certain per centage upon the assessed value.

"The Municipal Bonds are issued by the cities of Canada for the purpose of sewerage, public roads, &c. &c., and secured upon the whole property of the city, and generally repaid in twenty years.

* Upper Canada, 140,000 square miles ; Lower Canada, 200,000 square miles.

a person at home, aged twenty-one, to secure an annuity, under the Legacy Duty Act, of 100*l.* per annum, would have to sink a sum of about 1600*l.* ; here he could get the same income by investing that sum in Canadian securities, and save his principal.

"Again, a lady of sixty, at home, with a capital of 5000*l.*, could only get an income of 150*l.* per annum from the funds. She could get from hence, for the remainder of her life, when advancing years require increasing comforts, 400*l.* a year half-yearly in London; and thus be enabled to leave her little fortune to her relatives, undiminished by any of those attenuating processes with which your Chancellors of the Exchequer sometimes indulge you.

" To parties willing to lend money upon mortgage, the Legislature affords first-rate security. In regard to the investigation of title, a registry office is established in each county, for the registration of all deeds and wills relating to land there. Registration is so far compulsory, that unregistered deeds are valid only as between the parties, and may be disregarded in looking into a title. Thus, suppose that *A* sells to *B*, who neglects to register his deed, and *C* subsequently purchases from *A*, and registers; the title of *B* to the land is gone, and he can look only to his remedy against *A* for fraud. The investigation of title is also much facilitated by the facts, that land generally has not as yet changed hands very often, and that conveyances are very simple, and free from those questions of trusts and settlements which are often found to complicate and embarrass titles in England. With this safeguard fraud is almost impossible.

" With respect to the valuation of property offered as security, there can be no difficulty on this point : each farm in the country, and lot in town, is valued for the purposes of taxation by county officers regularly appointed, who are directed by the statute to estimate the property ' as they would appraise the same in payment of a just debt due from a solvent debtor.' The assessors' certificate can be obtained, and their estimate may be relied upon as clearly within the cash value. When the loan is large, and it is desirable to obtain more particular information, an agent is sent to a surveyor living in the county, and employed to report upon the value. When houses form part of the security, the borrower is required to insure to the amount loaned, and assign the policies.

"You must look upon this letter as a kind of text for future ones—a mere outline—which I shall fill in from time to time."

No. II.

"Toronto, Aug. 1855.

"MY DEAR WYNDHAM,

"HAVING told you the many advantages with which Providence has blessed this province, the very name of which you once told me used to make you shiver, I now tell you some of its drawbacks.

"The first of these is a long winter. This, however, is our Maker's will, and it does not become us to repine. It has, moreover, its uses and advantages as I will show elsewhere, and is yearly mitigated by clearing lands, draining swamps, and various other agricultural improvements. We want more places of worship—more pastors—representatives in the Imperial Parliament or authorized agents at home—trees for shade, shelter, and ornament—hedgerows—coal—access to public libraries—male and female agricultural and domestic servants—more money, or banks with more capital—more good beer and less bad whiskey—in the concoction of which filthy poison it is computed that 4,000,000 bushels of native-grown grain are annually consumed! In this latter matter we are without excuse. Barley produces admirable crops in both provinces—say 25 bushels an acre. Hops are indigenous, and grow everywhere. They are, too, less infested with the blight and louse than at home. I know an instance in the splendid township of Whitby, where a friend of mine, a Yorkshireman of the name of Ritson, sold the produce of three acres of hops for 1000 dollars—200l. of your money—and got a first prize at the Horticultural Show. What Mr. Ritson did can be done by thousands of others, and the country might become weaned from the consumption of a beverage of a most injurious character, and the fatal effects of drinking, which are painfully *numerous* among us.

"AGRICULTURE is progressing most satisfactorily among us, as you will see by the following products; Upper Canada alone, for one year ending January, 1852 :—

M

Wheat	. .	12,600,000 l	bushels.	Hops	113,000	lbs.
Barley	. .	6,000,000	„	Hay	680,000	tons.
Rye	. . .	479,000	„	Wool	2,700,000 l	lbs.
Pease.	. .	2,870,000	„	Maple Sugar .	3,500,000	„
Oats	. . .	11,000,000	„	Butter . . .	15,900,000	„
Maize	. .	1,600,000	„	Cheese . . .	2,200,000	„
Potatoes.	.	5,000,000	„	Beef	111,000	barrels
Turnips .	.	3,000,000	„	Pork	300,000	„
Carrots	. .	174,000	„	Tobacco . . .	760,000	„

" The amount of stock returned was as follows :—

Bulls, Oxen, &c. . . .	139,000	Horses	200,000
Calves and Heifers. . .	254,000	Sheep	969,000
Milch Cows	296,000	Pigs.	570,000

" THE PROGRESSIVE VALUE OF STOCK

may be gathered from the following table, and you must bear in mind that when I name the price of any Canadian produce, the sum named is in *currency*, unless I distinctly call it sterling value; the simple way to bring which into sterling money is to deduct one-fifth.

1833.

	£.	s.	d.		£.	s.	d.
Horses	10	0	0	to	15	0	0
Working Oxen, per pair . . .	15	0	0	„	17	10	0
Sheep	0	5	0	„	0	7	6
Cows . .	3	15	0	„	4	0	0
Pigs, of 300 lbs. each, per cwt. .	0	12	6	„	0	17	6
Lambs	0	3	9	„	0	5	0
Oxen for slaughter, per cwt. . .	0	15	0	„	1	0	0

1850.

	£.	s.	d.		£.	s.	d.
Horses	15	0	0	to	20	0	0
Working Oxen, per pair . . .	17	10	0	„	20	0	0
Sheep	0	7	6	„	0	12	6
Cows	5	0	0	„	6	5	0
Pigs, of 300 lbs. each, per cwt. .	0	15	0	„	1	0	0
Lambs	0	5	0	„	0	7	6
Oxen for slaughter, per cwt. . .	1	0	0	„	1	5	0

1853.

	£.	s.	d.		£.	s.	d.
Horses	25	0	0	to	35-	0	0
Working Oxen, per pair . . .	20	0	0	„	22	10	0
Sheep	0	17	6	„	*1	10	0
Cows	6	5	0	„	7	10	0
Pigs, of 300 lbs. each, per cwt. .	1	5	0	„	1	10	0
Lambs	0	10	0	„	0	12	6
Oxen for slaughter, per cwt. . .	1	5	0	„	1	10	0†

* Leicesters.

† The present price of stock, &c., will be found in another portion of the work.—EDITOR

"It is impossible to estimate the mischief and injury to themselves and the country arising from the retention of large blocks of land in this most favoured part of the province, to the extent of many thousands of acres each, by land-jobbers and speculators. Everything is retarded hereby—settlement, roads, schools, progress of all kinds. The Government, however, is about to meet this case, by surveying and offering for sale, on easy terms of payment and low prices, millions of acres of land in both provinces, quite as capable of successful cultivation as those held by these selfish people, who never again will realize the amounts at which they have refused to sell. They deserve no pity and will get none.

"You cannot conceive the singularly cold and dreary appearance of the whole country from the want of hedgerows, and clumps of trees for shade, shelter, and ornament around the homesteads. You may travel hundreds of miles and nothing meets the eye but the interminable snake-fences.

"With the early settlers every tree was a weed of gigantic growth. 'Down with it' was the universal motto. Many persons have wasted and burnt timber to the value of the fee-simple of their estate.

"I submit the following sketch very respectfully to the path-masters, and fence-viewers of Canada, and I leave them to consider which side of the road looks best.

A CANADIAN SIDE LINE.

AS IT IS.   AS IT MIGHT BE.

"The answer I invariably got during my early acquaintance with Upper Canada, 'Oh, sir, the hedges won't grow, our winters are so severe.' But there is also another reason—they are too lazy to try! There are plenty of plants growing at their very doors; the English thorn thrives with moderate care; the beech would form an impervious hedge in three years; the buckthorn (*Rhamnus catharticus*) grows with great rapidity, and has the advantage of forming a very thick hedge, and one which, from its medicinal properties, the cattle will not nibble at.

"Upper Canadian farmers are constantly abusing the climate of Lower Canada, but in the neighbourhood of Quebec there are luxuriant hedgerows for miles round and beautiful clumps of trees of every variety."

No. III.

"London, Canada West, Sept. 1856.

"My dear Wyndham,

"I have been spending a few weeks in this fine portion of Canada, and am much delighted with all I have seen, and see from day to day. I have not confined myself to the beaten track, but have wandered about beyond the regions of stage-coaches and crowded streets. While I continue to grumble at the absence of all taste for floriculture, at the abundant evidences of the most inconceivably-primitive state of farming, the utter ignorance, practically, of draining, or irrigation, still there is *progress*!

"You cannot imagine the painful silence which pervades the 'bush.' I have walked hundreds of miles at different times alone, and for hours together I never saw a living creature in the shape of an animal, a bird, or a butterfly. Yet there are many, and beautiful, and rare specimens of all to be found in Canada. Once now and then a *Vanessa antiopa* would cross my path—then, perchance, the scarlet tanager, *Tanagra rubra*, and the beautiful meadow lark, *Alauda magna*, would delight the stranger for a moment with a sight of their beautiful plumage. We have, among other rare birds, the white-winged crossbill, *Loxia leucoptera*.

"I suppose, however, the taste and the search for these beautiful objects will arise among us one of these days. I know throughout Upper Canada only one English gentleman, Mr. Cottle, of Woodstock, who takes any interest in ornithological pursuits and investigations.

*   *   *   *   *   *

"It will be hardly possible for

'You gentlemen of England
Who live at home at ease,'

to realize what has to be done and is *doing* here. That nearly

THIRTY MILLION ACRES should have been brought into gradual and productive cultivation—that the immemorial forest should have given place to the waving corn-field, the laden orchard, the pretty village, the thriving town, the stately city—that the placid lake should bear on its broad bosom splendid steamers instead of the birch-bark canoe of the poor Indians, and all within sixty years, is matter at once for deep congratulation to the people of Canada, and anxious attention in those who now, or may hereafter, direct her worldly destinies. That much was due, under Providence, to the steady good sense and discretion of Lord Elgin I am quite convinced, being able to look upon the events of the last five years with no party prejudice. I should really consider it as a serious evil if his lordship should not return to complete those plans of internal improvement, both social and intellectual, which *he* has indicated, and the government is *pledged* to.

" If the present moment be not wisely improved Canada must retrograde. It is indeed a period of anxious interest, and upon the judgment which those who ' bear rule' display in this crisis of her history much of the future welfare of millions depends. Canadian legislators should bear in mind that they are called upon to make laws for a future

"NATION,

" ENGLAND, IRELAND, SCOTLAND, CANADA !

a nation which I believe to be destined to fill a bright page in the history of the world,—a nation which, remembering her origin and her home, will take an honest pride in endeavouring to imitate, and emulate, and perpetuate the arts and sciences, the literature and the religion of Great Britain.

" You ask me about the Indians! Poor Indians! They are now ' a feeble folk' and dying out fast. It has been found that the annual gathering of these poor things to receive their ' presents' has led to a good deal of abuse and immorality. The plan suggested of selling the remaining Indian reserves, funding the proceeds, and giving them annuities, may perhaps be more useful to these poor creatures. In any and every case I hope they will be treated with kindness and consideration. England and Canada should never forget the time when the Red-man was their ally, did them good service in their time of need, shed their best blood in the fore-front of

many a stricken field, and contributed in no small degree to
save Canada to Great Britain.

"I happened to spend a St. George's day in New York, and
was gratified at the way in which it was celebrated there.
At a dinner, I heard the following anecdote about the Indians
which interested me much.

"In replying to a toast, Major Sprague, of the United
States army, said:—'Some years ago I was engaged in
removing some Indians beyond the Mississippi, and one day
when encamped I saw a party approaching me. I took my
glass and found they were Indians. I sent out an Indian
with the *Stars and Stripes* on a flag, and the leader of the party
immediately displayed the RED CROSS OF ST. GEORGE! I wanted
him to exchange flags, but the savage would not, for said he
—"I dwell near the Hudson Bay Company, and they gave
me this flag, and they told me that it came from my great
mother across the great waters, and would protect me and
my wife and children wherever we might go. I have found
it as the white man said, and *I will never part with it!*" I
could not,' added the gallant officer emphatically, 'but admire
the feeling of confidence and the sentiment.'

"Canada deserves to be better known than she is, and I
anticipate, at no distant day, that Canada will become the
fashion for tourists and sportsmen. The country which
Lords Derby, Carlisle, Ellesmere, Mr. Godley, and Sir Charles
Lyell visited with so much pleasure and profit, has attractions
for others besides these distinguished gentlemen.

"While I am alluding to this subject I must mention as
one of our most pressing wants in Upper Canada—a race of
country gentlemen, the sons of our native Canadians.

"Among the scores of young men whom I know, the sons
of persons of position and property, there is only one who
promises to belong to this class with whom I am acquainted.
What on earth these young men do with themselves I can
hardly conceive. Instead of bringing into cultivation some
of the waste lands which they or their fathers own, their
highest ambition seems to be lounging about streets or draw-
ing-rooms, becoming lawyers, clerks, doctors, or 'associate
coroners,' of which latter class, Upper Canada can boast more
than Great Britain with her thirty millions of inhabitants!
The young gentleman to whom I allude is Mr. H. J. Boulton,
who lives upon and farms his ample estate, near Toronto, and
there, by precept and example, he shows what *can* be done
upon a Canadian farm, and done with profit. He has spent

large sums of money in draining and various other improvements, for which he is entitled to the highest praise for the example he thus sets his neighbours, many of whom are becoming gradually convinced of the importance and advantage of the measures recommended by Mr. Boulton by the evidence of their own senses. The Members of the Legislature, during the last session, paid less attention to this neglect of draining than its vast importance deserves.

"Since the above remarks were printed, I have met with an Address delivered by the Honourable Mr. Moore, M.L.C., and President of the Agricultural Society of Missisquoi in the Eastern Townships, which expresses admirably my views upon this subject, and to which I invite the attention of certain young gentlemen now leading a life of little utility to themselves or to others.

"When agriculture, as a science (for it is now admitted to rank among the sciences) and as a profession, shall assume that station and position to which it is entitled, then hundreds, I may say thousands, of young men, who are now crowding the different professions, and seeking their way in all the avenues of trade in mercantile pursuits, will find employment in the more useful, and equally honourable occupation of agriculture. The more fully and clearly to illustrate the above sentence, I quote the language of Mr. Hutton, who says, ' that the very nature of the farmer's occupation, which leads him daily and hourly to contemplate the surpassing beauties of the animal and vegetable kingdom, and their striking adaptation to the wants and requirements of man, lead him more than the townsman, more than the mechanic, more than men of any other occupation, to look through nature up to nature's God: to admire his works and to look with grateful dependence to *Him*, for the continual supply of his bounty.' The beautiful vicissitudes of the ever-going and returning seasons, and the constant variations of climate, remind him, above all others, that though Paul may plant and Apollos water, it is God that giveth the increase. And is not this the great advantage of a farmer's life? Do not our gaols and our law-courts attest the fact that, above all others, the farmer's life is the moral, and therefore the happy life? If he is a benefactor of his country who causes two blades of grass to grow where only one grew before, how useful and materially important must be the life of the intelligent farmer. Agriculture, I may say, is of divine origin; in the beginning of the world the first man, Adam, was sent forth from the garden of Eden to till the ground. And a divine decree was made, that he and his descendants should from thenceforth live by tilling the ground."*

No. IV.

"Toronto, Canada West, Dec. 19, 1859.

"MY DEAR WYNDHAM,

"I AM not surprised that Mr. Caird's pamphlet shoul have caused you and your noble neighbours 'much anxiety about the welfare' of your old friends and parishioners, 'consigned' by you and them to me for settlement in Canada, and of whom several reside on the Free Grants, which, *without seeing them*, Mr. Caird pronounces 'to be too. poor, even when cleared, to be profitable.'

"A reference to Mr. Hutton's able and conclusive answer to Mr. Caird's book will show you official details proving that, on the very road named by Caird, 800 acres of land returned to the settlers on them, during *their first year*, products representing a market value of 5000*l*.

"And the return for 1859 shows that less than 9000 acres, cropped on this Caird-abused locality, produced crops of a market value of more than 140,000 dollars, or nearly 30,000*l*. sterling.

"I answered Mr. Caird's book, at the time of its publication, through the Hamilton *Spectator ;* he complained that my answer was written in a tone of 'acerbity.' I entertained no such feeling against Mr. Caird, but I felt that some decisive mode of expression was called for to counteract the possible effects of a work published by a person of his agricultural reputation, and written in a tone of such confidence.

"I might, however, have saved myself the trouble, for when it was known that Mr. Caird was a mere land-agent for the Illinois Central Railroad, and well paid by them to puff the prairies, his influence ceased, and the few who went from England or Canada to see this wretched district—this treeless, waterless, unhealthy place—returned in disgust.

"The publication of Mr. Caird has evoked many statements

* Let those who desire to see what can be done by skill and well-directed labour go to that part of the province which Upper Canadians look down upon as an inhospitable country and climate, and see what has been done on their respective estates by Major Campbell, M.P., Mr. D. Price. M.P., Mr. Baby, M.P., and the Hon. Mr. De Beaujeau, M.L.C.

from anonymous writers, the insertion of which I avoid. Too many of them are written from a selfish, personal, and purely Upper Canadian point of view, and in their zeal to advocate their own interests and 'puff' their own localities, they have overstated the advantages of this country, and also the disadvantages under which even American authorities admit the Illinois Central District to labour.

"I shall also avoid naming any one particular district or province of Canada, in preference to another, as suitable fields for European settlement. Each Province has its peculiar advantages and wants, and having visited all parts of it, I come to the conclusion that the choice of a future home must depend upon the requirements, the tastes, the former pursuits, and the *stamina*, physical and intellectual, of the intending settler.

"If I were called upon to state shortly the difference between the Upper and Lower Province, I should say Upper Canada was a wheat-growing, Lower Canada a grazing and dairy country. But you must not understand from this that Upper Canadians cannot raise stock and keep dairies, but that they *don't*.* Neither do I mean to say that Lower Canada cannot produce wheat. For many, many years that part of the United Provinces was visited with the midge or weevil, and wheat culture almost ceased. Now they are free from this pest, and Lower Canada, this year, has splendid crops of wheat, and continues to excel in root crops. Mr. Price, the Member for Chicoutimi, 200 miles below Quebec, assures me that he shall have upwards of 30 bushels an acre of fine wheat on his farm there. The accounts from the Eastern Townships are equally encouraging. In Upper Canada *all the crops*, except hay, exceed by 33½ per cent. the average of either of the two last years, and 20 per cent. above that of the last *seven years*. Wheat, wheat, wheat, year after year, seems to have been the *summum bonum* to which Upper Canadians aspired. There is no agricultural production which they are not able to raise quite as well, if not better, than our American friends on the other side the noble lake, lying in light and beauty at my very feet. Cousin Jonathan must chuckle over the fact that his Upper Canadian near neighbours on the frontier allowed him in 1857, and there is no doubt in the same proportion since, to carry off two million pounds in exchange for broom corn, ashes :—

* Seven first-class prizes for cattle were taken by Upper Canadians at the great United States Fair held last week at Chicago!

Butter,	£10,000	Indian Corn,	£100,000
Cheese,	41,000 ! !	Wheat,	600,000
Flax,	24,000	Hops,	5,500 !
Green Fruits,	39,000 ! !	Eggs,	4,600 ! !
Flour,	315,000	Wool,	10,000
Vegetables,	16,000	Cattle,	120,000

Meats of all kinds, £200,000 ! !

Thus the supineness and the want of enterprise and energy of the present race of Canadian farmers allows the Yankee farmer to beat them in their own markets!

" The agents of the Illinois Central are flooding the Province Show at Kingston with their books and pamphlets. It shall not be my fault if distant and ill-informed persons are not warned in due time to save them from disease, disappointment, and ruin. Families are returning by scores from Illinois to settle in Canada, and thus save the wreck of their fortunes. A few weeks since, a farmer and several fine young men, seduced by the glowing picture drawn by Caird of prairie farming, went thither, and returned dispirited and disgusted with all they saw and heard. The young men have wisely hired themselves out to learn the ways of the country, the farmer has purchased a farm of 100 acres in the Eastern Townships for five pounds currency per acre, with 60 acres cleared, a good house and offices, and has gone back to Ireland to bring out his family. Here then is an authentic evidence of the mischief done by this one-sided ' land agent.' The North of Ireland farmer has an undoubted title to his farm from the Crown; the titles to lands in the Illinois Central, I suspect, neither belong to the railway company nor the United States, but to certain bond-holders in England.

" Among a variety of letters which I have read in *American* papers, I subjoin two or three, which have all the appearance of authenticity :—

'Grayville, White County, Illinois, Aug. 31, 1859.
' EDITORS *Press* and *Tribune* :

' *The wheat crop here, when brought to the test of the threshing machine, has sadly disappointed the farmers, and cannot be set down at more than half a crop.* Oats and grass light. The late rains have revived late potatoes, and promises a fair crop : early ones, owing to the hot dry weather in June and July, are poor. Corn, especially in the Wabash Bottoms, is excellent.

' Yours respectfully,
' SYDNEY SPRING.'

'Sterling, Whiteside County, Illinois, Sept. 5, 1859.
'EDITORS *Press* and *Tribune:*

'As no one has reported the condition of the crops from this vicinity, we would call your attention to the fact that the prospect for anything but hard times is gloomy indeed. *The frost last week has damaged the corn so that not half the average yield will be realized.* Sweet potatoes and sugar-cane have " gone by the board." Farmers in this section did not estimate their wheat and oats as high as many did in other places, and yet, when they came to thresh, they were sadly disappointed at the result ; the yield will not bring one-half their estimate.

'Mr. Jacob Powell, near here, farms about four hundred acres, and had one hundred and thirty acres of wheat, and thought it a low estimate at twenty bushels to the acre; but when he came to thresh, *the yield was only eleven bushels to the acre.*

'It is so all through this section, and the farmers are in very low spirits, and look for another hard year.   'Yours truly,
'TERRELL & HARPER.'

'Carlisle, Illinois, Sept. 5, 1859.
'MY DEAR BROTHER,—

'I HAVE not written to you now for a long time—sorrow and sickness, and misery and disappointment, must plead my excuse ; and as they must have formed the only subject of my letters you may the less regret my silence. Indeed, I could not find in my heart to mar, with a detail of my own suf-ferings, so much comfort and happiness as seem to have fallen to your envied lot: my continued silence should still have saved you from the painful commiseration I know you will feel for me, had not the thought struck me that you might possibly be able to find some one in your neigh-bourhood who would exchange farms, &c., with me here, if the rage for coming to this *fine* country has reached you, of which I make little doubt, as it seems to have reached everywhere,

'If I cannot dispose of my property in some such way (selling it is out of the question), I am doomed, I was going to say, to live in this country, but rather to die ; I have had more than a hint of this during the summer : I have suffered dreadfully—you would hardly know me—I am literally and really an old man ; but this is not all, my farm has been totally neg-lected, as I could do nothing, and hiring being impracticable.
'C. W.'

" I could multiply these painful records an hundredfold, but I do not desire to do more than prove my case, which I can easily do from the sources named, and from Caird's own book.

" The sons of the country gentlemen of England, of their tenant-farmers, and the agricultural labourers, should remem-ber this, that Canada, the nearest and most important of British colonies, offers to them *all* prospects of independence (if not for themselves in all cases, most certainly for their families), which have been realized by tens of thousands of persons already here, and in store for others, if SOBER, patient, industrious, without which qualifications they must neither expect, nor do they deserve, to succeed.

"YOU GENTLEMEN OF ENGLAND

must bear in mind that, in Upper Canada alone, we have more than 150,000 landowners; that a tenant-farmer is a very 'rare bird;' that the taxes to which these landowners are liable, rarely exceeds five cents (3*d.*) in the pound upon the assessments made by themselves, and that even this small sum is applied to local purposes and improvements—road repairs, schools, &c. &c. They have no rent, no tithes, poor-rates, church-rates, stamp-duties; tea and sugar are cheaper than at home; and nothing is dearer except wearing apparel and bedding, and beer and porter.

"The last two years have been to Canadians a period of anxious solicitude. The usual results of a wild spirit of speculation in town and village lots and wild lands pervaded almost every class among us. Two successive crops of our great staple—wheat—deficient in quantity as well as quality, reduced us to a state of depression unknown before in our brief and prosperous national history; and the merchant at his ledger, the farmer in his clearing, and the back-woodsman in the deepest recesses of our forest solitudes, waited and watched for, with trembling anxiety and intense interest, the result of this year's cereal productions. But God, in his goodness, has blessed the work of our hands, and given us more than we could reasonably have asked, and far more than we deserve. In grateful and solemn acknowledgment of which 'blessings of peace and plenty,' His Excellency in Council appointed a day last month as a general holiday and Day of Thanksgiving throughout the Province, which day was observed with grateful and commendable solemnity."

No. V.

"Quebec, March 26, 1860.

"MY DEAR WYNDHAM,

"A QUEBEC Paper, *Le Canadien, &c. &c.*, in a sensible and temperate article on the very interesting and important subject of emigration, much approves of the wise and liberal policy of the Commissioner of Crown Lands in giving Free Grants (*concessions gratuites*) in the neighbourhood of the Colonization Roads now made or to be hereafter made; and further states that the success of this enlightened proposal will merely depend upon the zeal and honesty with which it is carried into effect by those Agents to whom the duty of directing emigration shall be intrusted. The writer recommends that Government should invite the attention of Norwegians, Germans, Belgians, Swiss, and even *French*, to the advantages afforded by Canada, with a view of bringing to this country the thousands of adventurers 'who now go to California, or encounter the murderous climate of South America.'

" Various causes have prevented an extensive emigration to this country for the last four years :—

" 1. The gold discoveries in Vancouver's Island ;

" 2. The large sums of money voted by the Governments of New Zealand and Australia for free passages, and other inducements, have tempted many persons to go there, and the result has always been severe distress and disappointment, because the parties who availed themselves of these offers were poor and otherwise totally unfitted for agricultural or domestic callings ;

" 3. During the greater part of the last three years there have been rumours of war, and actual war, and some of the Continental Powers have discouraged and *forbidden* emigration ;

" 4. Great Britain has enjoyed, especially in the rural districts, an unusual degree of prosperity, which has also tended to limit the number of emigrants to this and other countries ;

5. " Canada, of late years, has gone through the severe ordeals of self-induced difficulty and deficient crops, and the tidings which have reached home have happily postponed the advent of new settlers, whom we dared not invite during a time of depression. *Now*, the cloud which has long hung over Canada begins to show a silver lining. To God's good Providence we are indebted for one of the best cereal crops with which we have been blessed for twenty years—the finances of the country, embarrassed by over-trading at one time, and its inevitable result of diminished imports since, are rapidly recovering from the pressure of wild speculations and deficient harvests. We have had a stern, but just and salutary lesson, and it will be long before our merchants and farmers will allow themselves to be again seduced from their legitimate duties, by too great haste to get rich by very dangerous and equivocal means.

" The Honourable Mr. Vankoughnet deserves the highest praise for the prudent forethought which has distinguished his administration of the Emigration Department. Three years since he annóunced that he was not prepared to yield to popular clamour and invite ' a promiscuous rush of immigrants.' He first ascertained, upon authority, what classes of settlers were most needed, and then he gave his sanction to the publication of such works as gave a temperate and truthful view of Canada, as regards her climate and [resources. To other parties belongs the discredit of having, by unauthorized and untruthful statements, induced many hundreds, unfitted for any employment in Canada, to come here.

" It may not, perhaps be known to the Editor of the *Canadien*, that a work on Canada, translated into *French*, German, and Norwegian, has been circulated on the Continent, and now that the prospects of the country justify the step, additional industry will be used to disseminate this information. A map has been published, under Mr. Vankoughnet's directions, which shows every county and township of Upper and Lower Canada, and contains, by a novel mode of illustration, a vast variety of information about our minerals, fisheries, &c., &c. I look upon this map, and a pamphlet just now completed, as the very best of agents to be employed in making us known. A glance at this map, and proper attention to the pamphlet, will do more than a hundred lectures :—

> ' Segnius irritant animos demissa per aures,
>   Quam quæ sunt oculis subjecta. fidelibus.'

" The words of the lecturer are soon forgotten and unheeded ; the written advice and the many-coloured chart make a lasting impression, and can be again and again referred to with increased interest and continued instruction. A gentleman is now in Germany to carry out the important object of conveying information. Mr. Hawke (one of the Canadian Government Emigration Agents), whose experience extends over nearly fifty years of colonial life, has opened an office in Liverpool with a similar object, a step which I think will be attended with the happiest results. During the coming summer Canada will be talked of more than ever, and thousands will visit a country which only requires to be seen and known, to have her capabilities duly appreciated. It will be our own fault if we allow the coming opportunity of honestly 'advertising' ourselves to be neglected.

" CANADA now seems to be a land of kindling energies. The wonderful success which had attended her up to a certain period, led too many of us to neglect those pursuits, and that

steady course of toil and industry, our hereditary lot, without
which no one can or deserves to prosper—

—————— 'Deus ipse colendi
Haud facilem esse viam voluit.'

" The trials of these years have forced upon us attention to
enterprises which will eventually emancipate us from European markets, and from which we ought long since to have
become free. In manufacturing matters we hear of woollen
and cotton factories—in agricultural affairs draining is talked
of, and even the word 'irrigation' has been whispered
into wondering ears—the accumulations of manure which
had remained for a generation unheeded, are gradually
finding their way into arable lands impoverished by repeated
crops of the same grain—there is moreover, a merry sound of
returning prosperity in our crowded cities,'on our noble lakes,
in the deep solitudes of our forest homes,—que nous en pro-
fitons.

" Our Revenue returns are most satisfactory, the taxes
necessary for the due administration of the public service
are raised in such a way that the least possible pressure
falls upon the masses, the municipal and local taxes are
very small, the necessaries of life are cheap, and wages fair—
our great staple, wheat, has reached a remunerative price—
cleared farms with suitable buildings can be bought, or
rented with the option of purchase, on very favourable terms—
millions of acres of wild lands, most of which are covered with
valuable timber, can be purchased from the Government in
various parts of Upper and Lower Canada, at sums varying
from two to four shillings an acre, payable by instalments
extending over four years.

" The yeoman of Great Britain gives 3l. sterling per acre per
annum for land of less value than he can rent here for 15s.
currency, including all taxes! It is from this class we
should like to see a large immigration, for their sakes and
our own. Cleared farms can now be rented, all over both
provinces, on the terms I have named. There are hundreds
of farms in both provinces, provided with all requisite buildings, well watered and fenced, to be purchased at from 5l. to
10l. sterling per acre, upon which 30 bushels of wheat per
acre, and other produce in proportion (with firewood for the
chopping), can be grown. There never was a better time for
the British yeoman, with a capital of from 100l. to 5000l., to
cast his lot among us.

" Canada offers to large and small capitalists a great variety
of securities in which money may be invested with the utmost
confidence, and for which· interest at the rate of 8 per cent.
per annum, payable half-yearly in London, can be obtained.
These securities consist of mortgages upon cleared farms and
other productive property of ample value and undoubted title,
our system of registration of deeds and the sworn assessment
of value rendering fraud almost impossible. There are, also,
municipal debentures, some of which are guaranteed by the
Government, which will pay 8 per cent.—shares in some of
our banks pay even more. There is a class of persons at home
who, with a view of increasing their incomes, purchase annuities. By investing money in Canada, an equal income can be
obtained, AND THE PRINCIPAL SAVED !

" Canada possesses unrivalled railway facilities whereby
access is obtained to the principal markets of our own
country, and also to those of the United States. Our own
St. Lawrence promises to be the great highway of travel
from east to west—stately steamers and the white-winged
messengers of commerce are borne on her broad bosom
full-freighted with the necessaries and luxuries of life. The
recent commercial treaty with France affords a new field for
enterprise. With proper management, Quebec may recover
her lost trade with the West Indies. The Reciprocity Act,
between ourselves'and our cousins on the other side the frontier,
is attended with beneficial results in a commercial as well as
a social point of view.

" We Canadians entertain no feelings but those of amity
towards our American brethren. There is no desire on
either side for territorial aggrandisement at the expense of
the other, or for any closer political connection than that
which now exists. Each nation has before it a noble mission
over an ample field; and for the due cultivation of this vast
space, socially, morally, and religiously, we shall assuredly
have to give account. A talent of inestimable value is
commited to our joint keeping, which we cannot, without
guilt, allow to remain unimproved,—a jewel lent to us which
we are bound to keep untarnished, remembering that we all
had a common origin, have a common language, and a common
faith, and are treading a path which we pray may lead to a
common home, and a glorious heritage above."

No. VI.

"Quebec, June, 1860.

" MY DEAR WYNDHAM,

" IN a former portion of this book is recorded the result of the first year's experiment upon the Free Grant Roads, which, under the many disadvantages of a new mode of life, must be considered a great success.

" The result of the second year is still more encouraging. The number of adults on these lines now amounts to nearly 1000 persons of various nations, of whom about one-half are Irish. They are the owners of 100,000 acres of freehold land; every acre of which I verily believe will, in a few years, be worth twenty dollars an acre. The agents upon this road are highly respectable and trustworthy gentlemen, and they announce to the Minister of Agriculture that the valuation put by them upon the produce of this land is a very low one; that many of the settlers spent too much time in hunting and shooting; the results of which are mentioned in the following Table, under the heads of 'Fur, Deer,' &c. Fish, too, are omitted, although the district affords them in such quantities as to form no inconsiderable portion of the maintenance of a family, summer and winter. And yet these lands rendered to their owners produce, the money value of which is not less than forty dollars, 10l. an acre, upon the 4000 acres under crop last year.

" Now, these Free Grants are situated in the same district where several

" BLOCKS OF LAND OF 50,000 ACRES

are offered to the country gentlemen and farmers of England at two shillings an acre!

" These Free Grant Roads lead to many of them, and very much enhance their value. I allude now more particularly to those announced for sale, and marked on the new Map, in the counties of Victoria, Peterborough, and Addington. (See Table, page 178.)*

" You will observe that these returns do not include the many useful things which the forest and lakes produce in abundance—hops, wild fruits, fish, &c.

* In addition to the produce there classified, Mr. Perry records 11,025 lbs. of beef slaughtered; 127 yards of flannel; 67 yards of fulled cloth; and 158 bushels of rye.

N

"RESULTS of the FREE GRANT SYSTEM in UPPER CANADA.

"The SECOND YEAR.

OTTAWA AND OPEONGO ROAD.							BOBCAYGEON ROAD.	HASTINGS ROAD.
			Dolls.	Cents.		Dollars.	Dollars.	Dollars.
Wheat	8,515	Bushels at	1	0	=	8,515	1,620	4,350
Oats	8,420	,,	0	50	=	4,210	. .	1,990
Barley	395	,,	0	60	=	237	. .	167
Corn	202	,,	1	0	=	202	500	186
Pease	245	,,	1	0	=	245	. .	175
Potatoes . . .	22,450	,,	0	50	=	11,225	10,350	9,486
Turnips . . .	1,580	,,	0	15	=	207	3,080	4,219
Hay	149	Tons at	16	0	=	2,384	320	2,020
Straw	308	,,	5	0	=	1,540	. .	. .
Sugar	5,650	lbs. at	0	12	=	678	800	961
Molasses . . .	325	Gallons at	1	0	=	325	240	. .
Pork	164	Barrels at	16	0	=	2,624	. .	. .
Potash	85	,,	22	0	=	1,870	150	2,949
Soap	4,660	lbs. at	0	10	=	466	. .	. .
Ashes	9,100	Bushels at	0	5	=	455	. .	. .
Sawed Lumber			. . . .				300	1,000
Shingles . . .			. . . .				150	162
Deer			. . . .				700	. .
Furs			. . . .				1,500	. .

ADDINGTON ROAD.

Wheat .	{	472	Bush.	Winter Wheat.	Molasses . . .	748	Galls.
		2,432	,,	Spring Wheat.	Pork	13,295	lbs.
Oats . .		4,455	,,	Oats.	Potash	73	Barr.
Barley .		348	,,		Sawed Lumber	164,000	Feet.
Pease .		333	,,		*Shingles . . .	291,000	
Potatoes		11,655	,,		Deer	103	
Turnips		11,075	,,		Furs	416	Dolls.
Hay . .		319	Tons.		Vinegar . . .	893	Galls.
Sugar .		16,158	lbs.				

"I will conclude this letter with a warning upon a point, the want of attention to which is rendering many a fine farm almost worthless, viz., the impolicy of repeated wheat-crops without manure, and the experience of a Canadian farmer as to the periods for planting, sowing, and reaping.

* Exclusive of cooper-work, valued at 52,000 dollars, &c. &c.

" The inevitable result of continually planting the same kind of crop upon the same ground for twenty years in succession, with little or no pains to recruit the exhausted soil, has thus been alluded to in the valuable Prize Essay of Professor Hind on the ' Climate of Canada.'

" ' Within five-and-twenty or thirty miles of Toronto, the better class of farmers consider thirty bushels of wheat to the acre an average crop; and this return is obtained in spite of all the imperfections of a comparatively primitive system of husbandry. If half the care were bestowed upon the preparation of land for wheat which is devoted to that operation in Great Britain, fifty, instead of thirty bushels to the acre, would be the average yield on first-class farms. It must be borne in mind that subsoil draining is unknown among our farmers; that top-dressing in the fall with long dung is never practised; a proper rotation of crops scarcely ever adopted; frequent repetitions of the same crop general; farm-yard manure applied without any previous preparation; and yet, under all these disadvantages of ART, NATURE, with her fertile soil, and admirable *agricultural* climate, produces most abundant crops when she is not too grossly abused.'

" And again—

" ' One fact, however, appears to be certain, that in a very few years the farmers in the front townships of Western Canada will be compelled to pay more attention than hitherto to the cultivation of a *variety* of crops. Independently of that deterioration of the soil, which, as a general rule, must result from a frequent repetition of the same kind of crop, and the absence of cheap special fertilizers, the aspect of coming years induces the belief that the price of Canada's staple agricultural production—wheat—will not maintain even its present diminished range. It is, in fact, at the present time, a matter not only of individual, but also of national importance, that farmers should turn a careful attention to the agricultural productions of other countries, and endeavour to see how far they, by their introduction into this province, may be made to assist and develop its husbandry. It is equally a matter of individual and national importance that every earnest well-wisher of Western Canada should contribute his mite to elevate the industry of the country, and extend the knowledge of her capabilities to the tens of thousands across the seas, who would willingly, and even joyfully, make this fertile British Province their home, had they confidence in its climate and soil.'

" SOWING, PLANTING, AND REAPING SEASONS.

" Generally speaking, the snow is off, and the ground is fit for ploughing between the 25th April and 1st May.

" Pease may be sown up to the 20th of May.

Indian Corn	do.	do.	do.	do.
Spring Wheat	do.	do.	25th	do.
Swedish Turnips	do.	do.	15th	do.
Aberdeen	do.	do.	do.	10th of July.
Oats		do.	do.	1st of June.
Potatoes		do.	do.	24th	do.

" Cabbage Seed is planted in a box about the 15th of April, and transplanted to the open ground by 1st June.

" Haying (mowing) generally commences about the 12th of July. An acre and a quarter is the average quantity of meadow that a man will cut per diem. The expense of saving the hay is considerably less than in England. It may be judged of by the fact that light meadow has been known to have been cut and put into the barn on *the same day*. The more usual system, however, is to shake it out soon after being cut, then to rake it into 'wind-rows,' make small stacks of it by the evening, and next evening put it into large stacks or the barn.

" The reaping of the wheat that has been sown in the fall (autumn) begins about 1st of August. If it be not lodged it can be 'cradled,'—which means being cut with an implement called a cradle, resembling a scythe, and by means of which a man will cut at least four times as much as with the reaping-hook.

" *Spring Wheat* comes in about 10th August, and may also be 'cradled' if not lodged.

" *Oats* is usually fit for cutting by the 14th August, and is most frequently 'cradled.'

" *Pease* ripen by the 5th August, and are cut with the scythe and reaping-hook.

" *Indian Corn* is gathered in about the 8th September, and it takes about four men to the acre. Women and children are almost as useful at this work.

" *Potatoes* ripen according to the time at which they have been planted. They are taken out with the hoe, and at this work, too, the women and children are found useful. The taking out of potatoes costs nearly as much labour as the planting of them.

" By the 10th of October the harvest is generally housed, and then underbrushing—which cannot be done in winter in consequence of the deep snow—is commenced. Potash is now being made, and sleighs, &c., put in order for the winter's work.

"Potash is very remunerative to the farmer, and requires but little skill in the manufacture. The kettle and coolers necessary cost about 14*l.*; but they are always supplied on credit by the storekeepers in the neighbourhood, who are paid in potash or other farm produce. The ashes of 2½ acres of ordinary hard-wood land should be sufficient to make a barrel of potash, say of the *second* quality, and for this the owner should receive thirty dollars (7*l.* 10*s.*), after deducting all expenses of carriage, storage, &c."

No. VII.

"DIARY OF FARM OPERATIONS IN CANADA.

"MY DEAR WYNDHAM,

"I HAVE often been asked for a detailed account of the operations upon a block of wild land, or a partially-cleared farm. I have lately met with a little work, published in 1843, called 'The Emigrant to British North America,' which gives the desired information. Of course much improvement has been made in farming implements and other agricultural improvements since that time, but the same hard work has still to be done by the newly-arrived emigrant, who, however, now-a-days possesses advantages incalculably greater than could have been expected in so short a period as that intervening between 1843 and 1860.

"April 10th.*—Returned, with my hired man Richard, and a load, with a horse and ox-cart, from Montreal, forty miles, two days on the road, which is very bad, the frost not quite out of the ground—my loading all safe, consisting of the following items; a plough 17 dollars, two axes 8*s.* each—harrow teeth—8*s.* for a bush harrow, in shape of the letter A.—Two logging chains 10*s.* each—two scythes and stones 9*s.* 8*d.*—one spade 3*s.*—one shovel 4*s.*—one dung-fork 2*s.* 6*d.*—two steel pitch-forks 3*s.* 6*d.* each—three augers, 1, 1½ and 2 inches, 15*s.*—one barrel of pork 20 dollars—one barrel of N. shore herrings 5 dollars—two barrels of flour 27*s.* 6*d.* each—twenty apple-trees, and six plum-trees, at 2*s.* each—

* The first of this month may be considered generally as the commencement of the agricultural year.

sixteen gooseberry-bushes and grape-vines, at 1s. 3d. each, amounting to 21l. 2s. 2d.

"Put my apple-trees, &c., into a hole in the garden—got a good cup of tea, saw my horse and oxen well taken care of, and went to bed—thus ended the first day of my new mode of life.

"April 11th.—My man Richard fed and watered the cattle—got breakfast with some difficulty, owing to the want of many things we ought to have got in Montreal; we had no frying-pan, for instance—herrings superb—being Sunday, went to church, morning and afternoon.

"April 12th.—Up at daylight—reprimanded Richard for being out too late the night before, planted my apple, plum trees, &c., in what had been an apology for a garden—mended the fence round it—broke open our pork barrel, found it good —had some for dinner—knocked the spout off the new tea-kettle, of course cracked before—worse off than ever for cooking-utensils—borrowed a frying-pan, and boiled potatoes for dinner in a forty-gallon pot—two cows calved, and a ewe yeaned two lambs.

"April 13th.—Got a supply of cooking-apparatus at a shop in the neighbouring village—commenced ploughing for wheat, making garden, &c. Hired another man for the summer at ten dollars per month, same as I gave Richard, another cow calved. This was considered a very early spring, but I have since sown wheat, on this day, two years consecutively, and might have done so oftener, had it been otherwise convenient.

"April 14th.—Hired a housekeeper at four dollars a month —sowed onions, beets, sallad, &c.,—new man Charles, mending fences—drawing rails with the horse and cart—Richard still ploughing with the oxen—myself at the garden—bought four cows at 18 dollars each—two of them calved a month before—made a harrow.

"April 15th.—Sowed wheat after washing it with brine and drying it with lime—Charles harrowed it in with the horse— four bushels (our measure, which is nearly the same as imperial,) upon three and a half acres, according to the custom of the country—planted early peas and sowed garden seeds— Richard still ploughing—two ewes yeaned.

"April 16th.—Charles and myself making fence—one of the new cows calved—ploughing for potatoes and corn, first time.

"April 17th.—Same as yesterday, and same to the end of the month, except that we sowed about four acres of oats and peas mixed.

"May 1st.—All at work on the roads—finished our highway duty.

" May 2nd.—Sunday.—All to church.

" May 3rd.—One of the men churned before breakfast, with a swing-churn, lately invented—cut up a little fire-wood—too warm to plough with oxen in the middle of the day—all making fence.

" May 4th and 5th.—Wet days—made four rakes and handled and ground the new axes, one having been partially ground and a temporary handle in it before—cleared out and repaired the barn.

" May 6th.—Fine again—land too wet to plough—making fences—Richard went to the mill with a few bushels of oats to be made into meal—got the horse shod.

" May 7th.—Very warm and sultry—ploughing for Indian corn by daylight, left off at 10, and commenced again at 4 P.M., continued till dark—carting stones off the corn land—finishing my garden—got home the grist sent away yesterday.

" May 8th.—One of the principal farmers of the settlement killed by a tree falling upon him. Work same as yesterday until noon, when we all went to assist in raising a wooden building for a barn 40 feet by 30 for one of our neighbours.

" May 9th.—Sunday.—All went to church—I need not again mention this, as we never allowed anything to interfere with this duty. A tremendous thunderstorm.

" May 10th and 11th.—Drawing manure for Indian corn, ploughing it in, &c.

" May 12th and 13th.—Same work as two preceding days— and planting Indian corn and pumpkins—attended funeral of the neighbour killed on the 8th.

" May 14th and 15th.—Sowed more oats and finished planting Indian corn—killed a fat calf—sold one quarter for 5s. and the skin for the same.

" May 16th.—Sunday.

" May 17th.—To end of month clearing up an old 'Slash,' which term has previously been defined; drawing the logs together with the oxen; then piling and burning them. One wet day, sheared the sheep, which were got in before the rain came on. Commenced planting corn on the new clearing.

" June 1st and 2nd.—Sowing one and a half acre of oats on the clearing; Richard ploughing the potato land second time; Charles drawing out manure and spreading it before him; myself planting potatoes with a hoe after him: it may be here remarked, that before the stumps are all out, or nearly so, it is not possible to drill up land for this crop.

" June 3rd.—Finished the potatoes, and reckoned up my

crop—stands as follows: wheat three and half, peas three, oats five, Indian corn six, potatoes five and a half—in all, twenty-three acres—meadow twenty, pasture thirteen, partially cleared twenty, added to the twenty-three, makes seventy-six acres. It may be remembered here, that I said my farm contained about fifty acres of cleared land, whereas I make out seventy-six acres, but I did not then take into the account neither the twenty acres partially cleared, nor the six or seven I cleared myself.

"June 4th.—A holiday, which I have always kept in commemoration of the birth of good King George III., of blessed memory.

"June 5th.—Went to a *training*, as it is here called. All the men in the country, with some trifling exceptions, between the ages of sixteen and sixty, capable of bearing arms, are obliged by law to muster once a year; and this constitutes the militia of the province.

"June 6th.—Sunday.—I witnessed on this evening a splendid and gorgeous sunset, far surpassing anything of the kind I had ever seen at home. Even a sunset in Italy, as a commissariat officer, settled on a farm near me, who had served in that country, declared could not be compared to it.

"June 7th to 15th.—Finished mending and making fences. Made a road through a little swamp near the rear of my farm, where I had commenced a clearing—carting out upon it an accumulated heap of chips from the front of my wood-shed—put up a small building behind my garden, which, though not always to be found on a farm-stead here, is not the less *necessary*.

"June 16th to end.—Hoeing corn and potatoes—excessively hot, thermometer, one day, 86 in the shade; sowed an acre of turnips on my new clearing.

"July 1st, 2nd, and 3rd.—Finished hoeing Indian corn the second time, and making fences.

"July 5th.—Wet day—ground scythes and *hung* them.

"July 6th.—Commenced mowing.

"July 15th.—Finished haying without a drop of rain—very hot.

"July 16th.—A fearful thunderstorm—burned a log-barn in the neighbourhood, or, as some suppose, the accident happened from a man going into it with a lighted pipe, to prevent which has been a great source of trouble to me whenever I have employed Canadian labourers—killed another fat calf.

"July 17th.—Finished off my hay-stacks.

"July 18th.—Sunday.—To church—clergyman absent at a distant settlement—prayers, and a sermon read by the schoolmaster—weather quite cool, as is usual after a violent thunderstorm.

"July 19th.—Commenced hoeing corn the third time, or rather cutting up with the hoe whatever weeds had grown since the last hoeing—sold 200 pounds of butter, at 8d. per pound—cut first cucumber.

"July 20th to end of month.—Finishing hoeing corn and potatoes—commenced clearing new land, by cutting down the under brush, and piling it in heaps ready for burning—this I did upon thirty acres of woodland, during the rest of the summer, when I found I could spare a day for that purpose, and in the winter cut down the large trees, and then into lengths for piling in heaps to burn. The summer is the best season for commencing to clear land, because the brush is in full leaf, which, when dry, helps to burn it, all which a person soon learns when he comes to the country, but would doubtless like to know something about it before.

"August 2nd.—Attending a meeting of the principal inhabitants about repairing the roof of the church-steeple; gave a dollar towards the expense—bought a pew, 6l.—the two men underbrushing—first new potatoes—bought a sickle and a cradle scythe—made the cradle, having had the fingers blocked out before—a very difficult thing to make.

"August 4th to 7th.—Clearing part of the under-brushed land, for winter wheat—same until 10th, when I began reaping and cradling—continued till 21st—finished harvesting, except one and a quarter acre of late oats and the Indian corn—cut first melon, but I am very late.

"August 31st.—Resumed clearing land—killed a lamb.

"September 1st to 10th.—Same work, and sowed three acres of winter wheat—commenced making potash from the ashes I had saved when clearing the land.

"September 11th to 22nd.—At the under-brushing—continued at the potash till I made two barrels, which I sold for something over 15l.—my neighbour's cattle broke into my Indian corn, but did little damage.

"September 23rd.—Wet day—threshing and dressing up one and a half bushel of wheat and eight of oats—sent them to mill at night—oats weighed forty-eight pounds.

"September 24th.—Got home grist—oats produced 2 cwt. 0 qr. 14 lbs.—Got a certificate from the miller and a farmer of the weight of the oats—forty pounds being the general average weight of good oats.—Made a wooden box as a steamer for my boiler—box containing twelve bushels.

"September 25th.—Commenced ploughing—had a cow dried up and bled, and turned into the best feed to make beef.

"An ox, belonging to my neighbour, being one of the cattle which broke into my corn, died of a surfeit, as was supposed, of such rich succulent food as the green corn. This made him mend his portion of the line fence between my farm and his, which I never could get him to do before.

"September 27th.—Commenced steaming pumpkins for my hogs—shut them up—threshed five bushels of peas and oats, had them ground to mix with the pumpkins—fed the hogs with raw food for some weeks before—made a hog-trough, by hollowing out a pine log. Went to a squirrel-hunt, which I must give some account of.

"Some years, when the nuts in the woods are plentiful, the squirrels are so numerous as to do great damage to the Indian corn, when a conspiracy like the following is entered into, for the destruction of them, as well as of all enemies that may be met with, whose depredations are chiefly confined to this valuable crop. All the men, young and old, for miles round, form themselves into two bands, each under a captain, and whichever gets the least quantity of game, has to pay for a ball and supper, at the village tavern, for the whole—each kind of animal being reckoned according to its importance, thus the right paw of a bear counts for 400—of a racoon 100 —squirrel one—right claw of a crow, woodpecker, or blue jay, one, &c.—By daylight of the morning of the muster, the woods were all alive with the eager hunters, and in the after-part of the day, the fields were swarming with groups of women and children, with provisions and ammunition for their several partizans, and to disburthen them of their spoils—it was truly a season of merry and joyous holiday, in which all business and work was suspended ; many a small party spent sleepless nights watching for bears and racoons, for it is only then they come out—this lasted for three days, when we all met at the tavern to count up our spoils, in trembling anxiety for the award of two judges appointed to decide upon the claim for victory—the party I belonged to had 2 bears, counting 800— 4 racoons, 400—473 squirrels—27 crows—105 blue jays and woodpeckers—counting altogether 1,835, and yet we lost, as the other party had nearly the same, besides one bear more.

' The child may rue that was unborn
The hunting of that day.'

"September 29th and 30th.—Richard ploughing—Charles and I gathering Indian corn; at night had a 'bee,' a term used for a mustering together of the neighbours, to assist in any work which would puzzle an individual to do alone, when all the young men and boys in the settlement came to help me to husk it. Got the first premium for it from the Agricultural Society.

"October 1st and 2nd.—Same work—evening to husking bee at a neighbour's.

"October 4th to 7th.—Ploughing—finished getting in the Indian corn—cutting the corn-stalks—husking ourselves at night what little we had gathered during the day: collected and brought home pumpkins.

"October 8th to 9th.—Binding corn-stalks, and stacking them up to dry,—collected and got in pumpkins.

"October 11th.—Got in remainder of pumpkins and the onions.

"October 12th.—Stacked corn-stalks, and fenced them round together with the hay-stack.

"October 13th.—Commenced digging potatoes.

"October 14th to 20th.—Finished taking up potatoes—800 bushels—ploughed over the land to the end of the month—ploughing—clearing land, &c.—Hired Charles for the winter, for seven dollars a month.

"October 22nd.—The boundless, measureless forest—the stupendous wilderness of woods, which overwhelms the whole face of the country, exhibited, in the bright sunshine and the pure atmosphere of this lovely morning, a picture as novel as it was beautiful in the eyes of a stranger; for, instead of waving their luxuriant foliage over mountain, hill, and valley, in the same rich though monotonous hue of living green, the trees now had assumed a colouring which, in brilliancy and variety, exceeded all description. The soft maple is the first to commence this gorgeous display, by changing to a rich crimson; the sugar maple then follows in similar, though more sombre tints, variegated with the yellow of the trembling poplar, the orange and gold of the beech, and the sere brown of the butter-nut, while the sturdy oak still maintains his deep green, in defiance of those harbingers of winter.

"November 1st.—Same work, and getting in turnips and cabbages, and all other garden stuffs—took in the cows at night. 350 bushels of turnips.

"November 2nd.—First hard frost—could not plough till noon—clearing, &c.

"November 3rd to 20th.—Under-brushing—cutting fire-wood—cattle out all day and only the cows in at night—hard frost: no more ploughing, I suppose.

"November 21st.—First snow,—took in all the cattle.

"November 22nd.—A thaw and wet day—threshing more grain for the hogs—sent it to the mill.

"November 23rd to 30th.—Ploughing again one day—clearing—killed a sheep—hard frost again, but fine weather, called the Indian summer, with a slight smoky haziness in the atmosphere, through which the sun is seen with a deadened lustre—something like a full moon.

"December 1st to 4th.—Indian summer continues—clearing and chopping.

"December 5th.—Killed my hogs.

"December 6th.—Fall of snow—threshing—cutting up and salting pork.

"December 7th.—Drawing wood home for fuel, in the log, with the horses and oxen, not being snow enough to draw it on the sled.

"December 8th and 9th.—Made an ox-sled—cutting fire-wood.

"December 10th and 11th.—Drawing fire-wood as on the 7th.

"December 13th.—Snow-storm—threshing.

"December 14th.—Drawing in stack of corn-stalks to give to the cattle instead of hay, which I cannot yet get at in my barns, it being covered with grain, and not wishing to cut into my hay-stack till I should have room enough to take it all in at once.

"December 15th.—Commenced cutting down the trees on the land I had under-brushed, and chopping them into lengths for piling—cutting fire-wood and drawing it—cutting, splitting, and drawing out rails for fences, and timber for a new barn—threshing and tending the cattle—getting out hemlock logs for the saw-mill, for boards for the new barn—drawing them home, and making shingles, occupied our time all winter with the exception of my journey to Montreal with butter and a few bushels of grain, which I sold, and, with the proceeds, bought some groceries and other necessaries, preparatory to my anticipated change of circumstances.

"In the following spring it was the 20th of April before the snow was all off the ground, when vegetation commenced and progressed with a rapidity unknown to the British isles; it is indeed a disadvantage for the snow to go away earlier."

No VIII.

"MY DEAR WYNDHAM,   Toronto, Aug. 17, 1860.

"I KNOW of no reason why the two families you name, with the capital they have, should not come out at once. Let them go to ——— or ———, or some one of the small towns on the lake or river between Brockville and Cobourg, near which they have determined to settle, and they will have many opportunities during the winter, the 'horrors' of which are very much exaggerated at home, of finding some suitable farms. They can live cheaper in Canada than in England. Our harvest this year is the most abundant ever known, and is all safely housed. I have completed a conditional arrangement for the rental of the three farms for M—, T—, and L—, at 12s. per acre per annum for *the cleared part*, with the option of purchase within four years: the local taxes may amount to three more. I send a copy of the agreement, but I do not like the responsibility of concluding the arrangement until they have seen the property. There are good houses and buildings upon all the farms; and before the end of September there will be on an average thirty acres of fall wheat sown upon each, which they can have at a valuation, as well as any part of the hay, straw, and stock they like.

"I shall be truly happy to see these sons of my old school and college friends, and I hope their example may be followed by hundreds of the sons of country gentlemen and tenant-farmers. Canada affords more examples of success in commercial and agricultural pursuits than any other colony in the history of the world; and the longer I live here the more strongly I am persuaded of its value and importance as a field for emigration, and the more I am surprised that a colony presenting so many advantages from its fertility and wealth of various kinds, and unrivalled facilities of rapid communication with the United States and European markets, should not have attracted a larger number of Agriculturists, at all events, to occupy and improve the millions of acres of productive soil of which as yet 'the mower filleth not his hand, neither he that bindeth up the sheaves his bosom.' His hand who fed the multitude in the wilderness and the prophet in the desert is not shortened, and if duly sought HE will be as present a help in the backwoods of Canada as in the thronged mart or the crowded city!

"'" "Hitherto the vast wealth of Canada has scarcely been made known. The establishment of free ports at Gaspé and Saulte St. Marie, the former famous for its inexhaustible fisheries, second only to Newfoundland, and the latter for its mineral wealth, the abolition of the tolls on the St. Lawrence, &c., &c., show a degree of bold reliance upon our resources which does honour to the forethought and ability of our 'Chancellor of the Exchequer,' Mr. Galt.

"As to the minerals of Canada, we have one of great value which deserves especial notice. Lower Canada is, as far as is yet known, the only country which possesses a rich titaniferous ore capable of making alloys of great excellence, the influence of which upon iron and steel has lately been mentioned by your eminent metallurgist, Mr. Mushet, in *The Engineer.* The ore found in New Zealand only possesses 8 per cent. of the oxide of titanium, while that of Canada exceeds 50 per cent., and can be had in any quantity.

"We have, too, another almost unknown and entirely neglected source of wealth in the fish offal on the St. Lawrence, the annual value of which thrown away in the fisheries of the St. Lawrence is enormous. This offal properly prepared would supply the farmers of Great Britain with manure for a hundred years to come, and is within ten days' reach by steamers and three weeks by sailing vessels.

"As to manufactures in Canada I have little to say; we ought to have them; but as long as our leading merchants derive such enormous profits from imports they are not likely to promote the scheme your friends contemplate. There can be no doubt of its entire success. Flax and hemp thrive amazingly here, and the cotton from the Southern States passes our doors to be made up in the States or England and be returned here!

"I know of no place in Canada better suited to the objects sought than Cornwall, where there is an unrivalled water-power: it is very central, and, as you will see from the map and plan I have sent you, it has ready access to all parts of Canada and the States by rail or steam-boat, and to and from England by the St. Lawrence in the summer and Portland in the winter.

"In the Township of Delaware, a few miles from London, C.W., there is also a fine site for a manufactory; the owner of which, as well as the one at Cornwall, will contribute largely towards its erection. Our Canadian Thames, which is here pronounced as it is spelt, flows through this property in an ample stream.

· "The Prince will be welcomed with great enthusiasm, especially in Lower Canada, where a more Conservative tone of feeling exists than here. His visit will do us and *you* all a great deal of good in many ways, and among other things you will find out where Canada is! When the Prince landed at Newfoundland, New Brunswick, Prince Edward's Island, and Nova Scotia, *The Times* and other papers announced 'THE PRINCE IN CANADA!' When he *did* touch Canadian soil at Gaspé you at home seemed sorely puzzled!

"A lady of position in ——shire has commissioned me to buy some property for her younger sons. She first, however, desires to know how far the property is from the Black-foot Indians; and upon my announcing that I could not promise one within 2000 miles, she desired me to complete the arrangement.

"SPORTING IN CANADA.

"Let no man come to *settle* in Canada for the sake of sporting. He who has time for a few weeks' amusement will find a variety of game in certain remote districts, and for certain short periods of the year. In answer to the questions of —— on this point, I answer that the following are *some* of the kinds of game we have—I don't include deer, bears, wolves, foxes, moose, cariboo—all these *are* to be had, if diligently sought for, but are seldom found in the settled parts— viz., rabbits, pheasants, grouse, partridges, woodcocks, snipes, heath-hens, ptarmigan, &c., &c.

"Deer are found in almost every part of the province. Moose and cariboo generally in the Lower Province and even a few miles from Quebec.

"The rabbit is the *Lepus Americanus*. It does not burrow like our rabbit, but lives under the stumps of trees. It becomes quite white in winter, and hundreds may be had daily in the markets of Quebec. The prairie rabbit, found in the Western States, has very much the look and colour of a leveret three parts grown.

"Our pheasant is the *Tetrao umbellus;* our partridge is the quail, *Ortyx virginianus;* our heath-hen, the *Tetrao cupido;* our grouse, the *Tetrao Canadensis;* our woodcock, the *Philoheda minor*, and is not half the size of the English bird. Snipes and ducks are plentiful in certain districts and for short periods.

"Immense quantities of quails are brought to our Canadian cities from the Western States in the winter, packed in ice.

All the game in Canada, except the wild turkey, is dry and with little flavour. I have seen ptarmigan in Quebec as white as snow, and about the size of a pigeon.

"Sportsmen everywhere should feel much indebted to the Honourable John Prince, M.L.C., a thorough sportsman and English gentleman, for having introduced and carried through Parliament a bill for the better protection of game in Upper Canada, by which it is enacted that :—

"No deer or fawn, elk, moose, or cariboo, shall be hunted, taken, or killed, between the first day of January and the first day of September in any year.

"No wild turkey, grouse, partridge, or pheasant, shall be hunted, taken, or killed, between the first day of February and the first day of September in any year.

"No quail shall be taken or killed between the first day of February and the first day of October in any year.

"No woodcock shall be taken or killed between the first day of March and the fifteenth day of July in any year.

"No wild swan, goose, duck, widgeon, or teal, shall be hunted, taken, or killed, between the first day of April and the first day of August in any year.

"No deer, wild turkey, grouse, partridge or pheasant, quail or woodcock, shall be trapped or taken by means of traps, nets, snares, springes, or other means of taking such birds, other than by shooting, at any time whatever.

"Fish abound in almost every part of both provinces. There is scarely a township which has not in it lakes abounding with various kinds of fish, of large size and delicious flavour. The brooks in Upper Canada are said to have abounded with 'speckled trout,' but I never heard of any one using any steps to stock these streams with more."*

* Here again, as a sportsman, I must mention with pleasure and gratitude the efforts made by Mr. Nettle, of Quebec, the Superintendent of Fisheries, for the artificial propagation of salmon wherewith to stock the rivers near Quebec. Too much praise, too, cannot be given to Mr. Whitcher, of the Fisheries Department of the Crown Land Office, for his exertions, which have resulted in stringent regulations for the protection of the valuable fisheries of the Saguenay. Perhaps there is no place in the world where more abundant sport can be had than in the district to which the map at page 132 applies, and which is within about seven days' steam of Great Britain. The Rev. Dr. Adamson, I am told, caught here, this summer (1860), in five days, forty-seven salmon, varying in size from 8 to 18 lbs. each. Salmon-trout are also wonderfully plenty and afford capital fly-fishing. I heard of a party, consisting of Lord Keane, Dr. Adamson, Mr. Holyoake, and two other gentlemen, who killed one morning 240 brace of fine salmon-trout, a year or two ago, in the same neighbourhood.

APPENDIX.

LOCALITIES IN WHICH VARIOUS CANADIAN MINERALS ARE FOUND.

MINERALS.

THE triumph obtained by Canada at the Paris Exhibition, for her splendid display of minerals of all descriptions, tells its own tale. The grand medal of honour, awarded to Sir William Logan, the Canadian provincial geologist, by the Jurors of the Paris Exhibition, will do more in calling the attention of European capitalists to the vast mineral wealth of the country, than the most elaborate description of its distribution and extent. It was a prize won in a strife where all were strong, and tells of rare industry and success in bringing to light the hidden wealth of Canadian rocks.

The principal economic minerals of Canada, are stated by Sir W. Logan, to be :—

METALS AND THEIR ORES.

Magnetic iron ore; specular iron ore; limonite (bog ore); Titaniferous iron; sulphuret of zinc (blende); sulphure of lead (galena); copper, native, sulphuret of, variegated; copper pyrites; argentiferous do., and containing gold; nickel; silver, with native copper and sulphuret of silver; lead.

Magnetic Iron Ore.—Marmora, four localities; South Sherbrooke, Bedford, Hull, three localities; Portage du Fort.

Specular Iron Ore.—Wallace Mine (Lake Huron), Mac Nab, St. Arnaud, Sutton, three localities; Brome, three localities; Bolton. *Simonite (Bog Ore).*—Middletown, Charlotteville, Walsingham, Gwillimbury West, Fitzroy, Earldley March, Hull, Templeton, Vaudreuil, St. Maurice, Champlain, Batiscan, Ste. Anne, Portneuf, Nicolet, Stanbridge, Simpson, Ireland, Lauzon, St. Vallier. *Titaniferous Iron.*—St. Urbain (Baie St. Paul), Vaudreuil (Beauce). *Sulphuret of Zinc* (Blende).— Prince's Mine and Mamainse (Lake Superior).

o

Sulphuret of Lead (Galena).—Fitzroy, Lansdowne, Ramsay, Bedford Bastard, la Petite Nation, Ause des Sauvages, and Ause du Petit Gaspé Mamainse. *Copper.*—St. Ignace, and Michipicoten Islands (Lake Superior), St. Henri, native copper ; Prince's Mine (Lake Superior), sulphuret of copper ; Mica Bay and Mamainse (Lake Superior), sulphuret, variegated, and copper pyrites ; Bruce Mine (Lake Huron), Root River, Echo Lake, and Wallace Mine (Lake Huron), copper pyrites ; Inverness and Leeds, variegated copper ; Upton, argentiferous copper pyrites ; Ascot, copper pyrites, containing gold and silver.

Nickel.—Michipicoten (Lake Superior), arsenial nickel, with a hydrated silenite of nickel ; Wallace Mine (Lake Huron), sulpharseniuret of nickel ; Daillebout Berthier, nickeliferous pyrites ; Ham and Bolton, in small quantities.

Silver.—St. Ignace and Michipicoten Islands (Lake Superior), native silver with native copper ; Prince's Mine (Lake Superior), native silver with sulphuret of silver.

Gold.—Seigniory of Vaudreuil, Beauce, on the rivers Guillaume, Lessard, Bras, Touffe des Pins, and du Loup ; Aubert Gallion, Poser's Stream, and the river Melgermet. All these localities, in the county of Beauce, afford native gold in the alluvial sands. This auriferous region has an area of 10,000 square miles, and the precious metal has been found at Melbourne, Dudswell, Sherbrooke, and in the valleys of the St. Francis and the Chaudière. Native gold is also found in Leeds, at Vaudreuil, Beauce, &c.

Some of the Non-Metallic Minerals.

Uranium ; chromium ; cobalt ; manganese ; iron pyrites ; graphite ; dolomite ; carbonate of magnesia ; sulphate of barytes ; iron ochres ; stextile ; lithographic stone ; agates ; jasper ; felspar ; avanturine ; hyacinthe ; corundum : amethyst ; jet ; quartzose ; sandstone ; retinite and basalt ; gypsum ; shell marl ; phosphate of lime ; millstones ; grindstones ; whetstones ; tripoli.

Millstones.—Several kinds of stone, more or less adapted to the purpose, are employed in Canada. The best is a corneous quartzite of the Eastern Townships, and at Bolton.

Grindstones.—A sandstone, known as the gray brand, found in many localities of Western Canada.

Whetstones.—Madoc, Marmora, Lake Mazinan, Fitzroy, Potlow, Stanstead, Hatley, &c.

BUILDING MATERIALS.

Granites; sandstone; calcareous sandstone; limestones; hydraulic limestones; roofing slates; flagging stones; clays; moulding sand; fuller's earth;

Marbles—white, black, red, brown, yellow and black, grey and variegated, green.

Granites.—Large masses of a very beautiful intrusive granite are found in many townships of the East.

Sandstone.—A beautiful variety of yellowish-white sandstone occurs at Niagara, Hamilton, Nottawasoga, Terrebonne, Lac des Allumettes, and Fitzroy.

Limestones.—Malden, Manitoulin, Sydenham, Nottawasoga, Orillia, and many other localities.

Marbles.—White, black, red, brown, yellow and black, grey and variegated.

COMBUSTIBLES.

Peat; petroleum; asphaltum.

Many of the mines are now being actually worked, and the "raw material" only waits the application of capital and skilled labour, to reward enterprise and industry.

Sir W. E. LOGAN, F.R.S., &c.
Geological Reports.

LAND REGULATIONS.

In addition to the Free Grants, Government Lands are sold on the following terms:—

Lands are sold either *en bloc*, or in single lots, of 100 acres, to actual settlers.

Lands *en bloc* are sold in quantities varying from 40,000 to 60,000 acres, at 50 cents (about 2s. sterling) per acre, cash, in Upper Canada; and in Lower Canada, at from 18 cents and upwards, according to situation; on condition that the purchaser cause the block to be surveyed into lots of from 100 to 200 acres each, on a plan and in a manner to be approved by the Government; and that one-third of the block be settled upon within two years from the time of sale—one-third more within seven years—and the residue within ten years from time of sale.

This requirement will be dispensed with as to any portion of the land which at the last-mentioned period, is found to be unfit for settlement.

The settlers must have resided on their lots for two years continuously, and have cleared and cultivated ten acres of every 100 acres occupied by them before they can get absolute titles.

Lands are surveyed by the Government into lots varying from 100 to 200 acres, and these are sold to actual settlers at 70 cents an acre (about 2s. 10½d. sterling), cash, or one dollar, (about 4s. sterling), in Upper Canada; and 10d. sterling, or 20 cents and upwards, in Lower Canada, according to situation; one-fifth being paid down, and the balances, by annual instalments with interest.

Absolute titles will be given to the purchaser on payment in full of the price, and on his having resided at least two years on his lot, and cleared and had under cultivation ten acres of every 100 acres occupied by him.

Free grants of 100 acres each are made on Government roads to actual settlers. These roads are marked on maps, just issued by the Government, in red.

Townships for sale *en bloc* are marked in deep red on the Government map.

SURVEYED LANDS.

The quantity of ungranted lands in both provinces surveyed up to the present time amounts to nearly 6,600,000 acres; about 4,540,000 in Lower Canada, and 2,060,000 in Upper Canada, and is thus distributed:—

1. Below Quebec, east of the river Chaudière to Gaspé, about 1,310,000 acres; in Gaspé and Bonaventure 348,000; in Saguenay District 259,000 acres.

2. In Three Rivers District, 349,000.

3. In the Eastern Townships, 1,030,000.

4. In the Ottawa Country, north of the river, 1,200,600.

5. Between Ottawa River and the Georgian Bay, 1,740,000.

6. West of the French River and Lake Nipissing, about 160,000.

The price and conditions of sale of these lands will be found elsewhere in this book.

The abominable impositions and frauds practised upon emigrants reaching New York are commented upon by several witnesses. Complaints upon this subject have been so frequent, and the outrages committed upon passengers so gross, as to call forth the strong remonstrances of the United States'

Emigration Commissioners, and led the Imperial Commissioners to issue the following warning in their Colonization Circular, the too infrequent publication of which is to be regretted :—

" There is one piece of advice often given of great importance to the settler, but which is not so much attended to as it ought to be, viz., that settlers should *go out early*, and if they wish to avoid imposition should go viâ Quebec or Portland. If anything goes wrong with them, or their baggage, it is impossible to obtain redress if they go viâ New York."

And yet the British nation has subsidized a line—the Galway—to take British subjects away from her own colonies to a rival country.

Taking into consideration the discomfort and time lost in reaching Canada by sailing vessels, emigrants are recommended to come by steamers. The average length of time occupied in a sailing-vessel is FORTY-TWO days, and by steamers TWELVE DAYS !

REPORT OF THE SELECT COMMITTEE TO WHOM WAS REFERRED THE ANNUAL REPORT OF THE CHIEF EMIGRATION AGENT, QUEBEC.

This Report contains a vast amount of useful information and many valuable suggestions. Some of these, however, had been anticipated by the Minister of Agriculture and the Crown Land Commissioner—such as the publication of the new Government Map, showing the free grants, and the exact position of the lands offered on sale *en bloc ;* the appointment of Emigration Agents at Liverpool, in Germany and Norway ; the new system of field notes (a specimen of which will be found in this work) ; the intention of the Crown Land Commissioner to establish a lithographic establishment in connection with his office ; the translation of the new Government pamphlet on Emigration into German and Norwegian, for distribution in those countries.

The following table (page 198) shows in tabular form the statistics of population, and area in square miles, of countries to which European emigration is chiefly directed.

" The natural attractions or laws under which such a distribution has been steadily going forward of late years may be classed under these eight heads, viz. : of a kindred race—of gold—of cheap, or free land—of higher wages—of climate—of cheap and convenient access—of a familiar language and free institutions."

COUNTRY.	Date of Statistics.	Population.	Square Miles.	Average Population to Square Mile.
Canada, West . . .	Estimate 1860	1,409,428	147,832	9¼
„ East . .	,,	1,130,781	201,980	5₁₀
New Brunswick . .	,,	200,000	27,700	7¼
Nova Scotia . . .	,,	300,000	18,746	16
Prince Edward . .	,,	62,348	2,134	29
Newfoundland . .	,,	120,000	57,000	2₁₀
North-West . .	,,	..	180,000	..
Vancouver's Island .	,,	11,463	16,000	¾
British Columbia . .	,,	..	213,500	..
Cape Colony . . .	,,	285,279	118,256	2¼
Australia :—				
N. S. Wales . .	,,	310,000	536,000	¾
S. Australia . .	,,	110,000	520,000	¼
W. Australia . .	,,	15,600	1,040,000	₆₁
Victoria . . .	,,	500,000	162,000	3
Tasmania . . .	,,	84,000	28,600	3
N. Zealand . . .	,,	50,000	97,000	2
S. American States including Brazil }	1860	19,846,000	5,863,000	8¼
United States . . .	,,	23,191,876	3,306,834*	7₁₃

The Committee cannot omit to mention the neglect of steerage accommodation and prices on board ocean-steamers.

"The Canadian line," the Report proceeds to say, "secured as it now is for a term of years of a large annual subsidy from the provincial chest, could not in any way better prove itself worthy of that subsidy, than by putting down its steerage rates to the same figure with the New York lines. It is in

* This is a prodigious territory, but the British possessions in North America far exceed this.

The exact amount, according to Alison, is 4,109,630 square geographical miles, and the water in British America is 1,340,000 square miles—the whole terrestrial globe embrace about 37,000,000 square miles, so that British America contains nearly a ninth part of the whole terrestrial surface of the, Globe—the number of acres is 2,630,163,200. Alison remarks that a very large portion is perhaps doomed to everlasting sterility, owing to the severity of the climate—such is no doubt the case; but it should be recollected that as the country becomes cleared up, the climate improves, and there are at present twenty or thirty millions of acres, to the successful cultivation of which the climate presents no insuperable barrier.

In 1851, England had 332, Wales 136, Scotland 92, the Islands 363, to a square mile.

evidence that the Inman line and the Galway line charge but five guineas for a steerage passage, while our line charges seven guineas. This difference of ten dollars and a half per head, to a man of family with small means, must operate injuriously against our route.

"It ought also to be made by this Government, in the opinion of your Committee, an additional ground of objection, to the unfair competition imposed on our lines by the imperial subsidy to the Cunard and Galway lines running to New York, that these subsidies enable them to diminish their rates of steerage passage, thus enhancing the cost, and diminishing the number of British emigrants into these British provinces."

The Committee report their decided opinion that "German and Norwegian settlements should be encouraged and multiplied from Gaspé to Lake Huron, as *nuclei* of future strength."

The Committee bear cheerful testimony to the conspicuous ability of Mr. Buchanan, the chief emigration agent for Canada. They consider FREE OR CHEAP CULTIVABLE LAND as the greatest attraction to the settler, and upon this ground they recommend more intimate relations between the Emigration and Crown Land Departments.

The Committee remark strongly upon the subject of absentees' lands, of which there are in Upper Canada alone 3,431,800 acres!!

"The retention, in a worse than mortmain clutch, of such an immense quantity of the productive soil of Upper Canada —exclusive of the Canada Company's Territory—must exercise a highly unfavourable influence on emigrant settlement. These blocks of unused, unsold, untenanted waste, act as barriers against all improvement, hinder the making of roads, diminish the number of schools, and devolve the burden of taxation unfairly on the actual settler. The high prices at which they are held drive many thousands of men into the United States, while, when they are sold, the unfortunate stranger is frequently unaware that he is buying two, three, or four years' taxes, in addition to the land. Some alteration of the assessment law, enabling the municipalities to enforce the payment of taxes on such lands annually or biennially, and such other remedial legislation as the House might in its wisdom devise, ought to be applied to this enormous evil."

The Committee among their formal recommendations concur, on the advice of Messrs. Buchanan and Hutton, in opinion "that an untransferable land scrip, 'good for fifty acres of public land in any part of the province of Canada,' should be

issued through these provincial agents abroad, to intending
actual settlers, on certain conditions to be fulfilled within a
specified time, and that similar precautions to those taken by
saving banks, be taken by the agents to protect the province
and the individual from imposition and loss. The adjoining
fifty acres to those which the scrip would cover, to be also
reserved for a limited time, that the settler may have a fair
opportunity of acquiring it by purchase."

NATURALIZATION OF ALIENS.

Aliens, after a continued residence of three years, are
entitled to a certificate of naturalization. They are required
to take oath of residence and allegiance. Any woman married
to a natural-born subject shall be deemed naturalized. The
alien to have the same privileges as to real estate as the subjects of Her Majesty. Such privileges of naturalization to be
subject to the provisions of Imperial Act.

QUARANTINE REGULATIONS.

The Medical Superintendent of the Establishment at Grosse
Isle, immediately upon the arrival of any Emigrant Ship there,
forthwith inquires into their condition, inspects the list of
passengers, the Bill of Health, Manifest, Log-book, &c.; and
in case of the existence of any contagious disorder, the passengers are detained, and medical attendance and other relief
afforded at the expense of the province; in a word, no pains
are spared to secure the comfort and afford ample protection.

STANDARD WEIGHT OF GRAIN, SEEDS, ETC.

The following standard weight of grain, seeds, &c., has
been sanctioned by the Provincial Parliament, and shall in
all cases be held to be equal to the Winchester bushel of all
grain, pulse, or seeds, opposite to which they are set.

No. of lbs. to the bushel.

		No. of lbs. to the bushel.	
Wheat	60	Malt	36
Indian Corn	56	Carrots	60
Rye	56	Parsnips	60
Peas	60	Beet	60
Barley	48	Onions	60
Oats	34	Flax Seed	50
Beans	60	Hemp Seed	44
Clover Seed	60	Blue Grass Seed	14
Timothy Seed	48	Castor Beans	40
Buckwheat	48	Salt	56
Dried Apples	22	Potatoes	60
Dried Peaches	33	Turnips	60

BANKS IN CANADA.

TORONTO	. .	UPPER CANADA	T. G. Ridout, Cashier.
„	. .	Toronto . . .	Angus Cameron, Cashier.
„	. .	B. N. America.	W. G. Cassels, Manager.
„	. .	Commercial. .	C. J. Campbell, Manager.
„	. .	Montreal. . .	R. Milroy, Manager.
„	. .	City Bank . .	Thomas Woodside, Manager.
„	. .	Quebec . . .	W. W. Ransom, Manager.
„	. .	Molson's . . .	John Glass, Agent.
„	. .	Gore	Bank of Upper Canada.

Most of these banks have agencies in the principal towns of the provinces.

MONEY MATTERS.

Parties going to Canada are recommended to take no more money with them, in the shape of bank notes or cash, than is necessary for the voyage and the cost of reaching their destination. The remainder can be paid to their credit at any one of the above banks; or a letter of credit from a bank here will be readily cashed in Canada, when the party presenting has been identified.

Sterling money is brought into currency by adding about one fourth.

Currency is brought into sterling money by deducting about one fourth. (See pp. 112, 113.)

MONEY ORDERS ON CANADA are issued at all Money Order Offices in the United Kingdom of Great Britain and Ireland, on Money Order Offices in Canada, at the charge of 1s. for any sum not exceeding £2, and 2s. for any sum above £2, but not exceeding £5, beyond which amount no order can be granted.

VALUE OF ENGLISH COIN THROUGHOUT CANADA.

1 Sovereign	£1 4 4	. . . .	$4.85
1 Crown	0 6 1	. . . .	1.20
1 Shilling	0 1 3	. . . .	0.24

N.B. A good supply of clothing should be taken from home, as well as bedding.

COST OF NECESSARIES OF LIFE—STOCK, ETC.

The subjoined list of prices is reckoned in dollars and cents, the mode in which all accounts are now kept in Canada. (See tables at pp. 112, 113.)

	Dols.	Cents.		Dols.	Cents.
Flour, 196 lbs. . . .	5	40	Wool, per lb. . .	0	27
Wheat, per bushel .	1	25	Hay, per ton	15	0
Spring Wheat „ . .	1	10	Straw, „	6	0
Pease „ . .	0	57½			
Oats „ . .	0	30	Cart Horses . 60 to 120 dollars.		
Barley „ . .	0	67	Riding „ . 80 „ 160 „		
Potatoes „ . .	0	25	Yoke of Oxen . 60 „ 100 „		
Apples „ . .	0	50	Milch Cows . 20 „ 30 „		
Butter, fresh, per lb. . .	0	17½	Pigs . . . 3 „ 10 „		
„ tub „ . .	0	12½	Sheep . . . 3 „ 5 „		
Bacon „ . .	0	15			
Chickens, per pair . .	0	30	Sugar, per lb. . 5 „ 10 cents.		
Ducks „ . .	0	37½	White „ . 10 „ 15 „		
Turkeys, each . . .	0	75	Soap „ . 5 „ 6 „		
Beef, per 100 lbs. . . .	6	0	Candles „ . 15 „ 25 „		
	0	6	Tea „ . 40 „ 50 „		
Other meats, per lb. . { to					
	0	12½			

BOOK-POST TO CANADA.

The postage rate must be prepaid with stamps affixed outside the cover.

The packet must be open at the ends, to admit of the enclosures being removed for examination.

No communication in the nature of a letter allowable, unless such communication be wholly printed; but parties are recommended to put an entry as to the party sending the book, in case of the loss of the cover.

The packet must not exceed two feet in length.

				s.	d.
The rate of postage for a packet not weighing more than 4 oz. is				0	3
More than 4 oz., but not exceeding 8 oz. .				0	6
„ 8 oz. „ 1 lb. .				1	0
„ 1 lb. „ 1½ lb. .				1	6
„ 1½ lb. „ 2 lb. .				2	0

and so on; 6d. being charged for every additional half-pound or fraction of a half-pound.

POSTAGE LABELS are issued of the value respectively of Penny labels; Twopenny; Fourpenny; Sixpenny; and One Shilling.

Any head Postmaster having reason to suspect any infringement of these regulations is required to open and examine such packet.

OTTAWA.

THE SEAT OF GOVERNMENT.

THE QUEEN'S DECISION VINDICATED.

Quebec, October, 1860.

NEVER was a greater injustice done to a loyal and law-abiding people than in a recent editorial in the *Times* about French Canadians, and never was a more singular unacquaintance with facts exhibited than in those letters of its "Own Correspondent," which appeared on the 30th of August and 3rd and 6th of September. They who undertake to instruct others, and desire to guide and influence public opinion, should at least have truth and accuracy on their side.

I do not charge the distinguished English journalist, or his "able and experienced reporter," with wilful misrepresentation, but I maintain they have both done us a grievous injustice, for which we are entitled to all the reparation of which the case admits. The short answer to the sweeping condemnation of a whole nation, which appeared in the *Canadian News* of the 12th ult., shows that we have one friend at home sufficiently acquainted with us to defend us from an attack which had no better authority or foundation than the reported speech of a vulgar, French Canadian Councilman of Montreal, which a few days afterwards elicited an unanimous resolution "to record the names of the offending members in the Minute Book of the Corporation," as a signal mark of their disapprobation. Another resolution, proposed and seconded by two French Canadians, Messrs. Bellemare and Grenier, was also passed unanimously, to the effect, that they desired "to offer a reparation of honour by solemnly acknowledging their respectful devotion to their gracious Sovereign, their loyal attachment to her throne, and their indignant repudiation of the wanton insult recently offered in their Council Room."

Will the *Times*, after this, persist in its calumny upon

Lower Canada, or withdraw a charge which has not the slightest foundation?

In no part of the wide possessions of our Queen does there exist a people better satisfied with the institutions under which they live and prosper, and less inclined to scorn the connection which happily unites them to the British Crown; and, in confirmation of this feeling, they point with pride to the reception which the youthful heir to the proudest throne in Christendom met with, from the hour he set foot upon Lower Canadian soil to that when, amidst the cheers and good wishes and prayers of a million faithful subjects of French origin, he set out to visit the Sister Province.

In answering the statements so confidently made by the *Times* correspondent from Montreal, and the editor of the *Times* from London, about a district with which, personally, they were both unacquainted, I am neither influenced by any wish to underrate the vast commercial importance and progress of Montreal, nor have I, in attempting to show the wisdom of the selection of Ottawa as the seat of Government, that individual interest in Ottawa, which is erroneously attributed to the influence of "certain speculators," which led to its selection, and, as the *Times* asserts, to the "transference of the capital from Montreal to the upstart village of Ottawa."

Montreal never was the capital of Canada; and this statement is as purely imaginative as the picture drawn of the sufferings of the Ottawa lumbermen from "wolves, bears, cold, and hunger." The selection of Ottawa as the seat of Government no more makes that beautiful and "central" spot the capital of Canada than a similar distinction makes Washington the capital of the United States.

I have a far higher object in this answer, which is, to remove the prejudice which the countless readers of the *Times* may adopt against a part of Canada too little known at home, but which, from its vast extent, its various mineral, agricultural, and "lumbering" resources and riches, yields to no part of this fine province in value and importance. If I disprove the grounds upon which the *Times* rests its case, I maintain that, to some extent at least, I prove mine.

I have this advantage over my formidable opponent, that I know the district I desire to defend, or I would not write about it, and lived in Canada years before the last movement took place which led to that judicious compromise which resulted in the selection of Ottawa, on the part of the Queen's advisers, and solved a difficulty which might have remained a stumbling-block and bone of contention for a century to come, so powerful, so varied, so apparently insuperable, were the local, personal, national and political obstacles, involved in the question. There can be no question as, to the view which the Colonial Secretary, who has now seen the chosen spot, will take ; there can be no doubt that His Grace will adopt the recommendations made by Lords Sydenham and Elgin, Sir Edmund Head, and last, though far from least, " the great Duke," who, upon being consulted where the seat of Government for Canada should be, placed his finger upon Ottawa.

I proceed now to show the utter unacquaintance of the *Times* and its correspondent with the subject on which they have written with so much confidence. These errors I will first quote, and then answer. In the letter of the 30th of August, the writer says of Ottawa, *which he had not yet seen*, that it was " a miserable out-of-the-way place ; that its selection as the capital of Canada was a blunder, than which no greater could have been committed." " That every one in Canada, except a few speculators who bought largely round the intended capital, is indignant at the transference of the capital from Montreal to Ottawa ; that tents had to be sent down to accommodate the aides-de-camp, &c., for whom otherwise no place could have been found !" In the letter of September 3rd, we read of the steamer " nearing the new and very upstart village of Ottawa, and meeting the lumberers (lumbermen ?), whose adventures in the woods with bears and wolves, and cold and hunger, would fill a volume, and who make Ottawa, as being one of the wildest spots in Canada, their head-quarters—they are French Canadians, and constitute three-fourths of the population of Ottawa, which is about 12,000, being equal to Norwood or Sydenham—that all access to the stream above is cut off by the Falls," &c.*

" If Ottawa were fortified like Quebec—and it could be made impregnable for a few thousands—if it were not close upon the American frontier, if its inhabitants were English settlers, there might have been some reason for the extreme step of transferring the capital from Montreal to Ottawa ; to which place, in the present state of feeling on the subject, the Government or the people *will* re-transfer it. The Legislative members were placed in the front seats at the ceremonial, and

---

* The quantity of land capable of cultivation between Ottawa and the Georgian Bay is estimated at twenty million acres. The population beyond Ottawa and north of the river can hardly be less than 100,000.

decried the arrangements in every tense and mood. The Parliament Buildings will be grand, regal and ancient-looking enough to please Mr. Scott, and if ever finished will make an admirable lunatic asylum," &c.

In the letter of the 6th of September, the writer states that he considers it "a painful, a shameful truth, that less is known of Canada in England, even by public men and great colonial oracles, than of Peiho and Terai, and calls upon the Imperial Government to send some Livingstone to explore and explain the resources of Upper Canada!"

The *Times* "improves the occasion" afforded by its correspondent, and tells us that "the choice of Ottawa has united all in the province against the arbitration they themselves sought, and the decision which they pledged themselves to accept; that the buildings are of the straitest sect of architectural fanaticism; that the position of Montreal is commanding, and at the head of the navigation of the St. Lawrence; that Ottawa is the residence of a rough and disorderly set of *lumberers;* that it is reached by a branch of the Grand Trunk; that the river *below* is only adapted for vessels of light draught, and *above* rendered useless by rapids; that Ottawa is the *Ultima hule* of Canada, that nobody lives beyond it, and that everybody must go out of their way to reach it;* that Her Majesty's advisers, having been misled, should retrace their steps, OR, if the Colonial Secretary, having seen the spot, approves the choice, that no more should be said about it."

The *Times* correspondent says that Ottawa is the "headquarters of the lumbermen, because it is the wildest spot in Canada; that they are French Canadians, and constitute three-fourths of the population of the 'village,' which only contains 12,000 inhabitants." The lumbermen don't live in Ottawa—only 25 per cent. of the whole population is of French origin. The Irish in Ottawa exceed any other nation in numbers, and it is just possible that they may be the "rough and disorderly" set. It is quite certain that it is not the French Canadians, whose temperate and quiet habits are proverbial. It is only a month since that the *Times* denounced all Lower Canadians with bitter vehemence; *now* it insists upon the removal of the capital of Canada to the very city where the British and Irish and their Queen were so grossly

* The *New York Herald* says of Ottawa, that "it is a new city of 1,500 people, circularly and scatteringly built, with very muddy and wide streets and side walks, having no pretensions to be the capital *except its central position.*

insulted in the council chamber, and where there are 30,000 French Canadians and 15,000 Irish Roman Catholics.

The government buildings, which are admitted to be "grand, regal, and ancient looking," will one day do "for a lunatic asylum;" "they are of the straitest sect of architectural fanaticism," adds the *Times.* "The members of the Legislature decried the arrangements in every tense and mood."

Before leaving Ottawa, the Honourable G. Brown, M.P. for Toronto, and Dr. Tassé, representing a county close to Montreal, proposed a vote of thanks to the city of Ottawa, for their munificent hospitality, which was carried unanimously. The Press were the guests of the city; the aides-de-camp, and persons connected with the royal *suite*, were handsomely housed in a new hotel, and did not require "tents."

"Nobody lives beyond Ottawa—the river above it is rendered useless by rapids," says the *Times.* How was it that the Prince went by steamers, and canoes, and portages, 100 miles above Ottawa, "amidst the most exquisite scenery, where the almost devotional loyalty of the people was something quite touching, and where he partook of lunch at the residence of Mr. M'Loughlin, a lumberer,* which, for style and elegance, would have done justice to Trois Frères?"

So far from Ottawa being a miserable out-of-the-way place, it is accessible in more ways than any place in Canada. There is the river, "spanned by a bridge of singular beauty, and showing at Carillon a gem of Canadian scenery, and by which was reached a site the most picturesque I ever saw, except Constantinople." Then there is a railroad, not mentioned in the letter, which is *not*, as the *Times* asserts, a branch of the Grand Trunk. Ottawa is also approached from Kingston by the Rideau canal, and next spring the railway from Brockville to Arnprior will afford another means of access to this "intended capital."

Ottawa, "at a cost of a few thousands, could be made impregnable;" Montreal would take as many millions! So far from Ottawa being "close to the American frontier," it is much farther from it than Montreal, or *any* city in Canada, except Quebec!!!

The *Times* tells us that Montreal is at the head of the navigation of the St. Lawrence; we, poor colonists, say that the

* Lumberers are timber merchants, many of whom have very large fortunes invested in that trade. Lumbermen are the persons employed to cut down the the timber, and make the rafts, &c. They are sometimes, and more correctly, called axemen.

head of the St. Lawrence is 170 miles higher up, where lake Ontario ends.

A few words more about the Ottawa country, now beginning to be called, and very properly, Central Canada; which may be said to begin with the Bobcaygeon Free Grant Road north of Peterborough to the dividing line between Upper and Lower Canada. The government is yearly spending large sums in making colonization roads, and surveying new townships to the north of Lake Ontario and the river St. Lawrence. These townships are rapidly filling up, and the occupiers of them have had abundant agricultural success. The city of Ottawa is in the county of Carleton; the average returns of wheat from which have for some years past exceeded any county in Canada. Central Canada may not equal this for some time, but the *Times* correspondent admits its "fertility," and speaks of it as "a huge extent of rich uncultivated country." So far from there being nothing beyond Ottawa, it is *the* district from whence half the lumber used in, and exported from, Canada comes. The iron mines at Hull have been for years successfully worked, and not long since 8,000 tons of magnetic iron ore, of an unusually rich quality, went down the Rideau canal to be smelted in the United States! The Indians bring very rich specimens of lead ore down the Gatineau river, but as yet they keep their secret as to its locality with singular and characteristic caution. More than sixty years ago Mr. Philemon Wright explored the country near Ottawa, and settled at Hull, and in the year 1806 he obtained from the Royal Society in England a silver medal, having on one side this inscription, "Arts and Commerce promoted;" and on the other, "To Mr. Philemon Wright, MDCCCVI., for Culture of Hemp in Canada."

To write of Ottawa as an upstart village is unworthy of the writer and the occasion. The real property in Ottawa City was valued and assessed some years since at nearly 4,000,000 dollars. Eight hundred ships are laden annually at Quebec with timber from the Upper Ottawa country valued at 2,500,000 dollars. It has had, for many years past, churches, schools, scientific societies, mechanics' institutes, newspaper, and manufactories of various kinds. It has made more rapid progress than any city in Canada; its population having doubled in ten years. It is the high road to 25,000,000 of acres of land, as yet unsettled, but capable of successful cultivation, between it and the Georgian Bay. If the grand project of an union between the Atlantic and Pacific Oceans should ever be realized, and the best and nearest route taken, the *road* must pass near Ottawa. I say road, because no man but a lunatic would ever dream of a water communication which could be only available half the year.

Let the Canadian Government offer to the capitalists of Europe two or three millions of acres of the lands, now utterly unproductive, in alternate blocks of 20,000 acres on either side the road, chess-board like, between Ottawa and the free port of Sault St. Marie (close to the Bruce and Wellington mines), now the extreme north-west inhabited part of Canada proper, and I should not despair of seeing within three years a gravelled road between Lakes Nipissing and Opeongo, with lateral branches southward to connect with our great national boast, the Grand Trunk Railway, the full advantages of which will never be realized to the mother-country and the province until it has its termination at Halifax.

The duty paid to Government for the privilege of cutting timber, at ¼d. per foot for square timber, and 5d. each for logs, produces nearly 200,000 dollars per annum. More than 20,000 axemen are employed, whose wages and board average 26 dollars a month (more than five pounds sterling) each, and amounts yearly to 5,680,000 dollars, upwards of one million and a quarter sterling. There are more sufferers from bulls and bears, and cold and hunger, in the metropolis of England than among the well-clad, well-warmed, well-fed, well-paid-and-*piped* lumbermen of the Upper Ottawa!

I think now I have proved my position that the *Times* is ill-informed; that Ottawa is not the miserable out-of-the-way place it has been represented to be; that the country beyond and west of Ottawa has highly valuable mineral, agricultural, and lumbering resources.

I quite agree with the *Times* correspondent that the ignorance of Canada, among Englishmen, is deeply to be deplored, for their sakes as well as our own.

There is no need, however, for a "Livingstone to be sent out to explain and explore the resources of this part of Upper Canada." There is scarcely a square mile which has not been visited, and the result recorded in the Crown Lands Department. There is scarcely an acre, I was going to say, which has not been examined by the painstaking and earnest staff of Sir William Logan, whose love of geology amounts almost to enthusiasm, which he seems to have communicated to the able and accomplished gentlemen who serve under him. Nor has

P

the attention of those gentlemen been merely confined to geological researches, but the fauna and flora of Canada have been observed and recorded, as well as the fossils found in the various strata between Lake Superior and Gaspé. A geological map of Canada is now being prepared by Sir William Logan, the minute and accurate details of which will be deeply interesting to all whose attention has been given to this science. There are already detailed maps and reports of all this district, published annually, and obtainable from Sir William, or the officers of the House of Assembly at Quebec. Sir William Logan receives with willing courtesy, and welcomes all visitors to his valuable collection of Canadian minerals at Montreal.

The London *Times* has too readily adopted the opinions of its correspondent, however able and experienced he may be, who seems somehow to look upon Montreal through a *Rose*-coloured medium. The inhabitants of Canada, living at Quebec and Toronto, and other cities which competed for the distinction of the seat of government, may not perhaps, in their heart of hearts, be quite satisfied at the selection of Ottawa; but at all events they are silent—if they don't approve, they all acquiesce! For nearly two years past, during which I have associated very much with members of the legislature and the press, I have scarcely heard the subject alluded to with any feeling of asperity or disapproval.

Some few sturdy bucolics in the Lower House, acting under the influence of hot editorials from their favourite journal about "Lower Canada domination," vowed by more than Yea and Nay, that they would rather resign their seats than go among the *moutons* of Quebec. But they did *not* resign, and they *did* go; and during the whole session of 1860 I never saw a set of country gentlemen who seemed to enjoy themselves more among the warm-hearted people at the ancient capital, who talked English as well, and took as kindly to the inevitable pipe as themselves. And just as quietly and as gracefully will they fall in with their Queen's award about Ottawa, *which is nearer to the homes of a majority of the members of both Houses of the Legislature, and of the entire population of the two Canadas, than Montreal!*

The drab-coloured repudiators of Pennsylvania would be miracles of honour, and honesty, and good faith, in comparison with Canadians, if, after having invited their future King to lay the foundation stone of their Houses of Parliament on the site selected by that peerless wife and woman, their beloved Queen, they should seek to break the award they themselves agreed to accept, and thus cancel the "arbitration bond" by which they pledged themselves, as gentlemen, to abide.

Canada wants repose from mere party conflicts, in which no great principle of public policy is involved. We Canadians should begin to show more public spirit, and less self-seeking; more reliance upon ourselves, more personal attention to, and interest in, those measures by which our vast resources can be most judiciously and effectually developed. Humanly speaking, the great question of the day with us is, how this desirable end may be best accomplished; how our waste places can be filled by an industrious, God-fearing, law-abiding population.

Immigration and trade go hand in hand; a fact to which the statesmen and people of England give too little heed, as regards their nearest colony and best customers, but which engages the continual and unremitting attention of American statesmen, politicians, and speculators.

Let us, before it be too late, turn to good account the royal progress, which will draw an unusual amount of attention to this country, and endeavour to make this auspicious event ancillary to the permanent improvement and colonization of this vast and valuable appendage of the British Crown.

A CANADIAN.

THE CLIMATE OF CANADA.

THERE are many persons at home who apprehend that the climate of Canada is too rigorous for the production of such cereals and fruits as are grown in European latitudes. The following extracts from the Toronto *Globe* newspaper of the 21st of September, 1860, in reference to the Agricultural Exhibition at Hamilton, will afford some answer to these fears, and confirm the statements made elsewhere in this book as to vine, flax, and tobacco culture, and dairy products, in Canada.

"The display of fruit, in quantity and quality, surpassed what has been shown at any previous Exhibition. The results in this department were very satisfactory, proving that the climate of Canada admirably adapts it for the raising of many of the most valuable kinds of fruit. One of the principal exhibitors was Mr. Beadle, of the St. Catharine's nurseries. On

Q

one side of the central stand in the Crystal Palace he had 115 plates of apples, pears, peaches, &c., and 30 jars of cherries, currants, raspberries, blackberries, &c. Mr. Beadle exhibited ten varieties of peaches grown in the open air. Several of these varieties were of very large dimensions, and were much admired for the delicate richness of their tints. He exhibited also numerous varieties of apples; 41 in one collection of three of each sort, and 20 in another collection of six of each sort. He had also a large show of pears, comprising a large number of varieties. Among the varieties of open-air grapes shown by Mr. Beadle, were the blood-blacks, the Delaware, the Diana, the Northern Muscadine, the Perkins, Sage's Mammoth, and the Wild Fox Grape, a product of the Canadian woods, which has been domesticated and is marked by a strong musky flavour. Several of these varieties, Mr. Beadle states, are found to be well adapted to our northern climate. Mr. Beadle also exhibited a number of young fruit trees from his nurseries, comprising the apple, pear, plum, cherry, &c.

"Mr. Arnold, of Paris, exhibited a fine collection of fruit, tastefully arranged on a frame, bearing on a scroll the inscription: 'The fruit of the land.' This collection comprised apples, peaches, pears, clusters of grapes, &c.

"Mr. Benedict, of Clifton, showed some magnificent peaches, 20 varieties of pears, and specimens of a very large crab-apple, which he calls the 'Transcendent.'

"Mr. Reid, of Port Dalhousie, showed some results of experiments he has been making in improving the vine, and introducing new varieties suitable for Canada. By raising plants from the seed, instead of from shoots, he has obtained a number of new open-air varieties. Specimens of the fruit of these, very large, were exhibited. Mr. Reid also had on exhibition two bottles of wine, made from grapes of a native stock, brought into the garden out of the woods.

"Mr. Binkley, of Ancaster, had along with his fruit some bottles of grape wine and home-made sherry, the latter manufactured from currants.

"Besides the fruits already named there was a large show of melons. We observed, also, nectarines, apricots, crab-apples, cranberries, &c. The display of plums was very good, comprising many varieties of large and small size.

"Some one, whose name we did not learn, exhibited a collection of cigars made from tobacco grown in the province. They looked as well as ordinary Principes and Havanas; their flavour was a matter to be determined by the judges.

" Another exhibitor, whose name we did not ascertain, sent a collection, comprising some thirty bottles of pickles, home-made wines, apple brandy, and maple molasses.

" For the Canada Company's prize of £24 for the best 112 lbs. of flax, there were 5 entries.

" Best bushel of hemp seed, 6 entries. Best bushel of flax seed, 31 entries.

" Messrs. Alexander & Co. exhibited some specimens of scutched flax, which excited marked attention; they looked almost as if they had been dressed.

" DAIRY PRODUCTS, &c.

" These were in the northern part of the building. There was a good show of butter, and a number of splendid cheeses. Mr. Rannie, of Dereham, showed 200 or 300 lbs. of cheese, including some pine-apple cheese, a species of Stilton. Mr. Rannie carries on dairy operations on an extensive scale, keeping as many as one hundred cows. The honey exhibited, both in the jar and clear, looked exceedingly well."

LOVELL'S CANADA DIRECTORY.

A local and personal directory of Canada; containing a vast amount of valuable information as to routes, agricultural, financial, and educational statistics, &c., &c. It can be had at STANFORD'S, Charing Cross, London; MILLER'S, Stationer, 122 Ingram-street, corner of Hanover-street, Glasgow; OLDHAM'S, Grafton-street, Dublin. Price Ten shillings.

"That marvel of Canadian enterprise."—*Illustrated London News,* Sept. 28, 1860.

CANADA AND ILLINOIS.

CAIRD'S ERRONEOUS VIEWS OF CANADA, ANSWERED AND REFUTED. Price Threepence, postpaid.

ESTABLISHED 1856.

Published in London Every Alternate Wednesday.

THE CANADIAN NEWS,

NEW BRUNSWICK HERALD,

AND

British Columbian Intelligencer.

THE CANADIAN NEWS has been Established for the purpose of informing the English Public respecting the Progress of the vast Possessions of British North America, their capabilities, advantages, and resources.

Special Correspondence is received from the Principal Places, and original Articles are given on Current Colonial Topics.

BRITISH COLUMBIA and VANCOUVER.—The Latest News from these parts, *viâ* Panama, may always be found in its Columns, together with a Detailed Statement of the Export of Goods from London and Liverpool, with names of Shippers, &c.; this matter is Published on the Departure of a Vessel from either Port.

The Commercial Article of the Journal treats of the various Canadian Joint Stock Undertakings; Railways, Banks, &c.; together with the Prices Current, both here and in North America. This information is contributed by a Leading Authority on such matters. Proceedings at the several Meetings of these Companies are duly reported.

POST FREE 5*d.*, PER ANNUM 10*s.* 10*d.*

Post Office Orders to be made payable to MR. FREDERIC ALGAR.

Office for Subscriptions and Advertisements, 11, Clement's Lane, Lombard Street, London. E. C.

LOWER CANADA.

CROWN LANDS DEPARTMENT, FISHERIES BRANCH. —PUBLIC NOTICE is hereby given that the ESTUARY and RIVER STATIONS for SALMON and SEA TROUT FISHERIES, situate and discharging upon the shores of the river St. Lawrence and tributaries, and along the Baie des Chaleurs and tributary streams, are severally OPEN to PROPOSALS for LEASE during terms of three or five years, dating from the 1st day of May, 1861.

Applications should describe accurately the locality and precise limits required, distinguishing Net-fishing from Fly-fishing Divisions, and the rent per annum named for either of such privileges, separately. The names of two solvent sureties must be submitted.

Address proposals or inquiries to FISHERIES BRANCH, Crown Lands Office, Quebec; or through the Superintendent of Fisheries for Lower Canada; or P. FORTIN, Esq., Stipendiary Magistrate, on board of the Government vessel engaged in the protection of fisheries.

ANDREW RUSSELL, Assistant Commissioner.

Quebec, October 3rd, 1860.

TRINITY COLLEGE, TORONTO.

THE ANNUAL EXAMINATION FOR MATRICULATION, and for SCHOLARSHIPS, takes place Yearly in OCTOBER.

The following Scholarships will be open to competition :—

FOUR FOUNDATION SCHOLARSHIPS, tenable for three years, viz.:—One of 30*l.* currency per annum ; one of 25*l.* ; and two of 20*l.*

ONE CAMERON SCHOLARSHIP, tenable for three years, of the annual value of 25*l.* currency ; appropriated to the sons of Clergymen of the United Church of England and Ireland, who shall be at the time resident and doing duty in British North America, or who, having fulfilled these conditions, shall have been incapacitated by age or sickness, or removed by death. A preference will be given, *cæteris paribus*, to candidates intending to receive Holy Orders.

The holders of these Scholarships will be required to attend Lectures and Examinations in the Arts course.

All persons presenting themselves for examination must produce testimonials of good conduct. Candidates for Matriculation must have entered on their Sixteenth, and Candidates for Scholarships on their Seventeenth year.

The subjects of examination may be learned by application to the Provost of Trinity College, who will furnish any other information which may be required.

ONE WELLINGTON SCHOLARSHIP, of the annual value of 50*l.* currency, tenable for two years ; and one BISHOP STRACHAN, one ALLAN, and one DICKSON SCHOLARSHIP, each of the annual value of 30*l.* currency, and tenable for three years, will be awarded to Students commencing their College Course in October next, according to the result of the yearly examination in the following June.

N.B.—Students intending to study for Holy Orders will be eligible as candidates for Divinity Scholarships, either after having graduated in Arts, or after having spent one year at least in the Arts course ; provided, in the latter case, that they have entered on their twenty-second year and have been considered qualified for entering the Theological class.

FOUR DIVINITY SCHOLARSHIPS, one of 30*l.* currency per annum ; two of 15*l.*, and one of 20*l.*, tenable for two years, will be annually open for competition, in addition to one JUBILEE SCHOLARSHIP, of the value of 40*l.* currency per annum, tenable for two years, and restricted to the most deserving Bachelor of the year, who, having graduated in honours, shall have expressed his intention of studying for Holy Orders.

TORONTO, C. W., August, 1860.

LaVergne, TN USA
25 February 2010
174211LV00004B/53/P